FOUR WEDDINGS AND AN ENCORE

A life in rock with all its rolls, reflected from a Parisian window

AMANDA PELMAN

PUBLISHERS OF O.G AUTHOR GENIUSES

Published by E&R Publishers
New York, NY, USA

An imprint of MillsiCo Publishing, USA
www.EandR.pub

Copyright: © 2026 Amanda Pelman — All rights reserved.

Except for brief quotations in critical articles or reviews, no part of this book may be reproduced in any manner without prior written permission from the publisher. Write to: Permissions, E&R Publishers, 304 W 115th St PHB, New York, NY, USA.
Email: publishing@eandr.pub

ISBN: 9781966155232 Hardcover
ISBN: 9781966155249 Softcover
ISBN: 9781966155256 eBook
ISBN: 9781966155263 Audiobook

Library of Congress Control Number: 2025945852

DEDICATION

For you to be born today from 12 previous generations, you needed a total of 4,094 ancestors over the last 400 years.

Think for a moment — how many struggles? How many battles? How much difficulty and sadness? How much happiness and how many love stories? Expressions of hope for the future … how much did your ancestors have to undergo for you to exist in this present moment?

Let that sink in. It means everything I tell you in this story doesn't really amount to a hill of beans in this world but is all pivotal for my children to go on to tell their stories.

I dedicate this book to them: Olivia Elvie and Austin Pelman

"Love is like a tree: it grows by itself, roots itself deeply in our being and continues to flourish over a heart in ruin. The inexplicable fact is that the blinder it is, the more tenacious it is. It is never stronger than when it is completely unreasonable."

—Victor Hugo, Notre-Dame de Paris

CONTENTS

Foreword vii

Acknowledgements ix

Prologue. xi

Introduction: Sweet Little Rock n Roller. 1

Chapter 1: She Was Almost Right!. 3

Chapter 2: Radio Days. 23

Chapter 3: Walking in the Wild West End 33

Chapter 4: Every Little Thing She Does is Magic. 41

Chapter 5: Life's Locomotion 53

Chapter 6: Just One More Time Lovey 65

Chapter 7: Mental Monopoly Board 89

Chapter 8: The Call Sheet of Life 107

Chapter 9: My Interpretation 125

Chapter 10: Carrying a Torch. 153

Chapter 11: Broken Arrow 179

Chapter 12: By the Time we Got to Woodstock. 191

Chapter 13: Confusion Has its Costs. 201

Chapter 14: Paris, Something Greater. 231

Epilogue: A Girl Like You 237

FOREWORD

Amanda "Panda" Pelman has been my friend & associate for over 40 years. To say we have shared many magical and stressful moments would dramatically understate it.

Amanda is a rare woman, becoming successful in the man's world of music & entertainment back in the '80s. She has been a significant inspiration for many women who now frequent the upper echelon of the music world. A friend to many, she is acknowledged for her honesty, straight-talking, and incredible creativity.

All these factors are why I was drawn to her—and continue to put up with her!

Together we have created many major events—spending long days & nights giving each other a lot of shit. Amanda, or "Princess" as I sometimes call her, cajoled me into writing my own biography, *Hey, you in the Black T-shirt*. Now I am thrilled to read hers.

Four Weddings and an Encore, like the author, pulls no punches, and I'm sure a few people won't be happy, which is par for the course with my dear friend.

—Michael (Chuggi) Chugg AM
Australian entrepreneur, businessman,
concert tour promoter, and founder of Frontier Touring

ACKNOWLEDGEMENTS

My heartfelt thanks go to Simon Mills and Jeff Jenkins for their dogged determination to get me to the finishing line.

Love goes to friends across my wide world of wonder—

Michael Chugg, Russell Morris, Michael Idato, Clare O'Connell, Fi Seabridge, Snearky & Skippy, Ami & Spoony, Timmy the King, Angharad Start, Paul & Lorraine Young, and Didier Ducher.

And my 'extra' kids: Toppy, Georgia Beaumont, Luce & Corn, and Llama.

My gratitude and daily thoughts are with those gone too soon from my life — Gary Ashley, Michael Lang, Billy Thorpe, and Ira Yaeger.

PROLOGUE

I invite you to examine my tale of life, laughter, and loss.

What I refer to as The Circumference of My Existence.

I may be dead while you read my story — either killed in a bizarre boating accident or stabbed by a knife-wielding maniac (all husbands under suspicion). Worst of all, I could be considered 'elderly'. Picture propped up in a rocking chair, trying to remember my name, undoubtedly waiting for the day's first gin & tonic.

At the very least, know that I write this missive with all good-humored intent to entertain. Not to wilfully cast aspersions on any one person's character. Almost like Almost Famous. However much you may have loved, liked, admired, wronged, slighted, or fucked me over in the past … this is my story.

You can argue its truth and validity in your own minds.

So, let's get on with it, shall we?

INTRODUCTION: SWEET LITTLE ROCK N ROLLER

My Paris kitchen has no window. This feels unusual. Being unable to gaze from the sink or countertop into a wide blue yonder, hands under water, rinsing a cook's detritus away. Wondering what tomorrow will bring?

I take sixteen steps out from my kitchen towards a large window at the far end of the room. I gaze towards the Cathedral Notre-Dame and a welcoming wide Parisian skyline. This seems a fair trade-off to not having a window in my kitchen.

This is a lesson in perspective. In my little Paris kitchen, I think deeply about how far I have come to be here. The window may not be in my kitchen, but taking those sixteen steps grants me a world of clarity and perception I would not achieve by remaining at my sink.

Looking outward, I see multitudinous possibilities. Fraught with a mélange of danger and happiness, these ideas take shape in my mind — both geographically and psychologically.

My thoughtful gaze is interrupted with memories of the past.

Triggered by Spotify playing Kylie Minogue, I can be drawn back to first hearing 'Locomotion' on London radio, sitting in a Notting Hill hotel we shared on those frequent recording sojourns with Stock Aitken Waterman. I smiled at the sound then, as I do now, realizing hit records sprung in part from my labors.

iTunes shuffle contrasts next with Van Morrison's 'Precious Time'. I smile at the memory of him ad-libbing live, 'Precious time is slipping away ... love Amanda till the day I die', when he sang at Orangefield in Belfast during a private show. My labors with Van the Man are still to come to fruition.

The iPhone 'ping' signals Michael Chugg calling me with news of yet another death inside our rock 'n' roll cohort. These 'stage of life' inevitabilities echo through a stone from the gravesite of Michael Lang and a photo of Billy Thorpe adorning my desk. Neither token of memorabilia invokes sadness in me, but more a smile at the achievements in working with these industry titans who became friends.

I stood in a similar Parisian window many years ago. A hotel on the Rue de Turbigo in 1982, gazing from a 5th-floor garret, wondering what my future had in store. A photo from that time shows a girl full of hope and promise, filled with joy at the beauty that is, and will always be, Paris.

After 40 years, I am back in that physical and metaphoric window, surprised and elated at how my life evolved … and is still evolving.

CHAPTER 1: SHE WAS ALMOST RIGHT!

She was almost right, my friend LC. We were walking into school from where our parents deposited us each morning. This was a walk long enough to exchange arguments over skirt lengths, homework trauma and tuck shop lunch choices. This had been going on since we first met on Brighton Beach. But today was different. LC decided to predict my future. Not hers, just mine. She was adamantly convinced, whether through some psychic path or mental mumbo-jumbo, that I was going to be married five times. Sidebar marital predictions included me wearing mink coats, draped in jewels. As we approached our locker rooms before heading to class, my head somehow lifted higher in the deeply embedded knowledge that I was going to be fabulous!

We were 10 years old at the time. Despite this pre-pubescence, I was striding with purpose towards this monumental life that lay ahead of me. Surely there would be no detrimental ramifications to marrying five times.

Would there? From where did the furs and the jewels derive? All I knew was my head had to be held high. Breasts that were only just budding would march firmly ahead of me towards all five husbands, and I would be FABULOUS.

Our first impressions of ourselves are created from visual references. In my case via black and white photos taken hours after my birth by my photo-genius father. In these images, my mother looks genuinely shocked in equal measure by what she produced at the ripe age of 43 and the size of my nose.

The poor woman managed to give birth to her only child, a daughter no less, and I sprang forth with a hooter the size of Tasmania. This proboscis and dark shock of hair made me look like a mini version of my father.

I'm surprised my mother didn't ask for a refund. But then, my birth was my father's idea, so he had presumably put in an advance order with some higher power that I would look and think like him. Which I did, and I do.

In my first of many homes, I had a wooden cage set out in the garden. Only I was permitted in this cage, not the Shetland Terrier named Dougal.

Apparently if I had been born a boy, I was to be named Dougal, but the unsuspecting dog ended up with the abrupt Celtic moniker.

The smell of the wooden cage and the toys adorning it, in the garden on a sunny spring day, still fills my nostrils. The evocation of memory through smell is the subject of many a literary work, amongst them Patrick Süskind's Perfume and Jean-Jacques Rousseau's Confessions.

It lies in us all, and I urge you to personally explore it.

My mother at this point is 45 years young, and her business is booming. She is a preeminent fashion designer named Elvie Hill. While she might have forgotten to have a child until she was 43, through both circumstance and desire, she was ahead of her time in not allowing my birth to stand in the way of her remarkable career and professional drive.

Enter 'The Nannies'. From day one, a nurse accompanied the new parent home from the hospital. Dispensing advice on childcare and ensuring my mother's sleep schedule was not an interruption to her work schedule. 'Hymie' was the name of Nanny #1, watched over closely by my Aunt Annie – Elvie's much older sister who substituted as a grandmother figure.

My mother herself was a 'late in life' baby. Born in 1918 to Elizabeth Naylor Hill, with sparkling blue eyes to match her mother's. The few photographs I have of them give the appearance of sisters. I know very little of my mother's family lineage, save a cousin or two. They hailed from Bunbury, Western Australia, and moved to Victoria when Elvie was eight. My maternal grandfather's kin were from Wales.

The family members lived all in a row on Hotham Street, Elsternwick — next door to the mansion Rippon Lea. Visiting there years later, my mother recalled having seen kangaroos happily leaping around the grounds during her childhood. Her brother Clem moved to South Australia after their mother died, leaving the eldest child, Annie, to care for the household.

Eighteen years my mother's senior and with her mother dissolving in terminal illness, Annie became Elvie's maternal influence. Annie never had children. Her husband, David, was shell-shocked in WW2 and never spoke around others. He struck me as a haunted figure, given I was unable to imagine the wartime horror that plunged him into verbal silence.

Like her sister, my mother's life was forever scarred by that dreadful war. Her childhood sweetheart, Neville Seabrook, was called up when they had become engaged. They married hurriedly before his departure. Nevertheless, she was a most resplendent bride.

Elvie Joy Hill, as a little girl, cut up scrap paper to make dresses for her dollies. She took to cutting shears and seamstress scissors like a duck to water. This went beyond the yearning to have 'pretty things'. Her eye for detail could not have been learned behavior. In a home with a bricklayer father and homemaker mother, there was no finery to examine. She knew what she liked and how to express it. This is innately one of the things I have inherited from her, if not all.

Neville shipped out to a war zone that would remain unknown to his blushing bride for the first 2 years of their separated marriage. It was later learned that he spent those years on the island of Ambon in a troop of about 1,100 Australian men.

In 1939, young men across the Commonwealth dreaded the envelope in the mail telling them their number had come up — the birthdate that signified their impending doom. And their wives dreaded the arrival of the telegram announcing their husband's untimely demise. That knowledge came to my mother in the form of a knock at the door by one of the only surviving platoon members who witnessed her husband's fate. The soldiers had been lined up and beheaded by the Japanese. Each one of them hearing the swift blade's blow to their fellow officer before them. The dark horror of what is thought of in those moments cannot be replicated in the retelling. The wedding photo of Elvie and Neville reveals the joy in their all-too-few happy moments.

Of course, had Neville survived, my existence would not have come to be. And neither would a certain music industry recording legend, something I would discover many years later.

On the other side of the world, my father was fighting a similar enemy on different soil. Hector Campbell Pellicci was serving in His Majesty's British Army. Born in Dunoon, Scotland, Hector was the second son of Augusto Pellicci and Mary Elizabeth Campbell. Their first son succumbed to cot death, and the much-welcomed Hector was shortly followed by Betty, Rosa, Michael and Linda.

Hector literally means 'to act in an arrogant or intimidating way' — however, this was not my father's style. He certainly had an air of authority and self-assurance. This made him an admired gentleman and friend throughout his life. An athletics champion at Keil School in Dumbarton, he went on to study engineering on a full scholarship at Edinburgh University. During his boarding school days at Keil, he fell in love with a young lass at the adjacent girl's school. He called her 'Bluebird', and they would meet under the cloak of darkness. Maybe furtive kisses were exchanged, maybe more. 'Bluebird' went on to be a great actress — Jean Simmons. Hector swooned when retelling the story while watching her in televised reruns. In a 1955 studio photo, Jean bears a striking resemblance to my mother in her early years.

During WW2, after a tour of various European battlefields, Hector became a colonel. He was then stationed in the UK and received word that any undocumented immigrants of Italian heritage could be repatriated back to Mussolini's Italy.

My Italian grandfather had left his Tuscan village of Verni, near Viareggio, aged 16. The expensive passage by train and boat had been meant for his older brother Luigi, who fell ill just before the journey.

The ticket weighed heavily in my reluctant grandfather's pocket as he made his way to an unknown future in an unknown language. Augusto settled in a wee holiday resort in Western Scotland named Dunoon — thankfully in the summer months. This led him to recognize an industry yet to greet the shores of bonnie Scotland — soothing, cooling Italian-style ice cream: gelati. The sorbet would be made in the dingy bathtub of his second-floor walk-up.

Every Sunday, he toiled away on flavours never experienced by the Scots. Days were spent diligently sourcing lemons and expensive fruits, all reminiscent of his Italian childhood village life. Once tubbed, the delicious treat was flung into his ice maker on the back of a bicycle. His successful business led to renting his own café and meeting his future wife.

Nearly a half century ahead, it was my dad's job to keep his father safe and the family together. In 1941, he stood in a telephone box in London's Westminster, seeing his father's success going up in smoke unless he could manufacture a speedy name change. Keen to keep some semblance of nomenclature, he scoured the surnames with the derivation 'Pel', eventually coming up with Pelman, of which there was none in the humongous London phonebook.

So, my grandfather Augusto Pellicci became Angus Pelman, and the family unit was not cut asunder.

Unlike my mother's first husband, Hector thankfully ended his wartime tenure alive. He was billeted to Germany, where the Allied Armed Forces assisted Germany in rebuilding their industry. My father served in the Film Division. His interest in film was a hobby from his school days, and he went on to make several films in Germany, including 'Madonna in Ketten', about a woman giving birth in jail.

Hector lived in Frankfurt, where he was joined by his secretary and soon-to-be first wife, Eva.

The role my ever-so-suave father carved out for himself in Germany included many benefits, courtesy of the black market: cigarettes, alcohol, and a record player. 'Heck and Eve' had a son, Ashley Michael, my stepbrother.

Post-war restlessness grew, and Hector decided that Germany was not where he wanted to reside. With the guidance of a wartime pal, he turned his eye to Australia.

Needing a character reference as was required, I have a letter issued to my father from the Foreign Office in London in 1950. It reads that he was employed in the Control Commission for Germany (British Element) as a control officer between 1947 and late 1949. It indicates his conduct was satisfactory and that 'during the period he was not on any occasion in prison, charged with any offence or an inmate of a mental home'. Good to know.

The newly minted Pelman family sailed to Melbourne in late 1951 and took up residence in Simpson Street, East Melbourne.

In the apartment below lived a sparkly blue-eyed lady named Elvie Joy Seabrook. The recently widowed woman lived with her sister Annie and worked for Theo Denave as a dress designer and cutter.

After news of Neville's death, Elvie entered a period of mourning, resulting in her voluptuous black hair turning white. She wore the blank color as a badge of honor for her loss, long before turning prematurely grey was fashionable.

One evening, Elvie stood at her kitchen sink washing dishes. Looking up, she spied a peeping Tom glaring back at her through the window. The invader's huge nose masked his beaming smile; nevertheless, he was shooed away with a sharp rap on the window. Not to be deterred, my father rapped back, and the rest is history.

Elvie and Hector became lovers at the start of 1952, and as Frank Sinatra sang, love is lovelier the second time around. They basked in their discovery of each other while both building their professional lives.

Elvie became a fashion designer with Isabel Clayton in Flinders Lane. Hector started the Aluminium Roofing Company. Based in Bridge Rd, Richmond, they were the first company to build flat roofs across Melbourne. My father was always an inventor at heart. After flat roofs, he invented the car steering wheel lock and a swimming pool plastic bubble. Both patents were sold far too cheaply, which he always regretted.

After seven years of marriage, Hector reflected that if a child was going to emerge from this wonderful union, it better be quick smart. I often wonder if my mother's reluctance to give birth was due to her insecurity about how to parent. Having lost her own mother in her teens and her father just after her 21st birthday, her role model was her sister Annie, who herself was childless. But my father was exemplary in convincing her it would all work out.

My arrival came early April 1961 at Jessie McPherson Hospital. My paternal grandmother's birthday was April 5, and, on that day, far away in the Scottish Highlands, her cat jumped up on the mantelpiece. Nana Pelman said, 'Och-aey, that'll be Elvie in her labour pains'. And, sure enough, it was precisely when I was making my entry into this world.

In the first two years of my life, my paternal grandparents arrived from Scotland on a huge ocean liner called the Oriana. Nana was none too pleased by the Aussie heat, the beach sand, and the flies, but pressed on in this far-flung foreign land. She watched her beloved son build a dream home, with his own father pitching in.

The result was mid-century modern magnificence, built right on Brighton Beach. The smell of the bay was ever present, and everyone was abundantly happy.

I had teddy bears and dolls as siblings. There was never going to be a little brother or sister.

I was 4 years old in the joy of summer with my grandparents — Christmas filled with candy canes, hurriedly removed by my mother for fear I would turn out overweight.

Days whittled away in our new beach-bathing box, only steps across the Esplanade from our beautiful home. Yet Nana was restless. Within months, she and Papa were aboard the Oriana heading back to Scotland. For many years, the blue aerogramme letters were all that kept us in touch with our Highland folk. Telephone calls were restricted to birthdays and New Year, during which time all parties complained about how expensive it was to make the call.

My parents were full steam ahead in their careers and enrolled me at St Leonard's College: pre-kindergarten for the first 18 months. I was still far too young for actual kindergarten. Class began when I was five years old. I recognized my name on the 'peg'. Pegs were the precursor to lockers. a place for school satchels, hats, and blazers. On the adjacent peg was LC — she who was to be almost right many years later — and so began what should have been a lifelong friendship.

The school grounds were full of wonders. A fig tree so big I thought it reached to the moon. The enormous above-ground roots served to create cavities in which to conjure up mud pies as if we were cooking in a Parisian cordon bleu kitchen. Bright blue pinafores covered our uniforms to avoid dirt getting on our clothes. The pinafore would later double as a handy utilitarian item with which to tie boys to the shelter sheds. My new friend Leanne and I were the ringleaders of this lunchtime game of chance. If she could distract any of the unsuspecting boys and lure them towards the shed, I would spring out and use the pinnie-straps to secure them to a pole — long enough to kiss them. Amazingly, this early foray into bondage didn't result in any lifelong sexual kinks on my part. I cannot speak for Leanne.

I excelled at schoolwork all the way through my academic years. I relished learning, often pleading with my father on weekends to teach me any of the six languages he understood. A Japanese student joined our Grade 2 class. Kiko taught me how to count in Japanese, a skill I still hold, and opened my eyes to the wonders of other cultures. A lifelong travel bug may have started right there.

My parents were about to embark on a 6-week trip to Europe on a fashion-buying reconnaissance. I was not concerned with the prospect of time apart but more with where they were going… What, in fact, was 'Europe'? Driving down a steep hill with city lights twinkling, I naively asked, 'Mummy, is that the world in front of us now?' I clearly had a lot to learn.

On July 21st, 1969, our junior school congregated around a black and white television. Amidst the teacher's pleas for 'SHHHHH!', we heard a countdown with the echoed phrase, 'One giant leap for mankind'. Where were these men jumping in marshmallow-like white suits? What did NASA stand for?

I quizzed my father as he read the newspapers featuring Neil Armstrong. We gazed into the night sky as he pointed to where they landed, on that bright-white shiny globe called the moon. Even today, with SpaceX and Virgin Galactic, I find the concept mind-boggling.

Each time I fly, I do not question how it got off the ground or how high up we are — I am just consummately grateful to live and travel with ease.

Hector hit on the smart idea of conducting the bi-annual Elvie Hill fashion shows in our modern home. Invitations were issued to the loyal clientele, and Elvie's fashion consiglieri, Angela Brett and Phil McMaster, placed the women in their chairs. Probably not as strategic a place-setting as the Paris fashion shows for Chanel. Petite chicken sandwiches were served, and

Marie Antoinette's breast-shaped champagne glasses lined endless trays. Elvie started an additional label at this time called Young Elite. As the pièce de résistance, mother and I modelled matching outfits. Bright shantung silk adorned with rouleau fabric 'snail'-like flowers around the hems. Childhood modelling did not sit well with me. I did not like this kind of attention. Strange, given that in my career, I ended up on national television being watched by millions of people each week.

Those giddy modelling turns were not my first foray on the 'stage'.

At age 3, I was a flower girl at my cousin's wedding. During rehearsal and the pre-wedding photo shoot, I was very excited. In hindsight, this was due to the spectacle of the wedding and the event construction. I was a producer in the making. However, when it came to showtime — walking down the aisle, throwing rose petals ahead of the bride — I turned and ran like I was on fire.

Running out of rose petals and realizing I couldn't make it to the altar with enough floral detritus, I chose to turn and run instead.

My inner-Freud tells me this was a tell-tale sign of my attitude towards marriage and the act of walking down an aisle. After all, I had five of these moments to experience as a bride myself — didn't I?

Each Saturday morning, Elvie took me to swimming lessons. The smell of the chlorine is yet another olfactory memory. After class, I would accompany Mummy Dearest to her weekly hairdresser, cross-legged and impatient. My impatience was usually tempered by the purchase of a new doll or clothing item from the Mattel Barbie collection. There was Barbie, of course, but more importantly Skipper and Scooter and then… baby Tutti. I had to have her. I didn't have a sister, so I needed another doll.

Elvie said no.

It was six dollars. 'Do you know how much that is?' 'What is your point, Mummy?' Manipulative children kicking and screaming works in a public place — whatever point you are trying to get across. Tutti came home with me and joined her sisterhood with all the other Mattel characters, their wardrobes and accessories intact. And more than half a century later, thank you, Greta Gerwig, for realizing on screen those feelings for millions of girls.

My first recollection of going to the cinema was to see Mary Poppins at The Forum Theatre. I was dressed in a heavy wool coat with a velvet collar from Banbury Cross in Spring Street. Other than bespoke outfits from Elvie's own workroom, Banbury Cross was 'permitted' to dress me. Oh, what heady dreams my mother must have had for my future career in fashion. She was, except for a minor blip in the 1980s, left disappointed in that department.

As well as discovering cinema at this point, music made its most welcome arrival into my world. A little radio was closely followed by my own portable turntable.

My stepbrother Ashley was Beatles crazy. I gazed at the covers of 33 1/3 LPs and stayed quiet while he turned the discs. I vividly recall putting needle to vinyl for the first time, without scratching the precious disc. I can surmise that this early skill helped in proofing the hundreds of test pressings for releases on the Mushroom label years later.

Hector's first wife, Eve, had married a dashing surgeon, Stuart Esnouf. On learning of Elvie's pregnancy, Eve immediately ensured she too would soon deliver. Her daughter Durelle was born three months after me, so Ashley now had two stepsisters to contend with.

Elvie and Hector and Eve and Stuart saw each other socially — a modern European way of thinking. This egalitarian view never transferred to me wanting to hang out with any of my ex-husbands.

Meanwhile, Durelle and I occupied ourselves reading Enid Blyton's Famous Five and swimming in their pool.

Stuart Snr had a son, Stuart Jnr. He was a disproportionate six years older than me but the first boy I wanted to kiss. I was barely past double digits when LC's prediction of 'FABULOUS' started to emerge. My summer swimsuit was a halter-necked lime green Lycra one-piece. My budding boobs made me look more mature than my years, and I couldn't wait for Stuart to see me in this sizzling outfit.

He would surely appreciate my burgeoning 'womanhood' … until the swimsuit got wet. Only then did I understand the fabric was see-through and my other budding … in the pubic area … was on full display. He was never going to kiss me now as I blushed and ran inside. I hoped, like in the Famous Five, to find a cave to hide in and ride out this pubescent torment.

My father bought The Little Red Schoolbook, made popular in the early 1970s when parents didn't want to openly discuss sexual development with inquisitive children.

Shortly after my failed attempt at seduction with Stuart, I was walking with the Austrian nanny, Lonnie. I had been feeling uncomfortable at school in an unknowing kind of way. As I marched ahead, she exclaimed, 'Oh no, look sweetheart, you have blood on the back of your dress … die Schmach!'

We arrived home, and she marched me into the shower. Once cleansed, Lonnie dressed me in some bulky cotton padding, attached to my underwear with an elastic slingshot. I lay there, in my darkened bedroom, thinking

I must be dying. Lonnie thought I was sleeping, but I was inwardly dying, inside my young imagination. I lay in anguish until my parents arrived home. Mother rushed into my room in tears and gushed apologies. I did not know why she was apologizing, unless I was truly about to die.

The chapter on menstruation in *The Little Red Schoolbook* had alluded to me. Over the next few years, as my friends started to inherit this curse of womanhood, I was fully equipped to step up as their menstrual mentor and give them the drill. I taught Leanne about tampons — a long way from when we tied boys to the shelter sheds.

I took the book to school and read excerpts to the more 'mature' group of girls – the Beaumaris gang. They had older brothers; they must have known more than I did. We would debate what 'fucking' was and, of course, go on to do nothing about carrying out the unknown deed for years to come.

Across the road lived a sparky girl named Suzie, five years younger than me. I took my new guinea pig to show off. I was allowed this creature as part of a school experiment on animal welfare. The guinea pig was safely tucked in a shoebox.

I took the guinea pig out of the box, and Suzie's cat — quick as lightning — lunged. The crazed feline shook its victim with one dramatic sweep of its head, and that was the end of my guinea pig.

Time stood still. Suzie and I were both too stunned to move. Looking squarely like it had died of shock, my furry experiment lay motionless on the floor until Suzie's father came to the rescue. He ushered the lifeless guinea pig back into the box, blood dripping from its severed arteries, and accompanied me back home.

As adolescence blossomed, there were bike rides along the Brighton train line with the first boy I did kiss. Andrew had enveloping blue eyes. Those dreamy looks provided a benchmark for my 'type' going forward. Always look deep into a man's eyes — therein lies the truth. One of my husbands had cautious beady eyes — I dropped my benchmark with him.

Music defines eras of memory at every stage. This is a universal truth. Music soothes us as individuals in quiet times — through happiness and heartache. It serves us in unifying people across festivals and special family events. I feel privileged to have forged a career from one of humanity's most important tools.

I can recall where I was when I first heard an array of tunes that have become commonplace in my adult universe. The chapter titles of this book all indicate that.

I first heard Russell Morris' 'The Real Thing' by Andrew's house. It is with a touch of irony that my desire to play tracks repeatedly developed with a song produced by Ian 'Molly' Meldrum. Years later, when I moved into Molly's house, the mantra was 'Just once more, lovey!'.

My portable record player got a workout with The Monkees. For my birthday I received no less than seven copies of the same single — my friends knew me well. The local record store happily exchanged the duplicates for other chart hits. The Carpenters, The Jackson 5 and then The Partridge Family.

TV afternoons were filled with H.R. Pufnstuf, Gilligan's Island, Get Smart, The Monkees and then … him.

David Cassidy. My love knew no boundaries.
In the 1970s, there were no recordable VHS tapes or DVDs. It was 4.30 pm Monday to Friday or miss out. Each episode was a new explosive thirty minutes of … him.

Davy Jones and The Monkees had been a test run compared to this God of Masculinity.

I waited impatiently to get the latest issue of the fanzine Tiger Beat from America. Each photo of David Cassidy was carefully taped to the back door of my closet. I could speak to him at night of how someday we would meet and fall in love.

Around this time, my father was also broadening my musical influences. He bought a state-of-the-art sound system that dominated the living room, accompanied by huge headphones that resembled Princess Leia's hairdo in Star Wars.

His tastes were thankfully broad — Ella Fitzgerald to Little Feat. Lou Reed to Burt Bacharach.

One Saturday morning father handed me an album featuring a pensively handsome bearded man sitting at a piano. The only words gracing the black & white cover—in lowercase no less—read 'Brian Cadd'. It was 1972; I was pining for David Cassidy but had a new crush on Johnny Farnham's 'Don't You Know It's Magic'. I now learned this was the man who wrote the song. My favorite on the album became 'Fairweather Friend'.

I looked deep into the album cover and felt an extrasensory perception come over me. It had no name or time or words, just a profound feeling, different from the teen lust of my idols. Some internal 'knowing' of a connection that could not be fathomed in that moment.

Hector's musical taste extended to exploratory theatre. We flew to Sydney for 'Hair'. Opening in 1969, it played to sold-out houses curious to witness this progressive production. As we settled in, I smelt something unfamiliar. 'What is that smell, Dad?' I asked. 'Where is it coming from?'

Some switched-on patrons were smoking joints in the auditorium. This night unknowingly set me up for an open-minded future. If I didn't know what the word 'fuck' meant when I discovered The Little Red Schoolbook, I certainly found out after seeing Hair. A spellbinding woman named Marcia Hines had a skin color and funky attitude I had never witnessed before. How could I learn to be as magnificent as her?

I started to wonder if I could sing and perform. Gone was the shyness I felt as a flower girl. Now I wanted to be a girl wearing flowers in her hair and smelling that marijuana aroma again.

Casting 'Hair' for Harry Miller's revival 30 years later, I told the producing maestro my story and later to my friend, the divine Marcia Hines. Marcia came to Australia aged 16 and pregnant and forged an exemplary career for herself. I had the honor of working with her on Long Way to the Top and learned so much from her feminine energy and wisdom.

Before ABC TV's Countdown started in 1974, the must-watch music show was Hey, Hey It's Saturday. This originally aired Saturday mornings before switching to nighttime variety.

Hey, Hey held promotional competitions. I won Sunbury's triple live album– Mushroom Records' first long-form release, no less. Who was this musical monster yelling 'Oop Poo Pah Doo', and what the hell did that mean?

I had discovered Billy Thorpe. The Sunbury Music Festival had launched in 1972, only a couple of years after Woodstock had set the bar high for multi-act, multi-day music festivals worldwide.

The image on the cover of Sunbury Live shone like a beacon. The idea of rolling, open country fields and people shapeshifting themselves to frequency-bending music resonated in my very young brain. How is it we can visualize our future without really understanding what it is or when it will take shape?

I have not yet used the word 'precocious' to describe myself. Here it comes.

On March 8, 1974, I caught a taxi to Elvie Hill's Collins Street boutique. In that bastion of haute couture, I was outfitted in a navy & white gingham full-length ensemble. The occasion was the TV Week Logie Awards at the

Southern Cross Hotel. How did a 13-year-old get invited to the Logies? I didn't.

Trussed up like Cinderella, my parents drove me to the hotel. I instructed them to wait. Insert precocious with a capital P.

Celebrities were amassing outside the hotel's ballroom for the awards ceremony, televised on the Nine Network.

The reason for this façade of maturity, and the demands placed on my unwitting parents, was for one reason … David Cassidy.

My beloved had been brought to Australia to tour for Harry M. Miller. Cassidy, aka my future husband, was a celebrity guest at the Logies ahead of his show at the MCG. This was my one chance to have him confirm our love for each other, sweep me into his arms, and take me back to his love shack in LA. What could go wrong?

I milled around, trying to look important, taller, and thinner. Inside the vestibule by the ballroom, my eyes searched for David. He was nowhere in sight. All I got was a pinch on the bum by a Channel Nine announcer. Then came a flurry of excitement and photographers' flashbulbs. He was here! I raced out to the foyer as he descended the stairs in a white tuxedo with diamanté lapels.

Don't faint now, don't faint now.

But wait, who was that glamorous woman on his arm? Her uber-cool vibe is palpable, but her face is unrecognizable. This phantom lucky lady was wearing Ray-Ban sunglasses at night, just like the song goes.

Wow, I wanted to be her. What kind of job did she have that she got to be so close to David Cassidy? I knew it wasn't his girlfriend — he didn't have one.

OK, come on, I was only 13, and I could dream there was no one else but me.

Back to this feminine steel trap attached to David's side. How could I secure that job when I finished school?

The moment was at hand. I had to move fast. I lunged towards David, and as our eyes met, the back of uber-cool publicist-to-the-stars Patti Mostyn's hand met my neck and shoulder, pushing me aside. I reeled from the shock of the blow. I was right beside David Cassidy. David Bruce Cassidy — only to have it wrenched away from me by this … this WOMAN, even though I secretly admired her style.

I vowed revenge.

I waited many years, but eventually I got it — in spades.

I couldn't leave the venue. 'He' was now in the room, the same room as me. I was terrified. In my tiny mind, I had made up an elaborate story if anyone asked why I was there. I mentally manufactured a white lie that I was a distant relative of Ruth Aarons, David's American publicist. Then I found my mark. David travelled with his best friend, Sam Hyman, and photographer Henry Diltz. Not only was David in the room, but also the very man who took every luscious photo of my idol for Tiger Beat magazine. They both miraculously appeared minutes after Patti had swooped David away. Henry was a wide-eyed dude who appeared under the influence of 'God's herb', as he names it. His chosen moniker for marijuana was described to me in person after we became friends, 44 years later, through Woodstock and Michael Lang.

Dejected, but enlivened by the world of celebrity, I descended to my waiting parents. The drive home was a brutal reality check, only broken by my parents' occasional audible sniggering.

The ironic end to this tale is that also present in the Southern Cross Ballroom that night was Brian Cadd.

The guy in black & white on the album cover who looked longingly into my eyes in 1972, the very same. He possibly brushed past me. We will never know.

Soon after my Logies adventure, I got to realize my dream of international travel. Hector organized a round-the-world trip. This was, in essence, a fabric-buying trip for Elvie Hill. The only snag was my mother came down with the nervous disorder shingles, so Dad and I travelled alone.

My father saw an opportunity to publicize Elvie's label, contacting the media with the preposterous story of a 13-year-old schoolgirl embarking on an international fashion-buying spree.

A phone call came while I was in art class; I was to be taken to Elvie's Toorak Road boutique. There I was met by my anxious, PR-shy mother and the ABC film crew. Seeing myself on television was affirmation I was going to be FABULOUS. The Age and Herald newspapers followed the story in print.

Our first-class all-the-way trip commenced. LA was much more than Disneyland for me. Driving up Sunset Blvd, I marvelled at the size of the billboards – advertising Elton John's new Caribou album and movies like The Sting. The sun shone, palm trees swayed and at the ripe old age of 13, I had drunk the Kool-Aid and knew I wanted to make this my home, someday…

We arrived in London on July 29 as the radio reported Mama Cass had died. Salacious stories of the fabled choking on a sandwich riddled the airwaves. My father was reflectively sad at this news and pontificated about the musical legacy she left, something about 'Laurel Canyon'. He revised my musical education with Little Feat and Joni Mitchell by reminding me that Laurel Canyon was the hallowed musical ground above Sunset Blvd. Another cup of ephemeral Kool-Aid willed me to become part of that infamous artists' enclave.

At our London hotel check-in, Hector bumped into a chap he clearly knew. This jovial man had a broad Scottish accent. After much 'old times' backslapping, my father's accent became more broadly Scottish as the conversation evolved. We ascended by elevator, and the gentlemen bid each other adieu. As I had not been introduced, I asked Dad about his friend.

'Well, dear, that was an actor, Sean Connery. He plays James Bond; I knew him in the old days'. You're kidding, Dad, that broad-Scottish-accented, bald, out-of-shape guy? That was James Bond? Lesson #1 in appearances being deceptive.

We shopped in Harrods and took tea at Fortnum & Mason. To this day, I drink only Fortnum & Mason Earl Grey. We caught the train to Fort William and into the loving arms of my grandparents and extended Scottish family. We drove around the Highlands with my grandfather Angus, visiting Dunoon, where both Hector and the gelato business were born. Papa paid a visit to an old friend who ran the local newspaper, and our visit was put in print. On retelling tales of his time in Dunoon, the newsman reminded Angus of the beautiful black horse he had when he met his bride, Mamie. My grandfather stared skyward with a loving look and said, 'Aye, she was a beautiful horse'.

On the drive back home, Hector pointed out a tree growing from a large rock. He spun the tale that he had peed there as a boy and undoubtedly made the tree grow from the strength of his urine! After 38 years, on the release of the Bond film 'Skyfall', my stepbrother was convinced the very same tree was in a film scene. To give some credit, we did know filming took place in that exact Scottish location. Sadly, Hector didn't live to see his botanical creation on celluloid, let alone express an opinion on the 'new' James Bond.

We crossed the English Channel from Dover to Calais by ferry. The smell of Gauloise cigarettes made me vomit all over my newly purchased Burberry coat. As I infrequently partake of the same tobacco blend nowadays in Paris, its aroma only evokes happy memories.

My introduction to Paris was a cultural revelation as I made use of my schoolgirl French. 'Une baguette jambon et fromage s'il vous plait', I sprayed with confidence at Café Église Madeleine. That wistful 'flaneur' mentality hit me instantaneously in the City of Light. Despite its stark contrast to Los Angeles, I was overwhelmed by its beauty and cultural depth. My allegiances fluctuated. Could I live in this bohemian paradise? What would my future look like — a French husband, peut-être?

In Monte Carlo Hector planned to spend an evening at the Casino, as one does. Reminder: I was only 13 years old on this trip. I had bought a very daring backless summer dress in London. As we ascended the stairs to the casino, my father whispered to me, 'Take my arm and don't say anything, just smile'.

He confidently addressed security guards: 'Ma femme et moi avons une reservation pour le diner'. With my smattering of French, I knew my father just called me his wife. I smiled sweetly, and in we ventured.

The glamour of it all was intoxicating. I would repeat that walk with my son 47 years later, holding his arm and telling him the tale of his cheeky grandfather.

In Italy, we visited relatives in the hills above Viareggio, Tuscany. Solo pedo no veicoli … a town so small it is pedestrian only. The enclave of Verni was entered by a series of broad steps. The village hailed from the early 16th century, when its sister town Viareggio became the only gate to the sea for the 'Republic of Lucca'. My father had spent some months here as a young boy. I was not captivated by Italy as I had been by France. Relatives told long tales of the Pellicci and Grilli families as I imagined all their struggles during wartime and beyond. As mentioned in my introduction, imagine the historical hardships in decades before the technology that keeps us alive and connected today. I bowled in as a strong Pellicci young woman and stomped the maize to make polenta in the town square, grateful my grandfather's journey to Scotland had led to this moment here in my early life.

On to the business purpose of the trip, the next stop was Switzerland for fabric purchases. We were greeted at haute fabric house Schlaepfer by André Krechenski. A super-smooth European gentleman, like actor Curt Jurgens, I recalled him from his visits to Elvie Hill each alternate year with suitcases full of swatches. Velvet, brocade, delicate sheer silks … and now, by some strange fate, here I was in Switzerland choosing colors for next season's range. In hindsight, this trip proceeded without Elvie as a way of coercing me into the fashion industry. I was destined to take over the business my parents had toiled to build up. But the fact was — I am not Elvie Hill. I do not know an inseam from a peplum collar and had no desire to learn the difference.

Back home to Brighton and back to school. I planted my feet firmly in teen angst reality, but my head was in the American and Parisian clouds.

My interest in writing and turning music into visual representations led to a Super 8 short movie accompanying Elton John's 'Funeral for a Friend'. There was a fruit farm on the Mornington Peninsula my father was trying to buy. Dad and I filmed in the orchard's dilapidated house — no roof and bird shit all over abandoned furnishings. Eerie and spooky, the experience melded Hector's and my love of music and film. We spent hours splicing the footage together over that winter, and sadly I have no idea where the film is now.

My mother took a photo of Dad and me wandering the property. It instills the essence of our father-daughter relationship. That faded Kodak print has cropped up in my life in some very strange ways.

More music dominated these teen years — Gary Glitter, Suzi Quatro, T. Rex and The Sweet's 'Ballroom Blitz' were heard at Melinda's house. America's 'A Horse with No Name', Crosby, Stills, & Nash at Gretchen's house. Seeing Frank Zappa at Festival Hall with LC, closely followed by David Essex. Joe Cocker with the Mad Dogs and Englishmen tour at the Myer Music Bowl was a revelation. Materializing a life in music became a constant thought.

I hadn't fallen out of love with David Cassidy. I discovered more on the stylish lady accompanying him at the Logie Awards. She was Patti Mostyn, the leading publicist in Australia. I started to fantasize that this music PR game might be the career for me.

My education had taken an all-girls' turn into Merton Hall. I thrived. This school was everything, with magnificent teachers like Miss Deane Turner for English literature and Rev. Stuart Blackler for religious studies. It was quite the scandal when the school returned from summer break to discover they had married! Even more thrilling was a new set of friends at the reciprocal boys' school at MGS: Grammar.

Having completed a few years of Saturday morning drama at the National Theatre in St Kilda, I fell easily into drama groups on both campuses. We performed Shakespeare in the Quad. I made a great 3rd Witch in Macbeth. My friend Vivienne played the lead. She was magnificent.

I recited the poem 'I love a Sunburnt Country' by Dorothea Mackellar – dressed in my mother's bathrobe and hair curlers, smoking a cigarette on stage. Shocking. Not the cigarette but more my performance. A swift end to my acting career, affirmed by director Jack Keogh and thespian colleagues like Humphrey Bower, Michael Veitch and Tom Bishop.

I harboured a desire to sing. I listened to a wide range of music and still remember the lyrics to thousands of songs. I was fortunate to meet Evie Hayes. Madame Hayes was a judge on the TV show Young Talent Time, so she knew how to spot talent. I was her new pupil. YTT created superstars from their regular talent crew. From there sprang John Bowles, Debbie Byrne, Tina Arena and Dannii Minogue. It was hosted by Johnny Young, who had written 'The Real Thing' for Russell Morris. My father reasoned if Miss Hayes would tutor me, then I could achieve a spot on the show. This was way before American Idol or The Voice. One Saturday I was taken to Evie Hayes' home. Terrified, I sang for her.

At the end of the lesson my father was summoned to the room for Evie's analysis of my talents. Put simply, she said, 'Mr Pelman, it is my firm opinion you shouldn't waste your money on singing lessons for Amanda'.

I vowed revenge, just like I did with Patti Mostyn. More than 30 years later I got it. Worth the wait.

A girl I had been in kindergarten with was now at Merton Hall. Caro was a glamorous girl who had an older brother, Martin. They lived a kind of bohemian life with their mother in an apartment. We were all permitted to come and go from there as we pleased. This was an entirely different family and social structure from my home. The music memory arch here was Linda Ronstadt. A sophisticated girl named Deborah Conway was friends with Caro's brother. As early friendship bloomed, we were united in song. We sang in unison into our hairbrushes, songs from Ronstadt's Hasten Down the Wind album. I met Deborah again many years later, which proved those days were 'only the beginning' of a beautiful friendship.

I lost my virginity at Caro's house one Sunday afternoon. No romance, almost transaction-like. I only knew I wanted to understand what bodies together would feel like. Well, that didn't happen. All over in a flash, as they say.

The boy, who shall remain nameless, was even more nervous than me. On reflection, it was probably his first time. A memory that should be stamped with a hand-drawn love heart is recalled with his verbal dominance.

The importance of his masculinity had no doubt been put in his head by his father, a brother or a porno magazine. Was this meant to turn me on or just make him feel superior?

Moments like this in our lives should teach us to stop and ask questions. To quote Sherlock Holmes, 'It is easy to be wise after the event'. Why don't humans stop and reflect IN the moment instead of afterwards? It would surely avoid a hell of a lot of angst.

I know the whereabouts of this 'virginity thief', as we were in a similar business. I have absolutely no interest in discussing the ten minutes that took place and landed us in each other's sordid histories.

Such a shame for many; the moment you are supposed to launch into an entirely new branch of your being, you are left underwhelmed and under-gratified.

Thankfully, I was to make up for that very soon afterwards. And I still am….

CHAPTER 2: RADIO DAYS

My final school years were magical. I was in love with two boys in extremely different ways. I hesitate to call it a love triangle, as there was never any hint of group sex.

They were best friends, and then I came along, in a good way, I believe.

Humph and I were BOFs — birds of a feather. We related on every cerebral level. Our music was Peter Gabriel and Genesis, Cream, Brian Eno, Pink Floyd… the list went on. Our words were Kahlil Gibran. Our handwritten letters to each other were written daily. The depth and love in these missives make me against conducting relationships by text in these days of WhatsApp. I still have the packaged bundles of inky revelations four decades later.

My relationship with David was entirely different from the get-go. It was carnal and seductive and secretive.

David and I were able to walk between our homes via back streets after dark, when that was both safe and a 'thing'. I conveniently had an external door leading to my bedroom. Designed by my father as the laundry outlet for the maids, not for clandestine teenage meetings. I could sneak out and visit David in his bedroom bungalow.

David and I pursued many an 'afternoon delight' in bed and on the watermelon carpet, ending before my parents would arrive home.

We were in love, so when he took a study trip to Germany over the Christmas break, I was devastated. This time, however, served to solidify my relationship with BOF Humph. We spent time at his family's holiday home in Red Hill — our minds and hearts both full. His parents were devastatingly handsome people, physically and intellectually. His father, Herbert, was a psychiatrist who consulted with transgender patients to assist in gender reassignment. In the late 1970s, this was a groundbreaking new field. His mother, Roz, was a journalist who sadly succumbed to cancer.

Ensemble a tout, we would sit outside in the blazing Aussie sun, smeared in baby oil lotion as a tanning device, drinking rosé wine from a cask, and reading the afternoon away. I saw this as the height of sophistication and vowed to live my adult life evoking their 'joie de vie'. Sans baby oil, less cask, I definitively do.

Reading Kafka, Rousseau and Maupassant had me attracted to the cerebral side of life. Vivienne was a dramatist who had a quirky bent — she only wears yellow. Angharad was English with Welsh heritage. She was everything I could have hoped for in a sister. She remains so to this day. Emblazoned with a similar wit, 'Harry' was the only contemporary I knew who was in no doubt about her future. We both had a take-life-by-the-balls attitude and a desire to live outside of our adolescent Melbourne bubble.

Having missed out on our family trip in '74, my parents and I had a great American journey in '77. I was back in the land I wanted to adopt as my home. We met a cosmopolitan Australian couple and explored California and the Grand Canyon. Barbie was a dynamo who became a mélange of older sister and confidante. Her husband Richard flew us in a small aircraft over the Canyon — a mesmerizing experience. They lived opposite my school in South Yarra.

Barbie gave me my long-standing nickname, 'Amanda the Panda'. Her dearest friend was Olivia Newton-John. Olivia's mom, Irene, was a force of nature. I met Olivia as an impressionable young teen, not imagining how our paths would cross again many years later. Her beautiful smile and abundant happiness were what made her not only a music superstar but also an admirable friend.

Barbie was also friends with a restaurateur and TV personality — aka car salesman — Dennis Gowing. Kevin Dennis' New Faces was a TV show in the milieu of Young Talent Time and a forerunner of Idol and The Voice. Dennis owned a mansion in Toorak named Whernside. Built in 1876, it was one of Melbourne's first European-style mansion homes, overwhelming both in size and the style of its owner. Barb and I would visit frequently — after Dennis' divorce, she became a surrogate sister. My inkling for 'Fabulous' was enthralled by the collection of Sidney Nolan paintings and old-fashioned Chubb safe, re-fashioned as a champagne chamber.

Dennis had a rule: he didn't drink on Wednesdays. His daughter, Samantha, was 14 at the time. That summer she got a terrible sunburn, so Barbie and I swathed her back in chilled tomato pieces to calm her down.

Dennis and I became quite flirtatious with each other. I felt a huge desire towards him as an older man. After the first lost-virginity stumble and the heated passion with David, Dennis promised more adult excitement and certainly surprise. He was 49, and I was about to turn 18. His celebrity had nothing to do with my attraction; he was simply enigmatic. In bed together it felt wonderful as well as transient. I must emphasize I was not 'groomed'.

In today's horrendous environment of Epstein, Weinstein and #MeToo, I can honestly say in my case this was NOT the case. I knew what I was doing. Dennis would drive me to Grammar on an odd Sunday morning for Quad Drama rehearsal. In his Rolls-Royce. I don't think my fellow thespians even noticed.

I never let on.

There was no big parting of the ways with Dennis; it just waned. I do thank him for giving me an 'anything is possible in life, kid' attitude to live by. In his eyes, I was becoming FABULOUS.

As most young girls did, I kept a diary. I wrote poetically about standing in a Whernside window wearing Dennis' robe looking out to the grounds.

My mother became suspicious with the amount of time I was spending at Barbie's home. She betrayed any confidence we could have held between us by reading my diarized thoughts without permission. She confronted me when I went to her Flinders Lane workroom. What could I say that was not a lie to her vitriolic retelling of my diary to my face? She threatened to jump off the fifth-story stairwell to a certain death if I didn't vow it would end. I turned to look at my father for some level of support, and I got it. I reassured my dramatic couturier mother that it was a passing phase, but she was welcome to jump if it was too much to handle that her daughter was sexually active.

My next 'relationship' was the opposite of Dennis Gowing. From mature and humorous to immature and sullen. He was the son of theatre owners whose parents had built the Princess Theatre.

There were always lots of marvellous theatrical types around their home. Actors and actresses and designer John Truscott, who won an Academy Award for Camelot. One other delightful attendee was Loretta, who went on to marry GJ's best buddy, Michael, many years later. She was the essence of groovy and a little older than us.

GJ loved dope. He smoked joints day in, day out and this would be the only time in my early years that I indulged periodically in weed, 420, the devil's lettuce … His father smoked as much as he did, and GJ was the official family joint roller. His mother, Annie, on the other hand, loved a drink, so I joined her in champagne and American L&M cigarettes, the height of sophistication.

Our soundtrack to this ill-fated liaison was Fleetwood Mac's Tusk. Emanating from his parents' room was the hefty smell of smoke aligned with a TV flickering repeats of Mel Brooks' The Producers. Garnett Snr watched this film over and over, and I wondered how Annie ever got to sleep with the TV blaring in the bedroom, her eye mask firmly pressed over her beautiful face.

Year 12 was filled with prep for exams and drama rehearsal. I became exhausted. Directing and producing plays at school was my drug. Arguing with the teachers that I needed a bigger budget was so much fun and, as it turns out, a taste of things to come.

I didn't quite know how exhausted I had become until a blood test revealed I had glandular fever. Being highly contagious, I was not allowed to attend school for the last few months. Early in senior year, everyone contemplated their advanced education choices. I had decided to attend a new course at RMIT — 'Media Studies'. The fallout from no exam results would potentially end any college degree. My headmistress spoke to the Dean, Jack Clancy, and submitting my aggregate grades, I was granted a place. We met on campus and discussed Luis Buñuel and the merits of Werner Herzog.

RMIT was marvellous. There was student radio, and as a communications major, I thought it prudent to go and check out the scene. The radio signal had been 3RRR, and a license had recently been granted that meant they would become commercial, after which the in-campus signal became known as 3ST. It was essentially three large rooms atop Building 6, facing onto Swanston Street. In there was a transmission studio, an office and an audio library that looked woefully understocked. All our music was on vinyl, not even cassette. I felt useful here; I subliminally knew how to create organizationally.

I sought out local record company reps to add to our music collection and our interview hours. One of the first people I met was a PolyGram Records rep, Michael Shephard. 'Mimi' was one of the sweetest, kindest and most caring souls you could ever know. And boy, he knew how to laugh. I would visit his office and leave with the week's chart-toppers. Our friendship was cemented by the toss of a 12-inch EP into an elevator. I paid an eager visit to PolyGram the week 'Fade to Grey' by Visage was released in the UK. This new disco glam fabulousness was yet to hit Aussie radio, and I pleaded for a copy. Mimi was adamant I couldn't have it before Molly Meldrum at Countdown. I couldn't compete with our music institution, let alone its host. I left dejected as Mimi rushed towards the elevator and threw the Visage

12" to me. Mimi was the first person to put belief in me that I could break a record on the airwaves. He played a pivotal role in my life up until the day he died in 2014.

Slowly, more labels and PR people took our radio station seriously as we had a good captive audience on campus. We needed more 'staff'. First there was Tony and his mate Les. New on campus, they were eager beavers and added huge technical skill to the station.

I wooed and met the publicists. Suzie Howie, who not only covered music PR but also musical theatre. A total firebrand of a woman, her passion for her work was off the Richter scale.

Then came my old nemesis: Patti Mostyn. What good luck made it possible that I would meet the woman who stole David Cassidy away from me in 1974? Here was my opportunity to remind her of that night, when my dream of a future life in LA with my idol was laid bare by her swift hand.

Boz Scaggs was all the rage. He was touring, and a media scrum was to be held at fashionable Mietta's Restaurant off Collins Street.

This time I did not need to attend my mother's boutique to be dressed for combat. I was FABULOUS of my own making. Long brown hair, a jean jacket and suede boots — in I strolled. Patti came to greet me. All smiles, glistening white teeth and more gold bracelets than Mata Hari. 'Darling', she swooped, 'haven't we met before?' Yes, I replied — 'on March 8 1974, at the Southern Cross Hotel … the Logie Awards, when you smacked me in the face to prevent me from talking to David Cassidy'.

Boom. Mic drop. FABULOUS.

As fate would have it, Boz Scaggs heard the whole exchange. He stifled a laugh, made some clever comment and I watched Patti's face drop like a stone.

My relationship with Patti Mostyn gained much broader depth as the years went on.

Other than the radio station, I wrote for the college paper, Catalyst. I interviewed Joan Armatrading and Janis Ian, women with musical integrity and female purpose. I vowed to be more like them. I juggled my coursework with radio and print interviews. Suzie Howie mailed fake Ansett Airlines boarding passes to announce the arrival of The Tourists on tour — Annie Lennox and Dave Stewart. Annie was a woman with piercing eyes and Scottish determination that made you feel enervated just by being in her presence. On the opposite side of the spectrum was Debbie Harry — sadly, a drunken mess, dancing on tables in the Southern Cross Hotel. Truth be known, I hoped I would morph into a mixture of all the amazing women I interviewed. While I had no ability as a performer, I sensed their combined feminine energy had something to teach me. Their devil was in the detail and their deeds. They dressed for themselves with daring panache. They fronted causes that previously had no voice. How could I not be guided by them down my very own yellow brick road….

In my second year, I focused on film work and wrote a piece on Woody Allen, specifically his newest cinematic masterpiece, Manhattan. After I discovered Woody Allen, every one of his films left me reeling. The wit, comedic timing and characters — it all played out to me as a life yearned to be lived. Somehow, someday. I wanted to be Annie Hall. I was Annie Hall. La de dah. La de dah.

My obsession with Woody Allen lingered, and in 1985, I would get to meet my film hero.

I was procuring records for the radio archives and granted film preview tickets. I liked to focus on Australian film and met a gifted actress, Tracy Mann, when she starred in Hard Knocks. We did a lengthy interview and got on famously. She invited me to stay at her home if I should ever venture to Sydney. I took her up on the offer, garnering more interviews and material for the radio station.

Adding to the allure was hanging with Tracy in her Bondi apartment. After drinks and lively discussion, she bade me goodnight with an afterthought, 'Oh, if a guy tries to get into bed with you later in the night, don't worry, it's only Steve; he is on a night shoot'. Cool! This I am going to stay awake for. Unfortunately, sleep got the better of me, and 'Steve' never materialized. It was only in the morning that I learned I had missed the chance of 'sleeping' with Steve Bisley, who had been out filming Mad Max with his friend Mel Gibson and director George Miller. Many years later, Steve and I became Balmain 'neighbours', so I told him of this near miss in our lives.

Mimi from PolyGram Records and I remained firm friends. We shared a love of music, hairdos and going out to dance. I didn't understand at the time that he had issues with alcohol. I had grown up in a house where I was given a glass here and there, with no frequent wine at dinner. His environment had not been the same. He had a friend known as Uschi. As a hairdresser, she made us look beyond fabulous; we could have adorned magazine covers.

Barbie took me skiing. In an après-ski nightclub, I met Molly Meldrum, the special guest DJ. Of course, like all decent music-loving adolescents, I had grown up watching Countdown on Sunday nights. Molly was born

Ian Meldrum in country Victoria. He was affable and totally lived in the moment, more than anyone I had ever met.

For one fun-filled night we really hit it off as I helped unwrap the discs he was spinning. Here was another spellbinding moment in my early life, much like the 'Brian Cadd' album cover moment. I could not shake the feeling Meldrum and I were going to meet again.

Mimi nurtured disco music imports for PolyGram. One huge hit was 'Stars on 45'. The track didn't have a video, so Mimi created a dance troupe to perform it 'live'. I went to the studio to support him. My friend LC tagged along.

When time came for taping, more than half the dancers had not turned up. Here I was again in a room with Molly Meldrum.

Molly turned to me and said, 'If you don't dance, you will never work in this town again!' Dance I did.

Stars on 45 remained at #1 for six weeks.

Every week I got to see myself dancing on Sunday night TV. Over the ensuing years I went on to dance anytime, anywhere, to any tune or whim Molly Meldrum ever told me again. Period.

It was the beginning of a beautiful friendship.

Michael Shephard employed me for 'work experience' with PolyGram. This led to meeting a band I truly revered.

Dire Straits released Communiqué in 1979, which became part of my life soundtrack. Purists amongst my friends wouldn't accept them as reverentially as other '70s prog-rock icons, but I loved the poetic-like songwriting.

'Wild West End' — I visualized walking down Shaftesbury Avenue with Mark Knopfler. In the lyrics he sang about a 'go-go dancing girl', adding, 'Here's Mandy for ya'. Yes — I could be that 'Mandy'. Despite the fact I despised the name. For all my teenage dreams of Los Angeles and Paris, I started shifting my life cycle mind's eye towards London.

My musical mind's eye reverted to making my own movie to Elton John's 'Funeral for a Friend' in 1973. With the release of Making Movies in 1980, promoter Garry Van Egmond announced a tour. The number of shows swelled with the success of the album. Every show was stand-alone amazing, the crowd enraptured with the advanced arena sound system the band perfected.

In Melbourne after the first of five shows, the band, crew and hangers-on repaired to the Southern Cross Hotel. This was the very hotel that was the scene of the David Cassidy near-miss in 1974. Now I was walking through the halls with Dire Straits. Mark Knopfler drank red wine; he loved the Australian heavy, earthy reds. Guitarist Hal Lindes had split his jeans — mid-crotch and mid-song — so I became a willing seamstress. Joop de Korte, a man of many touring talents, was the court jester and kept us laughing until the early hours.

I continued the rock 'n' roll road with them to Sydney, this time at the Sebel Townhouse Hotel.

Garry Van Egmond was a charming gentleman with a sophistication that belied his profession as a rock 'n' roll impresario. He thankfully accepted my PolyGram tag-along status. I spent my 20th birthday with Dire Straits on the road in Sydney. Mark had started writing an opus called 'Telegraph Road', which he noodled away at after shows. Clocking in at 14 minutes, it became a clarion call for the next album, Love Over Gold.

I was nearing the end of my Bachelor of Arts degree and began to formulate a thesis. As my college years progressed, I had grown restless to begin my life in the wider world.

I figured if I chose a topic that included travel, I could vamoose out of Melbourne. I submitted the topic 'Comparison of album release marketing strategies between record companies in Australia and the UK'. Boom! Genius.

I had wanted to write my thesis in Los Angeles, but my father rejected the idea of any move to the US. I felt powerless to argue. That one decision on his part totally changed the course of my life. Literally for better and for worse.

London 1974

The Fur and Jewels as Predicted

Clive Hodson and Michael Shephard PolyGram Records days

Elvie Hill Collins Street

Graduating Bachelor of Arts

With my father on Mornington Peninsula 1971

David Cassidy and Patti Mostyn

Angharad at Botanical Gardens at MCEGGS

Interviewing Boz Scaggs for Radio 3ST

Inner Hippie

CHAPTER 3: WALKING IN THE WILD WEST END

Arrangements were made, and I flew to London, into the unknown. Before departure, I penned a letter to Dire Straits manager Ed Bicknell, heralding my arrival and begging for a job. I wrote, 'I will dust the gold albums and make the tea …' I lived in hope I could work in their management office.

Michael Shephard arranged for me to meet and interview various record company personnel attached to PolyGram UK. I went to Bell Records and loved the fact that this was David Cassidy's record label.

Luckily, Ed Bicknell responded, saying that I could indeed come and sort out all the band's press clippings and perform any other secretarial and menial tasks required. I was ecstatic. For initiation into Damage Management, he took me to lunch at the Ho Lee Fook restaurant on Kings Road. I was introduced to the demi-monde of rock & roll London society. Ed Bicknell's reputation precedes him. At times I wonder if the Spinal Tap character Ian Faith was based on Ed, given the film was released in 1984. He was generous and funny and gave me a great life lesson in how to be a manager and treat your clients. I may not have turned out as successful an act as Dire Straits, but I will always relish my time with those lucky lads.

My school friend Angharad had moved back to London ahead of going to Oxford. We hatched a plan to get an abode together and stumbled on a top-floor apartment on Hyde Park Square. Humphrey had been accepted into Oxford, so we occasionally drove out into the countryside together, all the while singing Peter Gabriel's 'Solsbury Hill'.

I submitted my thesis and figured I better get on with life.

The Hyde Park apartment was one bedroom and cheap.

My time with Dire Straits came to an end; they were on hiatus, so no more office work.

Together before Christmas, Angharad and I marched up Oxford Street trying to find work in retail to pay the bills.

She landed a job at Selfridges. I stumbled on, turned right at Regent Street, and went into Jaeger — a high-end fashion store.

If I had turned left, my life would have been very different.

As George Michael sang, 'Turn a different corner and we never would have met'.

I landed a job as a Jaeger salesperson. My mother was thrilled I was giving the fashion industry a chance. In the Jaeger basement was a stockroom for replenishing the frilly blouses and accessories we sold. People who worked down there were not permitted on the sales floor.

In my first week I descended in the elevator to re-stock. As I collected a bunch of belts and bags, a male voice said to me, 'Belt up … ha, ha … get it?!' I looked up to see a sheepish boy who was one of the delivery van drivers.

I responded, quoting the Chrissie Hynde lyric, 'Bad boys get spanked'.

Sometime later, this man-child named Clive asked me out on a date. He was barely out of acne and clearly had never appreciated a professional haircut. He offered to drive me home, claiming his car was his first love. I was not to know all his vehicles would remain in that lofty position for life.

Angharad and I threw a party in our Hyde Park hovel — fancy dress, no less. Through the winter cold, forty people arrived and trudged up our four flights of stairs. That night certainly gave birth to my love of entertaining and flowing good times. Clive arrived, never imagining he would end up in a room full of Oxford intellectuals. Clive confessed his surname was Goose. The timeline of our relationship started there — a boy from 'the other side of the track' and an upper-middle-class Melbourne girl living in New Romantic London in the early 1980s. Of course, everyone thought I was mad; I must have been mad. What did he have to offer me? Well, only one thing comes to mind. Surely, I would tire of him soon enough.

Elvie was thrilled when I telephoned from the red phone box on Regent Street to tell her what the next season's fashion colors and styles were going to be. Clive and I would go to the movies and McDonald's once a week, which was the limit of our entertainment expenditure. I achieved a salary raise from forty-three pounds to sixty pounds a week, and we were made in the shade.

Then Master Goose took me home to meet his parents. I decided to rally against the bourgeoisie. While my parents imagined me 'To the Manor Born', I was visiting a council flat where Clive was braised (not a typo). Betty was a 'home maker', in and out of mental institutions all her life. Her significantly older husband, Charles, had been a window washer. His days were resigned to sitting in a filthy armchair, chain-smoking cigarettes, coughing and cursing at the world via the TV. When Clive started to talk swiftly about us getting married, I don't think I fully comprehended I was a meal ticket out of this juggernaut of poverty. He was a nice guy, and he loved me. The night we called my parents in Australia to say we were becoming engaged, the first thing my mother said was, 'Well, don't imagine you'll get an engagement ring marrying a pauper'. She was right, but being a defiant 20-year-old, I marched straight down to Mappin & Webb and used my savings to buy MYSELF an aquamarine engagement ring. That would show her.

No, it didn't.

I admitted to myself I was unsure of this next step. I went to Melbourne for my graduation, leaving Clive and his ridiculous surname behind for a while.

My ambition of living in the US had not waned. I wanted to attend university for a master's degree in LA. The tuition bill alone was problematic — more than ten thousand dollars a year. My application to UCLA was rejected, so I attempted enrolment at USC — the University of Southern California — for an MA in Film Theory. Patience has never been a virtue of mine. Before my application had been processed, I packed my BA degree and my toothbrush and headed for LA.

A funny thing happened at the airport before my flight to become an LA Woman …

Waiting for QF 11 to board, there were two groovy-looking guys standing against a wall talking to each other. They were 20 feet away from me. I recognized one of them as Michael Gudinski. Mushroom Records was entering its teen years. Gudinski's persona already shone brightly in the music world. The other guy was staring at me intently. His name was Gary Ashley.

As we were boarding the flight, Gudinski disappeared, turning left into First Class. A tall blonde hippie-like woman had joined Gary. Jenny Keath was a Mushroom Publishing PR I met while at Radio 3ST. I recalled a Split Enz album launch at the Palais Theatre and conning my way backstage. As I stood on the side of the stage, Jenny came up to me and said, 'How the hell did you get in here? I don't want to know'. She added, 'But I admire your chutzpah'.

As we lined up to board the plane, Jenny said hello. Introducing us, Jenny recalled the story to Gary. We locked eyes and smiled. We took our seats — far, far apart.

I felt happy and confident — both from her recollection and from the sense I got from this guy. Gary and Gudinski would go on to become my new, post-Dire Straits, Brothers in Arms for many years to come.

A friend was living in Downtown LA and offered me a room. He picked me up from the airport, and we headed out to a nightclub, but not before making a crucial stop.

The dealer. Here was another new world opening to me.

I had never seen powder drugs before, and as the dealer weighed out the grams on the scale, I wondered if this was a good idea. My buddy suggested I just rub some on my gums, which would at least get me through any jet lag while we partied the night away. Boy, did it. I was in heaven — in LA, with friends, on campus, rocking out — what could go wrong?

What went wrong was I missed Clive. His dog-sad letters arrived at my new LA home. I attended lectures while my application was still pending because of student visa issues. Charlton Heston was one of the guest lecturers. He pushed a party line about the importance of the NRA (National Rifle Association) and his hardline Republican, almost fascist mantra. I looked around the room at a bunch of indulged, preppy Cali' kids who seemed to be doing a master's degree as a way of avoiding entering the real world. Maybe I had been wrong; I should go back to London and earn a living in the fashion industry. My father had been granted a scholarship to Edinburgh University, so I could understand his reticence in wanting to spend hard-earned thousands of dollars for me to end up knowing the difference between film noir and neo-realism.

NO — NO, DON'T DO IT, I can hear my inner voice … but I did. If only I had turned a different corner there in Los Angeles and met some significant other or started throwing the I Ching or doing EST, how different life could have been. Memory moments like this are not a pause for regret. Our imaginations should run wild at all ages on what could have transpired from those 'corner' decisions.

Back in London, I found a sweet little flat off Eaton Square. The lady downstairs was thankfully as deaf as a post to our music and parties. We kept a stockpile of 50-pence coins to feed the electricity meter. Clive was at Jaeger.

I went back to selling frilly blouses. What had I done? The dread I felt going to work each morning reminded me I didn't want to be in the fashion business.

On the flip side, I did like being in a love nest, in a great city, with a guy who cared for me. Back again on the other side of my brain … I wanted to be FABULOUS. My gypsy instincts won the coin toss.

I would plan weekends away. 'Mini breaks', as Bridget Jones dubbed them.

Clive and I ventured to Paris on the ferry, way before the invention of the Eurostar train service. This time I did not throw up. We stayed in a pensione on Rue de Turbigo in the 3eme Arrondissement. Hedonistic joy was a warm baguette and coffee in the mornings, inside the threadbare sheets of our garret room. Clive took a wonderful photo of me from the window. I was at my happiest. The photo remains my favorite representation of 'me'. LA be damned.

Paris was where it was at.

This was beyond immeasurable joy resulting from 'young love'. The City of Light envelopes you in its arms with a warm and sensual depth, truly felt as you stroll bridges overlooking La Seine after dark. If I had told Clive to take the boat back to London and leave me behind, would I have made a life there? Would I still be there now?

As I write, I am.

My second employment round at Jaeger grew more mundane. The only great thing to come out of it was meeting Nikki. I was her pal 'Panda', and she was my pal 'Snearky'. Friends for life. The type of friendship where it doesn't matter how many years transpire between meetings, you revert to the core of that precious relationship, always.

I was approaching my 21st birthday in London, alone with Clive. My parents asked what I would like as a gift, and, much to their relief, I asked simply for a bottle of Château d'Yquem Sauterne. Having first experienced the delicious nectar with Dad, it seemed a fitting celebration tipple in their absence. Clive and I dined at Hilton on the Park, ending the evening with the demi-bottle of d'Yquem. Feeling delightfully drunk, in the way only great French wine can elevate you, I mistook '21' for being mature enough to make lifelong decisions. Granted, my parents had raised me in an environment that endorsed advanced thinking, but here I was in London with every opportunity ahead of me, about to make a huge mistake.

Clive continued to drone on about getting married and moving to Australia. He also wanted us to have a baby. This was certainly not in my mind's eye at 21. I devised a scheme and bought a doll. I handed Clive the doll and a beer. I told him, 'If you look after this like a real child from now through Sunday, then I will consent to having a baby'.

Doll was in the trash by Saturday.

My parents were excited for me to return to Australia and take over the business. With that added pressure and Clive's lovelorn demands, I gave in to what seemed best for everyone. Everyone else.

This act of selflessness has reverberated throughout my life. My primary concern is always for the other person in 'the mix'. Be it friend, family or even foe, I cannot seem to recognize my own needs before others. I may have been becoming FABULOUS, but emotionally clever did not appear to be a subset of that consciousness.

I made it clear if we were to marry, I would NOT become Amanda Goose. I gave Clive a list of surnames I would be happy to bear. They included Windsor, Hilton and Rothschild. The transaction, in hindsight, was trying to turn a sow's ear into a silk purse. It certainly made the decision to remain with my maiden name easier.

Nuptial plans were made. Elvie Hill's incredible seamstresses created a dress. Miles of pink taffeta for the bridesmaids. 'Baby's Breath' gypsophila floral garlands for the headpieces. A scene right out of Muriel's Wedding. Except the bride had a little less enthusiasm. We confirmed Stuart Blackler, my spiritual advisor from Merton Hall, to officiate. Having not been raised religious per se, or a churchgoer, there was no loyalty to one venue for the ceremony. My sense of the theatrical kicked in, and we booked St Paul's Cathedral in Melbourne. The only date available happened to fall on VFL Grand Final Day, the last Saturday in September.

As our wedding day approached, Elvie was silently apoplectic. It was best we stayed as far away from each other as possible. I eschewed the tradition of dressing as a bride in the family home, opting to dress in the hotel where the reception would take place. Elvie and Hector arrived at the bridal suite for photographs. My mother, crying up a storm, had to be ushered into the bathroom to have her makeup reapplied. I was reminded of the Woody Allen joke when he tells his parents he is converting to Catholicism; his mother tries to commit suicide by an overdose of Mahjong tiles.

While my bridesmaids took control of getting Elvie to the church, Hector and I took a white Rolls-Royce a couple of blocks to the church. I don't know who was more nervous. My gallant father mumbled some comment. Undoubtedly my mother had drilled him:

'Talk to her! Talk to her in the car on the way there! It's not too late!'

The premise was they wouldn't mind if I backed out; don't worry about the expense, people will understand, you can do better, you are only 21, yadda yadda …

All of which was completely correct, but it was too late.

We exchanged Woody Allen and Monty Python jokes for the rest of the tortuous drive to the gangplank … sorry, the church.

We stepped tenuously out of the Rolls-Royce onto the church steps, pausing for photos. Deep breaths to begin our walk up the aisle. All I felt was my high heels sinking in between the tessellated tiles on the floor. Somehow this served to transfix me and send me into fits of laughter. I composed myself by the time we reached the rows of guests. The Reverend Blackler gave me a look that confirmed he had also been badgered by my mother. His huge black eyebrows sternly shifted, appearing to beat out some Morse code message: 'don't … go … through … with … it'.

I waited for someone, anyone, to yell, 'NO!' at that crucial 'does anyone object' moment. No warning sang out this time; it did on my second innings.

It remains incredulous to me — as the child of a happy 'forever' marriage– that I thought so fleetingly and disrespectfully of the institution of marriage. My mental background 'music' was reassuring me I could just leave it behind. Brian Cadd's song 'Let Go' comes to mind; how ironic.

My husband went off to work each day, and I fumbled around, employed by Elvie Hill. I tried to convince my parents/employers that we should remodel the Collins Street boutique to house Jaeger as their exclusive Australian representatives. Elvie Hill was already stocking Aquascutum and Burberry, so why not expand to additional prestigious British labels. In business terms, they could not see the upside when there were other larger stores like Georges.

I said, 'Mark my words, one day the whole Paris end of Collins Street will be luxury brand stores'. I wish my father had lived to see that become the reality it is today.

The Elvie Hill atelier in Flinders Lane had other wholesale fashion traders in the building. A dramatic step down from Jaeger saw me hocking nylon Osti housecoats. By now I was positive I had made a mistake in every single category of my life.

CHAPTER 4: EVERY LITTLE THING SHE DOES IS MAGIC

It came time to forge the career I aspired to in the music business.
I summoned my 'inner-Patti Mostyn' and started Amanda Pelman Publicity.
I designed a cool logo of a panda bear holding a telephone.

I found an office with a swish new Telex machine, a typewriter and phone system. I set about gathering my first group of clients. Mimi Shephard was working away at PolyGram Records and helped in client introductions.

First came Chris Gunn at Redgum Management and then promoter Jon Nicholls. Both became clients. A swinging chick named Gaynor Crawford also worked for Chris and Jon. She became my new work-life pinup girl. All style and decorum, her PR partner was a rollicking rotund called Rob Goldstone.

I learned a lot from Gaynor in the early days.

Richard Branson's Virgin Records set up business in Australia and sublet my office space. I did additional PR work for Virgin during the musically magnificent days of Culture Club and The Human League. Mimi visited most afternoons with his chosen tipple — a cardboard box of port wine. His addictions were in full swing, though he would soon tackle them head-on, becoming sober. Before then, we were back to nightclubbing around Melbourne and visiting Molly Meldrum at Countdown.

The independence I felt working in the media business was exhilarating. I wish I could say the same for my marriage. Clive had become sullen and resentful of my success. I made every effort to be the good wife, despite his 'home at six, dinner on the table' mentality.

I received a call from Jenny Keath at Mushroom Publishing. We had no contact since our chance meeting on the plane to LA years before. Mushroom was looking for a new in-house PR, so could I come in for an interview with Michael Gudinski?

You bet I could.

The Mushroom building in Dundas Lane, Albert Park, had recently been acquired after a move from Wellington Street, St Kilda. The company and its staff were growing in leaps and bounds, with a booking agency, music publishing division and numerous record labels. Jenny and I chatted before I was summoned to MG's top-floor office.

He sat casually behind his huge desk, rolling a joint.

The phrase 'larger than life' is not adequate to describe Michael Gudinski's persona. In his presence you had a resounding feeling he was thinking twenty paces ahead of you, about twenty things more than you. The man was perennially distracted, caused by those twenty ideas ruminating around his brain — a truly remarkable phenomenon and what contributed to his enormous success. Michael lobbed a burst of questions at me through a cloud of smoke:

Are you married?

Yes.

Are you going to have a kid?

No.

Do you have a car?

Yes.

What is it?

A BMW.

OK, you've got the job. MARY!

This last piece of the interview was a sound I would become all too familiar with over the next 13 years. Michael would call out for his 2IC, his left hand, his right brain — Mary Tarn Bainbridge — and she would appear, with a cigarette in one hand and a notepad in the other. We installed an intercom system throughout the building so he didn't have to holler. Nothing changed.

I vividly remember my first day at Dundas Lane.

Monday morning meetings were the most structured we ever got in the working week. In the early '80s there were no 'breakout groups', Zoom meetings or constant confabs that went on for hours. Monday morning was the only diarized corporate formality we held to in an era before every workplace ran on formal timetables.

The cast of Mushroom Records characters was amongst the best you could wish for, all taken under the Gudinski wing and given 'carte blanche' to fly in whichever direction we saw fit. Chief chefs MG and Gary Ashley mixed the secret ingredients in the Mushroom sauce — Jenny Keath and

Jacqui Dennis, Simon Young, Ian James, Janine Kerr, Hilary Quinn, the 'runner' Scott Murphy and a firebrand called Michelle Higgins. Michelle ran the show as far as I was concerned. On the phone for Monday conference calls was Gary Ashley. Based in London, he had set up the publishing company and was signing label deals for products to release on the newly formed Liberation Records.

In my first Monday meeting, Gary told us he had acquired the recording rights to Divine — the transvestite actor extraordinaire featured in John Waters films. I shrieked with excitement, maybe a little too loudly.

Gary giggled down the line and said, 'Who was THAT?'

I meekly introduced myself. He admired my enthusiasm and told me I could handle the Divine release rollout. We wouldn't meet in person for some time after that telephonic introduction, but I knew then and there it was the beginning of a wonderful working relationship.

The camaraderie in Dundas Lane was exuberant. There was no one-upmanship — everyone got on with making Mushroom the #1 independent record label, under the stewardship of Festival Records' Alan Hely.

I got a call from Gudinski at home on a Sunday morning, much to Clive's annoyance. It is hard to imagine in our 24/7 world now that this was unusual.

'Come into the office', he chimed with excitement in his voice.

I was hooked. 'We just signed Jimmy Barnes, and we need to do a press release'. I tingled from head to toe, imagining the string of #1 records to come. This was going to be a wild ride for us all.

My marriage was anything but a wild ride. So, we split up.

He moved to an apartment in St Kilda, with his beloved Holden Commodore to keep him company.

Mushroom was now the preeminent Australian record label. No one had specific labels in Dundas Lane. Every staff member's first love was music. Everybody could rise within the company with good old-fashioned hard work, ingenuity … and a little bit of crazy.

One of the label imprints was the White Label. Its genre was more alternative acts than Mushroom Records itself. Early signings were Hunters & Collectors, The Triffids, Dynamic Hepnotics, The Stems and Painters & Dockers. Michelle had Paul Kelly's demo tapes from his manager, Stuart Coupe, for what would become the Gossip album. She was keen to see this album released on the White Label, but for some inexplicable reason

Gudinski did not want to re-sign him. This was out of character, as MG gave us our own way 99 per cent of the time.

Michelle was in Sydney, staying at the Sebel Townhouse. She could not make the boss see reason, so she locked herself in her room for three straight days. My much-admired co-worker vowed not to come out until Gudinski agreed to re-sign Paul. Her hotel stay was racking up a hefty bill with room service, booze and room charges, so MG had to give in. Just one of the great fabled stories of A&R at Mushroom.

Mushroom's party ethos was front and centre in my life. Gigs and launch parties to celebrate #1 records, to herald the Mushroom label and our dedicated teamwork.

A pivotal move Gary Ashley made during his time in London was creating relationships with developing labels and production houses.

The Liberation label was created to release international acts, and a distribution deal was done with EMI. Mushroom was distributed through Festival Records. The first wave of Liberation artists enjoyed 10 out of 10 top hits. Harking back to my first day in Dundas Lane and the thrill of working with Divine, we brought him/her — there was no non-binary 'they' at that time — out to Australia for a PR trip.

MG had recently married a gorgeous, effervescent blonde woman named Sue, who was working at 3XY radio when they met. They became the best example of an enduring rock 'n' roll marriage in Australia, alongside Jimmy and Jane Barnes. Michael & Sue lived in a smart townhouse in South Yarra. It was here we took Divine and his manager, Bernard Jay, for a luncheon one Saturday afternoon. I baked a cake. Even though my mother had never taught me to cook anything, let alone a layer cake for a gay icon, I baked a cake. It was a somewhat stilted sunny afternoon in their garden. Mr & Mrs Gudinski were short on words. I rabbited on about every nuance of every John Waters film. Divine and I got on famously. Their performance that evening at Inflation was stellar. We were all golden. Molly was the guest DJ. I would periodically sneak into the DJ booth and coerce him into playing our Liberation dance product.

Molly and I laughed at his warning me that had I not danced on ABC's Countdown, I would 'never work in this town again'. Well, here we were drinking together … and dance again I did. The disco era soared.

Dancing at nightclubs was such a welcome release, with or without sex at the end of the night. Adam Ant 'Antmusic', David Bowie 'Ashes to Ashes',

The Human League 'Don't You Want Me', Duran Duran 'Planet Earth'. We were enlightened by music, and nothing else around us mattered.

Proving the demented diversity in Liberation Records signings, the next project I worked on was Les Patterson.

Barry Humphries alter ego, other than Dame Edna Everage, was an Australian diplomat of questionable morals. All cucumber-in-the-pants dick jokes — sexual innuendo obscenity before it was politically incorrect. Barry was a comic genius, doing radio interviews where he could morph from one characterization to another with ease. I was delighted to be re-acquainted with him again, as his date, in October 2006.

The Mushroom work ethic was fantastic — the team building was led by Michael and Gary, who had recently returned from London. I looked deep into Gary Ashley's eyes, as he had done to me at Melbourne airport years before. I was smitten. He was newly single, devilishly handsome, witty, boyishly cheeky, and slightly on the short side, which suited me. He was hugely impatient in all things but dedicated to the development of the Mushroom brands. I instantly knew we could create wonderful music together, literally and figuratively.

I fluttered my eyelids at him but wasn't sure it was going to amount to anything. Until it did. It started slowly after an album launch party.

It was delightful and illicit. There was now a Mushroom apartment in Foveaux Street in Sydney, required for the frequency with which we all travelled. Gary and I often commuted together. I crawled right in — to his heart and his bed.

We didn't make it obvious. There was no need. We were having fun. Then along came Donna from New York. On the eve of a Christmas party at Gudinski's home, she materialized. He was now the one smitten, and I was clearly out of the picture. It was a hot summer night in the garden of Michael and Sue's newly acquired Toorak mansion.

I cured this seemingly interminable heartbreak by becoming close friends with Molly Meldrum. The most important job I had at Mushroom was getting video clips played on TV shows like Countdown.

The hour-long show started in November 1974 and eclipsed Hey, Hey as the most important music information source. With the creation of MTV in America in 1981, it became obligatory for artists to make videos. This tool became as important as radio airplay had been in the 1960s. Molly had an encyclopaedic knowledge of music. His A&R antenna was beyond compare.

He was responsible for the groundbreaking production of the Johnny Young song 'The Real Thing' for Russell Morris in 1969. Molly's career has been well documented. A fun fact was that Ian Meldrum started out as a roadie with The Groop, featuring Brian Cadd. And that truly is a whole other connection story.

Molly permitted us record company flunkies to visit his home in Richmond every Monday between 10 am and 12 pm.

It started out with fixed appointment times so that each label didn't know what the other was pitching. It ended up being a free-for-all, a knock-down-drag-out fight between 'the reps' to get as many clips played, ensuring a solid chart position the following week.

For a while I was the only chick in Melbourne's A&R scene. Thankfully through the 1980s more women joined the bigger international labels.

Molly's household was run by a devoted woman named Lynne Randell. She had been a pop singer in the '60s. They were like brother and sister. When Lynne wasn't there, I found myself tidying up, emptying overflowing ashtrays and scooting around the kitchen making something for Molly to eat. He never ate. From the beginning of our friendship, I had a strong desire to look after him. This never bordered on sexual in any intent; I wholeheartedly revered Molly, and we got on famously. My nickname for him was Mouldy Mildew.

Liberation label mates for Divine were Billy Ocean, Bananarama, The Bangles and that's only the Bs! Moving on to the Cs … Joe Cocker.

I saw The Cock 'n' Bull Band perform at the Myer Music Bowl in '75. Joe's I Can Stand a Little Rain album from 1974 remains on my Top 10 list. This crazed vagabond spoke to me, one of the most dynamic performers I ever witnessed. He channelled his oeuvre from African-American spiritualists and freeform contemporary choreographers.

Now on Liberation Records, we were releasing Joe's new album. His manager, Michael Lang, was the creative visionary of Woodstock '69 fame. The fact that Joe ended up at Woodstock was a miracle solely down to Michael. He heard Joe's demo and signed him for the festival, sight unseen. Michael confessed later he thought Joe was a black soul singer. This is one of the great stories further elaborated on in his book Road to Woodstock.

Michelle and I had calls with Michael Lang to devise the album release strategy. International calls were a big deal. No Skype. No Zoom. No internet. We were lucky if the telex had gotten through to Michael's office to confirm the time of the call to Melbourne.

My earliest memory of Michael Lang was the dulcet, velvet-like tone of his voice. He sounded so calm for someone managing a wild man like Joe Cocker. He sounded weirdly young even in his 40s. I could never have imagined that voice would become a part of my everyday life many decades down the line.

The next Billy Ocean release, 'When the Going Gets Tough', was the soundtrack for The Jewel of the Nile. I decided if we tied in tight with the film company, we could sell a bunch more albums and participate in the opening events for the movie.

The first time I took to the stage in front of an audience was the opening night at Hoyts Cinemas. I stood confidently in the spotlight. I felt the heat on my face and the oblivion of anything beyond that light.

In that moment I understood what performers go through for their 'hours upon the stage', how they manifest their entire being into those moments.

I bought a townhouse in South Yarra. My friend LC returned from her travels abroad and moved in. We were seeking partners, and the clubbing prowl continued. Turning 25, our birthdays a week apart, was enough reason to throw a blowout party. We hired a warehouse in Prahran and charged $2 entry at the door. The word spread organically across Melbourne's social landscape. More than 200 people, both known and unknown to us, turned up for an amazing night. The concept of warehouse parties had not become popular; we were ahead of the curve. I hired a PA sound system from Hunters & Collectors, employed a DJ, bought massive amounts of booze and we danced till dawn.

Attendees were a conglomeration of Mushroom recording artists, 'beautiful people', office buddies, school friends, new friends, ex-lovers and hopefully soon-to-be lovers.

Other than getting clips played on Countdown, securing covers on rock magazines was my #1 priority. The concept of free weekly street press publications was new, and one of them was 'born' in my house.

On the night of our 25th birthday party, LC met her future husband. They started dating, and he became a fixture in our swinging singles pad. Rob had the idea for a street paper and mulled it over with me. I introduced him to a journo who was new to the game and super-intelligent. Off they charged, and BEAT Magazine was born.

Michael Gudinski and Gary Ashley were making huge inroads with the Mushroom group on the international scene. There were global talkfests and conferences around the world each year. In 1986, we headed to New York for the New Music Seminar. The day I joined Mushroom years earlier coincided with the same first day for a young punk called Gerard. A superstar agent in the making, he called me Pelm. We flew to New York along with Neil Bradbury, who was managing Kids in the Kitchen. The band played a showcase gig at CBGBs — the Bowery club synonymous with discovering the Ramones, Talking Heads and Blondie.

During the day, Neil insisted we take a helicopter flight over Manhattan. I pointed out that he was probably high enough for all of us, but off we went.

I had never been more terrified.

One night I accompanied the boss to Radio City Music Hall to experience Sting in concert. This was the Dream of the Blue Turtles tour. Gudinski was warming up for Frontier to promote the tour in Australia. Radio City as a venue is a knockout itself, but nothing could ever beat the vision of Sting – post-show, backstage.

We were ushered into the artist's inner sanctum, offering our verbal frankincense and myrrh at the phenomenon that was his performance. Sting appeared from his dressing room with only a towel wrapped around his waist.

I recall time standing still. Sting's glorious blond locks arched with light emanating from the dressing room ... I didn't know where to look. God knows I couldn't speak. The vision of Sting in a towel remains with me today. I conjure it up when needed.

On our only night off in New York, I arm-wrestled Gerard to accompany me to Michael's Pub. It was a Monday night, and Woody Allen was playing clarinet with his New Orleans jazz band.

I was long past dressing as Annie Hall, but this was Woody Allen, in New York. We got a table, as Woody would have said, far away from the action. I could still see my hero play. If only there were a mobile phone, the moment would have been captured.

When Woody took a break, he sat with his manager, sorting through mail. Now was my chance. After all, I had the 'pounce on the celeb' experience with David Cassidy. I was not going to let some agent muscle me out of the action this time. Gerard wished me luck. I sucked in my gut, pushed out my tits and strode forth to Woody's side.

I started the conversation with 'I have come from Australia to meet you. I wrote a thesis on you in university...' The rest of what I said is a blur to me. Gerard was too far away to capture the narrative. The last thing I recall uttering through pursed lips was, 'And will you marry me?' What the heck, right? I was only going to get the chance once. He could have had me removed, forcibly or otherwise, but no.

Woody Allen smiled and coughed with his hand in front of his mouth as a kind of time interlude — just like in all his movies. This gave him pause while he thought about how to respond to this crazy Australian chick. Still holding his pen, he looked up at me and said, 'Did you pass?'

Did I pass?! My thesis? Well, I had somewhat gilded the literary lily here, as it was a lengthy article on his film Manhattan for the college paper, not quite a thesis. I mumbled a yes as he autographed a menu for me.

That framed menu, advertising its $17.99 soft-shell crab, is one of the dearest things I own. In his next film, Hannah and Her Sisters, I could have played the part of Lee with ease.

In love with Max Von Sydow and seduced by Michael Caine: older guys, right up my alley.

So, between Sting in a towel and Woody Allen on the clarinet, it was a hell of a trip.

Michelle Higgins and I worked well together; she was my mentor. Feisty with a capital F, she focused on dominating the radio charts while I looked after print. We split duties on TV as she also had a magnificent relationship with Molly. I learned a marvellous story from earlier Mushroom days, when the label and agency had their first office in Wellington Street, St Kilda.

One day Michelle was on the phone to Molly, berating him for not promoting a certain act. When her tirade began, unbeknownst to her, Molly jumped in his car and drove the few miles to Wellington Street.

He jumped out of his car and ran into Michelle's office while she continued screaming down the phone. He snuck up behind her and screamed back.

Classic Molly.

Michelle had won the battle for Paul Kelly and was instrumental in making him the Australian music icon he remains today. Next came The Angels, whose handwritten logo was Michelle's handwriting. It was lucky her musical bent was hard rock and mine was pop because that division of genre labor served us well. Rose Tattoo's Angry Anderson had a true soft spot for Michelle. I loved watching her giggle and blush over his 'advances'.

One day a tall, balding guy walked into Michelle's co-joined office. She yelled, 'Ooo maow ma maow maow!' I realized this must have been Russell Morris, whose 'Real Thing' I had worn down to melted acetate years before. He had recorded for Mushroom as Russell Morris and the Rubes right before my tenure there. Little did I know what a bigger role he would play later in my life.

The roster grew along with the staff. Our Sydney office was run by Lizzi Dayney, followed by Sue McAullay, Nina Frykberg and Lisa McDiarmid.

Mushroom Music MD Ian James had an 'in-house' nickname.

Gary Ashley was a highly impatient traveller. If you checked baggage for a flight, it better come out first or he will leave the airport without you. No exceptions. Arriving in Cannes for MIDEM, Ian James' bag didn't appear … Gary reluctantly agreed to wait. The tardy suitcase appeared as its wheels caught in the conveyor belt. While Ian struggled to free it, we laughed at the Monty Pythonesque scene unfolding in front of us. 'Wheels' was his moniker from then on. A true music man, he played a pivotal role in the Mushroom landscape for more than 40 years. A loveable rogue, I adore him.

Michelle decided to leave the company and move to America. She handed our intrepid mail boy, Scott Murphy, a green folder with seven pages in it. This contained the foreign retailers that were buying Mushroom product. Like a Colonel addressing the troops, she told Scott, 'Go make something of this, son'. Scott built it into a company — Mushroom Exports. That's how it rolled there — just get in and do it.

Signing Jimmy Barnes was a huge coup for Mushroom and the beginning of an amazing friendship between Michael and Jimmy and their wives, Sue and Jane. Jane Barnes is a formidable woman. Her detractors in the industry derided her as 'the Yoko Ono' of Cold Chisel. Apart from this being a disgraceful racial slur, nothing was further from the truth. She and Jimmy were — and happily remain — two parts of a forceful whole. Their marriage and family are an inspiration, along with all the trials and tribulations they have now admitted to in the public arena.

Jimmy's second solo album, Working Class Man, was a blockbuster, selling more than 500,000 copies after it was released at the end of 1985. The Mushroom team and our distributor, Festival Records, put Herculean efforts into making the album debut at #1. The Monday morning chart announcement saw Michelle and I fall into a pride-filled faint. True to form, we issued an intercom building shout-out with the news. These days that type of excitement is sent via an email or a tweet with no human emotion on display.

I sure miss those feelings of engagement.

Jimmy and Cold Chisel were managed by Dirty Pool Management, formed by John Woodruff and Rod Willis, and personally overseen by Mark Pope. They created the groundbreaking video of Jimmy marching through burning cane fields in Far North Queensland. We had no trouble getting that clip played repeatedly.

Gudinski had gotten his #1 wish and was determined to make Jimmy his first American chart-topper.

The Liberation label was doing massive business with Joan Jett, Bananarama and The Bangles, amongst others. Then came an out-of-the-box UK signing by Gary — Samantha Fox.

The early Liberation releases could be bookended by Divine's 'You Think You're a Man' and Samantha Fox's 'Touch Me (I Want Your Body)'. Three decades later, today's mashup would be Sam Smith and Kim Petras' award-winning 'Unholy'.

Sam Fox in 1986 was the London newspaper Page 3 topless superstar. Her breasts were plastered on every mechanic's wall, from Portsmouth to Manchester. She was managed by her father, Patrick, who reeked of 'dodgy character'.

Unfortunately, my instinct was correct, as he embezzled from Sam for years and was finally caught. Her other dodgy mate was Australian Peter Foster. He sprunked herbal tea as a weight-loss remedy. We arranged a promo trip.

The media spot I was thrilled to secure was a Mike Willesee interview. The merits of her pop stardom aside, it was clear the interview was going to drill down into Miss Fox's endorsement of Foster's herbal remedies. Entering the TV studio, I told Sam I was going to position myself under her interview desk to help with appropriate responses if required. I made sure no production staff could see where I was hiding. Feeling slightly uncomfortable, I realized I was within inches of Samantha Fox's most intimate parts. And not the parts newspaper readers saw on Page 3 every week.

Willesee commenced the interview, and it was brutal. Sam wasn't coping, so I lobed a few lines we had previously rehearsed. It was like watching a dolphin out of water.

I whispered to her, 'Get out! Leave! Get up, walk out!'

Samantha confidently got up, paused like a true diva with the flick of her head, and departed. It was the best move we could have made. The next day she made media front pages worldwide. I created t-shirts that said:

'Will-e-see
Who is he?
He didn't see
The best of me!'

CHAPTER 5: LIFE'S LOCOMOTION

Michael Gudinski and I were personally never termed 'close'. That is not to say he wasn't a magnificent boss; he was. We had as many arguments as we had professional scores on the board. Inside the Mushroom camp there was a strange unspoken, but widely acknowledged, rule: you were either a 'Gary person' or a 'Michael person'. I was certainly deemed a 'Gary person' in one way I have already described. Maybe the disconnect with Michael was my pop genre drive, as that was not how he saw Mushroom's worldwide development.

Case in point — Samantha Fox.

It was never discussed, but I know it rankled MG to have the Mushroom name attached to bubblegum pop. Those 'one-hit-wonder' singles made money to support massive recording budgets for Australian artists. We were a commercial enterprise and early leaners into the 360-degree model.

I contributed generously to the company with my A&R acumen and my 'take no prisoners' attitude.

Most evenings we put tools down around 6pm. Some of us congregated in Michael's office to recap the day's events and 'shoot the shit' on ideas. This time was shared with the touring company stalwarts. 'The Old Man' Philip Jacobsen, Frank Stivala, Gerard, along with Michelle, Mary and I, would debate new releases and touring artists.

Occasionally, this included a jolly, fun-loving Sydneysider, Michael Chugg. Everyone loved Chuggi, and when he was in the building, you certainly knew it. Almost louder than Gudinski, when Chuggi yelled 'MEY-ARY' for Mary Bainbridge, it was impossible to tell their voices apart. Joint-rolling duties were spread around, and sometimes a few drinks were enjoyed.

During these hours I would ferret around on MG's desk, going through the plethora of cassette tapes submitted to Mushroom to become the 'next big thing'.

One fateful day, Michael did the converse and dropped a cassette on my desk to garner my opinion. It was pure pop and from a universe he neither cared for nor understood. It combined TV exposure and a bona fide '60s hit song.

The song was 'Locomotion', sung by Kylie Minogue.

The omnipotent Gudinski stood over my desk and motioned to the cassette. 'I don't have an opinion — tell me what you think. It's your thing'.

This is when our working relationship truly worked. Amongst the myriad of miracles Michael Gudinski gifted the Australian music industry, the faith and trust he put in his staff came first. From that business principle came an empire of success.

I love a challenge.

I thrive on the thrill of discovery. Be it in the professional arena of music or theatre or in my personal life — being open-minded and visualizing optimistic outcomes is my adrenaline.

Backed by her television co-stars — Jason Donovan and Guy Pearce — Kylie's voice was effervescent like Alka-Seltzer.

I knew Mushroom could make this work.

In Gary Ashley's intelligent observation, he inked a deal with UK production team Stock, Aitken and Waterman and their PWL imprint. Mushroom Publishing secured the PWL catalogue rights, Liberation the bulk of their record output, and a 'first look' at the pop acts we signed. This would give PWL rights outside of Australia/NZ — standard practice.

Neighbours was Kylie's star TV vehicle, produced by the Grundy Organization. It was a huge hit in the UK. Every afternoon, the British public would tune in to witness a big shiny blue-sky world of Australia — seen through the lens of the fictional Ramsay Street. This became a tourism calling card for life in Australia and painted a societal picture of middle-class prosperity. A stark contrast to Britain's own EastEnders.

Gary floated the idea of pitching 'Locomotion' to Pete Waterman.

We invited Kylie and her father, Ron, to Dundas Lane. I made sure the building was spick-and-span and the staff enthusiastic and welcoming. Michael was not in Melbourne when the meeting took place. Gary and I were on the front line.

This would not be the first goal we had kicked together, but it had the potential to be the biggest.

The Minogues arrived as I lunged into Gary's office to make sure he was primed. Ever nonchalant, he muttered 'So … what do you want me to say?' Jesus, Gary, convince them we are the right label and mention the PWL idea … OK? OK.

Ron Minogue was an extremely intelligent gentleman, apparent at first sight. A no-nonsense protective father who had up to now guided both his daughters' careers in the entertainment industry. Kylie was wearing a mauve mohair sweater, high-waist jeans and fashionable Reebok sneakers. Her mass of blonde curls added a modicum of height to her tiny frame. She radiated innocence and was a determined young performer.

Meeting a young Taylor Swift in 2009, at our Sound Relief concert, gave me a similar feeling to the first day I met Kylie. The inexplicable sense that these young women were the visionaries of their own careers.

Gary gave an overview of the label — sitting behind his desk, rocking in his chair, folding little pieces of paper into concertina shapes — a long-time habit. You always knew where Gary had been in the building, or elsewhere, by discovering these mystical paper objects. We introduced Kylie and Ron to Simon Young, Mushroom's COO, on their way out. Simon added a conservative business edge to the deal we were proposing.

All seemed positive, and a contract would be drawn up. I was thrilled at the idea of helping make this girl a star.

My enthusiasm was met with Gudinski's uncertainty about having Kylie on his label. He wanted the proverbial second opinion. I was prepared for the biggest argument we were ever going to experience. I was having my Michelle Higgins and Paul Kelly moment. I would not let this deal collapse because MG did not prioritize the pop genre.

Gudinski was visiting his sister in London and asked Tania and her kids how big a deal Kylie could be outside Australia. Need I add more?

Additionally, Neighbours had shot a storyline at Molly Meldrum's house in Richmond. Both Kylie and Jason charmed Molly, and he in turn convinced Gudinski we were onto something big. He has always publicly attributed Kylie's early success to my pushing hard with the 'we are doing this, Michael' end tale.

I invited Kylie and Jason to see Bob Dylan at Kooyong Stadium. This was a Frontier tour and I wanted her to experience the broader team at the Mushroom Group of Companies. Chuggi helped ensure Kylie was treated accustomed to the TV royalty she and Jason had become. MG finally met his potential new star and I was confident we were all on the same page.

In their London stable, Stock, Aitken & Waterman had a young blood engineer Mike Duffy. Gary confirmed him on secondment to produce tracks for some of our artists. SAW, still sceptical that Kylie could even sing, gave the go-ahead for Duffy to produce the track. 'Locomotion' became that first single.

Mike was a corker, in the true English sense of the word.

He was everyone's image of a younger brother — part Cocker Spaniel with a gee whiz-golly gosh attitude to life.

He moved to my house in South Yarra. Totally house-trained, it was great to have a guy around who cooked and who I worked well with during the day.

Nothing more.

As time was of the essence to get the single recorded, I needed to find a track for the B-side. Mushroom was recording again with Kids in the Kitchen. I asked Craig Harnath and Claude Carranza if they had songs to present to Kylie. The B-side to 'Locomotion', 'Glad to be Alive', earned those guys as much in royalties as Goffin/King received for the A-side — that's how single royalties work.

Now to the important selling tool — a bright and shiny video.

Kylie worked with different directors on neighbours, and together we secured the charming Chris Langman to direct. Andrew McVitty produced it. We hired Tania Lacy to choreograph.

A budget was set showing Kylie 'fly on the wall' style in the recording and dance studios.

McVitty presented me with a budget for $10,000, and Gudinski hit the roof. Gary left me hanging out to dry. 'You are on your own, baby!' On average in this era, videos cost $3,000.

I struck on a solution to have 'product placement' in the clip, indirect advertising to obtain funds to cover costs above the 'five grand' MG had promised me. Impulse Body Spray came on board for a few bucks. I used my old contacts at Sportsgirl to procure the required wardrobe. Kylie and I went into their flagship Collins Street store. Owner David Bardas dropped in to say hello to me and our protégé. The staff laid out next season's range. Wow, $500 leather jackets and more rah-rah skirts than you could count.

The video shot at Platinum Studios has two bobbing heads behind the recording desk — Mike Duffy and me. Vika Bull worked on reception and asked what all the fuss was about. I confidently told her we were recording the next big Australian female music star, who would be as successful as Olivia Newton-John. Kylie admitted to being influenced by ONJ. Given I knew Olivia through my friend Barbra Ward, I placed a call to ask her to give Kylie some encouragement.

I applied the same 'behind the scenes' principle for the stills photo shoot. Mushroom Art Director Yolande Gray knew photographer Andrew Lehmann. A new designer in Melbourne, Alannah Hill, had a store by Andrew's studio. So much was done in a hurry because of Kylie's production schedule at Neighbours.

I dashed into Alannah's, gathering up her new collection, and back to Andrew's to complete the shoot. Kylie is a petite girl. Even Alannah's small-size garments were too big. For most of the shots I hid behind Kylie, trying to disguise the photography pegs we had to make do with to cinch her waist to make the clothes sit properly.

The whirlwind of the release, both in Australia and the UK, was phenomenal. At last, Gudinski was taking notice. It was #1 in Australia for seven consecutive weeks. 'Locomotion' became the highest-selling single of the 1980s and Mushroom's biggest single.

The next hurdle was Kylie's availability to go back and forth to London for promotional appearances and recording while filming Neighbours.

Brian Walsh was in charge at the Ten Network and did not make it easy. After all, Miss Minogue was contracted to him first and foremost, and wasn't this little 'singing escapade' just a 'flash in the pan'? Well, no.

Michael Gudinski wasn't the only one now taking notice. Simon Young's friend Terry Blamey had offices in the Dundas Lane building, promoting cover bands and comedians. One afternoon he pulled me aside at the stairwell and asked if I would introduce him to Kylie's father. Up until then, Ron Minogue had been managing Kylie's business affairs, and Terry certainly saw an opportunity.

People often ask me why I do what I do — in terms of A&R, management, concert producing, etc.

My answer is simple: I relish the thrill it gives me seeing joy on the faces of audiences and artists alike. Helping facilitate both on- and off-stage dreams is my drug. Kylie was so happy in the early blush of her success; that meant I was doing my job and reaping a personal reward. She often talked of loving her acting career but really wanting to sing and emulate Olivia Newton-John, without ever imagining it would become a reality.

It was the beginning of a long, illustrious career. I am glad to have been a part of its gestation.

I had been feeling generally unwell, moody and physically uncomfortable. My intuition was right: something was wrong.

I was referred to a gynaecologist, Claire Peterson. A magnificent woman with a shock of wild red hair and a take-no-prisoners attitude. I praise her for facilitating three of the most important events in my life — delivering both my children and saving me from a premature death from cervical cancer.

Claire discovered my Pap smears had missed a cancerous growth. She scheduled surgery and promised me a successful recovery.

Being wheeled into the operating theatre, all I could think was whether I would be able to bear children in the future. Unlike my mother's lack of maternal instinct, my inner vision saw babies as a bounty, not a burden.

There were many trips back and forth to London in those days; I lost count. It could be Gary, Terry, Simon, me, or any combination of us all.

I vividly recall sitting at our boutique hotel in Notting Hill hearing 'Locomotion' on the radio for the first time. It was a watershed moment, and thankfully one that has been repeated many times over in my career with #1 hit songs.

The next tracks Kylie recorded were 'I Should Be So Lucky' and 'Got to Be Certain'. A speedy follow-up to 'Locomotion' was crucial. Much has been written about SAW's production style and how rapidly they wrote hits. They may have turned Rick Astley from their teaboy into an overnight star, but they were not renowned for treating their artists with deserved respect. It wasn't called the 'factory' for nothing. Kylie would sit and wait for hours at the studio because Mike Stock and Matt Aitken hadn't finished writing the songs she had flown from Australia to record.

The UK release of 'Locomotion' received massive press — both positive and negative. One so-called 'journalist' labelled Kylie 'a singing budgie', claiming she arrived in London off a flight looking 'like a worn-out Qantas blanket'.

The knives were out.

I wrote to the editor and gave her a piece of my mind. Over my PR career I built up a reputation for fighting back on negative press. Years later, when Melbourne journalist Nui Te Koha rubbished my band, Indecent Obsession, I sent a stinking rotten egg by courier straight to his office desk.

As Kylie's success grew with the release of 'Locomotion' worldwide, PWL took all the credit for her discovery. It was obscenely apparent in meetings with international label reps how Pete Waterman framed it in the press. He was a master at publicity, and this drew Gudinski's ire. Now Michael Gudinski wanted acknowledgement as the one who discovered Kylie Minogue ….

Kylie and Jason were very much an item. The press was ever eager to have this fact confirmed, but the lovebirds were careful never to be seen in any compromising light. By nature, celebrities have a love/hate relationship with media. One day you can't get enough column inches, and the next you are suing them for defamation of character.

One morning Kylie and Jason called me to say there were paparazzi outside their house when they left for the Neighbours set. They were worried about anyone jumping the fence, seeing photos of them together or just generally snooping amongst their things.

Jason was not as 'innocent' as Kylie, and there were a few plants in the garden that needed hiding. I raced over and ensured I wasn't seen entering the house. I foraged in the garden, hid the stash, slithered on my knees through the main house hiding photographic evidence, and made my getaway. Jesus, the things you do. I went to Molly's home and dissolved in laughter, regaling him with the story while we had a couple of stiff vodkas. Day drinking was entirely acceptable in the 1980s.

Terry had taken on Kylie's business affairs, with control of KDB — the company named for the Minogue siblings: Kylie, Dannii and Brendan.

Deals were being ironed out alongside photo and video shoots for singles at breakneck speed. I received the finished mixes of both 'I Should Be So Lucky' and 'Got to Be Certain' on cassette direct from London — hand-delivered by Gary with an 'OK, do your thing' grin.

I started to formulate script ideas.

It was imperative that Kylie's 'girl next door' image coincided with her character on Neighbours. This had been made abundantly clear by Grundy's and the Ten Network. As a label, we felt her image should represent the genuine Kylie, not Charlene. Sweet and kind, with a touch of cheeky thrown in. Hence the bubble bath scene in 'I Should Be So Lucky', which was deemed risqué. Every red-blooded teenage boy fell in love, and every young girl wanted to be Kylie.

The day of the shoot we were short on indicative props. Typically saving on budget, I filled my car with lamps, photo frames and other household items to make the set look more homely. I had a habit of giving Kylie something of mine to wear during filming as an 'ode to Hitchcock'. This time it was my diamond earrings for good luck. It worked — 'Lucky' was a worldwide number one and topped the UK charts for five weeks.

By the time we released 'Got to Be Certain', PWL decided they wanted creative control over the imagery. I wrote the video storyboard for 'Certain' while sitting in my car. It was the only cassette machine I had at my weekend Red Hill retreat. The idea was to feature the best of Melbourne to give context to where Kylie originated from, other than Ramsay Street! The half-dozen locations started out at Luna Park in St Kilda.

On shoot day, the parcel with shoes and clothes provided by PWL had not arrived from London. We had a film crew sitting around waiting for hours. I was about to pull the pin and suggest she wear something else when the package arrived. Good thing, as David Howells, PWL's general manager, was a difficult man to please. We ended the shoot at dusk, just as a full moon was rising, and Andrew Lehmann took some spectacular shots of us all.

Chris Langman and Andrew McVitty remained the production team making all the clips zing. After being single and enjoying it, I struck up a relationship of sorts with McVitty. He was a prickly pear, prone to fits of depression brought on by alcohol intake. You never knew which Andrew was going to appear day in, day out. He would go on documentary shoots to bizarre places, and the gifts he brought me were invariably ceramic animals. At least I enjoyed his sense of humour, as did my father, who deemed this a more suitable match than my hapless husband.

The first ceramic was a koala filled with port wine! The koala spent many years up a tree at my Red Hill property. Andrew and I spent time at his beach house, enjoying a silent drive there one weekend listening to Van Morrison's Poetic Champions Compose. Turned out I was more entranced with Van than I was with Andrew. By the time we got to make the video for 'Certain', I figured it was time to move on.

Before that longer wrong turn, I made a right one.

There was a team of journalists at Rolling Stone magazine who were fantastic; John O'Donnell, Ed St John and Toby Creswell were like the three musketeers. Great writers and arguably the best collective set of musical ears in the whole of Australia. Both John and Ed went on to have stellar record industry careers after putting their pens down.

Toby was simply gorgeous. I adored him. He had a way of speaking intimately, which felt like being covered in a warm blanket. I soon knew him as a generous lover.

Toby wrote a biography of Jimmy Barnes, so we spent time on the road with Jimmy and Jane. Neither of us placed any demands on the other, and when we were together, it was so much fun. As an editor of *Rolling Stone Australia*, Toby commissioned the first classy cover shoot of Kylie, shot by Grant Matthews. For that I was truly grateful. Spending so much time convincing the media that Kylie was the real deal and not a puppet was exhausting. Toby's story gave her early career some much-needed gravitas.

There was always Molly to give Kylie credibility; he was arguably her first media champion. Molly and my friendship grew over the years. I would cook dinners at his Highett St home and hang out. 'Lovey, lovey', he would call to me, 'make me an orange juice, will you?' The orange juice was one part orange and six parts vodka.

Ian 'Molly' Meldrum had the strongest constitution of anyone I have ever met — like ten bulls, not one. He was a brilliant sounding board for everything we were undertaking in Kylie's early career.

On release of 'Got to Be Certain', I asked Molly to consider having Kylie on Hey, Hey It's Saturday to sing live. Molly loved a challenge and loved an orchestra even more. Additional players were brought in to augment the band, run by Red Symons and Wilbur Wilde, whose trademark cynicism did not exactly fit the brief!

There were members of Dundas Lane who thought her live performance was a terrible idea, but together, Molly, Kylie and I proved them wrong. The version she performed on the show was certainly different from the single.

It showed her in a warm vocal light. Captivating television.

And then she was gone … on a whirlwind PWL junket of Asian and European PR, then on to London to finish the album.

I received welcome professional applause for having the foresight to sign Kylie, as much as for handling Michael Gudinski's initial dislike for the idea. Offers to move to another company came from a few areas, but the one that nearly saw me jump ship was to Richard Branson's Virgin Australia. Virgin's local boss, Michael Manos, outlined a very attractive deal.

Loyalty to Mushroom and Michael Gudinski won out.

I found it hard to get my cancer scare out of my mind. I hadn't let on to anyone, apart from Gary Ashley.

He and Donna had married and started a family, so our working life was purely platonic. Nothing felt certain, and as Kylie sang, 'Got to Be Certain'.

My first marriage had been a disaster from day one; my relationships with Gary and Toby had gone nowhere. For the first time, loneliness crept in.

I fled to France. Why France?

Whatever the human phenomenon is that gives us a telepathic sense that we have dwelled on Earth before — lived life as another person with or without the same soul, in another era — whatever that phenomenon is, I have it in spades.

It would be valid to ask, if I am so perceptive, why have I made so many wrong turns in life? Why do any of us?

My love of France stemmed from a sense that 'I' existed there during the 1800s. My relationship with France remains today, having made Paris home multiple times, as I do now.

But first to 1988.

I packed like it was forever and went to a lawyer to make a will — just in case it was that kind of forever. Michael Brereton was legal counsel for many artists across the entertainment industry. Our first meeting was one of professional convenience. I needed a will. I handed him a one-page dossier.

Full of positive attitude and joie de vivre, I made for France.

My first mission was getting a car — my little red Renault.

I plotted a trip south, deviating off motorways to stay at various Château, decades before Airbnb, let alone digital roadmaps or mobile phones. I had one travel book that pinpointed elegant-looking places to stay. I figured I would drive until it felt right to stop.

After weeks of tooling around, I grew tired, reminding myself this journey was meant to overcome both my cancer surgery and mend my broken heart and mind.

The place that stopped me was Fayence in the Provencal hills above Fréjus. I lived a sublime summertime in a pensione run by a charming couple who indulged my awkward French. Days were spent writing and reading, accompanied by the occasional glass of rosé.

Once revived, I shared my whereabouts with my parents and Gary.

Dad would send blue aerogrammes with news and multiple questions.

No, I did not know when I was coming back, or if I was going back. Wouldn't some sexy Frenchman run me off my feet, and I would live happily ever after in France? Was this another premonition of my future evolution?

As summer progressed and this wished-for man did not materialize, autumn turned cold. Rosé made way for a bold Bordeaux as reality took hold.

I had writer's block.

What if the cancer returns?

What if I never have children?

What am I achieving living here?

French radio assisted my French-language skills. Occasionally I heard Kylie tracks played on local radio. It was entirely surreal, as that world seemed very far away.

How many times could I reread Jean-Jacques Rousseau's Confessions?

I was becoming lonely as the cold weather drew in. I decided to make my way back to Paris and live out my inevitable spinsterhood there.

Then came the phone call. Director de Pensione called from le terrasse, 'Dépêchez-vous, Amanda, il y a un appel interurbain de l'Australie'.

It was Gudinski.

'Come back, we need you. Are you OK? When can you be here?'

I recall this command as the same question volley experienced the first day I met Michael Gudinski.

Indeed, it was no different the last time we spoke in 2021, weeks before his untimely passing.

And just like the first time, I was hooked.

Come home, he cried! So, I did.

I drove my little Renault to Paris, gave away my clothes and typewriter, and got the big bird in the sky to take me home.

I left part of my heart in France that time… waiting for me every time I return. Maybe one day it will be for 'ever', if the piece of my heart I still carry stops being so relentlessly restless.

CHAPTER 6: JUST ONE MORE TIME LOVEY

Molly, Marriage and Mayhem

If I didn't have a boyfriend, I had Molly Meldrum.

I moved into his home on my return from France. He was my 'Mouldy Mildew'. I was his 'Attila the Hen'. The fact that he nicknamed me after a 4th-century Hun, a feared enemy of the Roman Empire, is both hilarious and insulting.

We both got a great deal from cohabitating.

I cooked, made drinks, and listened on repeat to new tracks he was sure were hits. He made me laugh, and caring for him gave me a true sense of purpose.

He had an idea for a new label: Melodian Records.

I praised his A&R sensibility — from the groundbreaking hits he produced in the late '60s to his championing of ABBA and Madonna before anyone else worldwide knew how iconic they were going to be. Back in Dundas Lane, Simon Young drew up an agreement for Melodian Records. It felt good to be back in business, back in the feathered Mushroom nest with my favorite people. Michael Gudinski wasn't the only music industry icon receiving cassette demos. Molly's front room was full of them.

Every day we lived in laughter. Molly is a major Egyptophile. Everything in his home relates to Egypt. Even more amazing is that when he first saw the house that would become his home, he had no idea its name of origin was 'Luxor'. The name plaque had long been hidden and was quickly re-established when renovations commenced.

In designing a logo for Melodian, we looked to Egyptian symbolism. Molly and I presented a graphic image to Gudinski. Michael looked at us and, in all seriousness, commented, 'Ever been to Egypt? I haven't but I reckon the sand is lighter'.

Our first signings were Indecent Obsession from Brisbane, Roxus from Melbourne and Joanne Guilfoyle from Perth.

Who?

One evening when Joanne came to the house, Molly and I were undoubtedly in our cups, listening to demo tapes for hours. I blurted out, 'Listen up! For God's sake, we're not putting someone called Joanne Guilfoyle on our label. Let's call you Jo Beth Taylor and create a PR story that you are the illegitimate grandchild of Elizabeth Taylor'.

Preposterous.

There was another act Molly was insistent on signing.

Peter Andre. In fact, he offered him a record deal live on TV — when Peter was a contestant on New Faces. I found Peter immature, both musically and personally. My 'Attila the Hen' persona rose up to Molly and suggested he check his motives for signing someone who looked like a Calvin Klein underwear model.

Molly and I saw Peter perform in a Gold Coast shopping mall.

Truly horrible. I never saw a smidge of talent in the guy. But Molly was determined to turn a sow's ear into a silk purse. I had to eat my words when Peter Andre scored several Number 1 singles and a Number 1 album in the UK once we opened the Mushroom office.

Juno Roxas was pedigree music industry and a savvy guy. His style was early Bon Jovi meets Twisted Sister, and he looked the part. The other members of the band were not exactly stellar musicians, but one of them, the drummer Darren Danielson, had a good head on his shoulders and knew how to manage Juno's temper and unreasonable demands.

Indecent Obsession flew to Melbourne to record.

Lead singer David Dixon was 16 years old with a cocky attitude that belied his years. Michael Szumowski was tall and cool as a cucumber. Together they formed the writing team. The other two band members — Daryl Sims and Andrew Coyne — were contracted as 'sidemen', a status that rankled them and ultimately led to musical divorce.

At Melbourne airport I took a long hard look at David and said, 'Well, that mullet haircut is going to have to go'. He told me to fuck off. I made it clear he didn't get to tell me to fuck off, as I was in charge. He never did it again.

As most artists we were signing did not have management representation, it seemed a logical step to look after them — outside record company obligations. The first imprint was MAP Management — Miss Amanda Pelman. Later this dovetailed into MGM — Michael Gudinski Management.

I was working on Melodian's development simultaneously for Mushroom and Liberation. Dundas Lane was like a never-ending jigsaw puzzle with our growing number of staff. It has been architecturally re-configured more times than an old button factory should have had to bear. I commissioned a new interior design for Michael's office, which was featured in design magazines. Always a PR, PR sweety.

After Samantha Fox, the next crazy British broad onboard the SS Liberation was Mandy Smith … cor blimey. Mandy was 18 years old. Blimey x 2.

I fought to not be called Mandy and asked her why she didn't keep her christened name of Amanda. Her response: 'Aaaaaawwww … aaaahhhh … (insert thought bubble above head) … I don't knooooowwwww …'. End of conversation. That was about as deep as it got.

Mandy's claim to fame on this record release was her engagement to Bill Wyman, latterly of the Rolling Stones. Remember — she was 18. He was 52. Clearly, I should have had empathy here, harking back to my liaison with Dennis Gowing.

The track was titled 'I Just Can't Wait'. No kidding.

Her video tickled me the most. There were multiple setups as a direct rip-off of our Kylie 'Locomotion' clip. As Kylie once taught me, 'Imitation is the sincerest form of flattery'.

From Mandy Smith to Jimmy Barnes is a HUGE stretch.

The Freight Train Heart album release was a huge priority.

Gudinski had done a US deal for Jimmy with Geffen Records, giving the sound an overarching American influence. There was a lot going on, particularly Gudinski's play for Jimmy's management. I went out on the road with Jimmy and the crew. This became the moment that touring and live performance tattooed them on my soul. Occasionally Jane Barnes sent their first-born daughter, Mahalia, on the road with us. I became PR and Nanny rolled into one, which suited me just fine. I loved Mahalia and the relationship she had with her father on the road. Now Mahalia is a wonderful performer in her own right, with and without Jimmy.

The crew included two people dear to my heart — true Road Warriors, the pair of them — Peter 'Sneaky' McFee and Howard 'How-Weird' Freeman.

Howard was irascible, psychic and psychotic in the same moment. The funniest man on the tour. I loved their company.

The Jimmy Barnes Freight Train tour was a huge success, celebrated with a boat cruise on Sydney Harbour. Mushroom staff were dynamite — Sue McAullay, Eleanor McKay and Lisa McDiarmid were a terrific team, backed by the powerhouse distributors at Festival Records. Warren Costello was soon to be enticed away from Festival to Mushroom.

Gudinski was elated at the success for his #1 artist.

I was tired. I had been checked again for cervical cancer and received an all-clear. I needed a few weeks off after a mind-bending tour and multiple album releases.

Imagining a quiet beach somewhere? Wrong.

I went to Egypt.

As the Barnes cruise ended, I told Gudinski, 'I'm going away for two weeks, I promise only two …. sensing Michael thought I may disappear to my beloved France again!

I told him I was headed to Egypt. He said, 'Yeah, sure. See you Monday'.

Living with Molly created my love of Egypt. The antiquity fascinated me.

So off I went on another brief but spectacular adventure.

I landed in Cairo out of my mind with jet lag and tour fatigue.

As Billy Thorpe taught me years later, I was decompressing.

I was escorted to my hotel, and the driver, a young athletic boy, enquired if I needed 'anything else, Madam?'

Well, yes, I responded — hustle up some hash and some vodka. He returned an hour later with both and stayed for several hours to help with my 'decompressing'.

Refreshed to say the least, I headed to the Khan el-Khalili market for food and sensual stimulus. If you have never experienced an African or Middle Eastern market, 'do yourself a favor', as Molly would say, and put it on your bucket list.

Egypt links northeast Africa to the Middle East and dates back millennia to the time of the pharaohs. The Pyramids and the Sphinx outside of Cairo in Giza, Luxor's hieroglyphic-lined Karnak Temple and Valley of the Kings, and the Aswan Dam are all breathtaking.

In the market I feasted with a Bedouin family. In any remote foreign journey, you lay your trust down and pray you don't end up writhing with food poisoning. I ate cautiously and drank fragrant Karkade tea made from hibiscus flowers. The patriarch of the family watched me intently.

I can hear my mother's stern travel advice: 'Don't wear jewellery; you're asking to be robbed'. Quite the opposite occurred, as the kindly gentleman offered me one hundred camels for my hand in marriage to his son.

Now we're talking.

Molly provided the Egypt to-do list.

I arranged a trip 'up' the Nile. The tour was conducted by a renowned Egyptologist from Cairo University — Dr Said Gohary. Handsome and highly intelligent, he looked like an Egyptian Gary Ashley.

We hooked up during the boat trip. He took me to places I could otherwise never have reached — geographically. Hidden markets off the shores of Luxor where antiquities were surreptitiously sold.

I admit to buying a few Coptic pieces I intended to bequeath to Molly. Once we had floated as far as Aswan, Dr Said got a flight back to Cairo, and we planned to meet up again. The heat in Aswan was stultifying, but floating in a pool for a few days was what the doctor had ordered. Back in Cairo, we attended a chamber concert and restaurants, my lover regaling me with the history of Egypt. I was hooked in a delightful holiday romance. Said had his cousin drive me to Alexandria to stay with his extended family.

I visited the oldest library in the world. Established during the reign of Ptolemy II, it dates from around 285 BC. Its foundation was dedicated to the Muses, the nine goddesses of the arts. If I couldn't find inspiration here, where could I?

Back to Cairo for the last few days spent at Mena House, under the watchful gaze of the pyramids. I was to visit this place again many years later, under extremely different circumstances.

I would never see Said again, grateful for time spent in his academic and loving thrall. I did, however, stumble across 'seeing' him again in 2009. My son, a committed Egyptophile, was watching a documentary including Dr Gohary. I sat quietly so as not to be questioned by my inquisitive children.

Back at Molly's I retold my Egyptian adventures and got back to work.

One thing life with Molly offered me was the opportunity to experience all people as equals. Celebrities, footballers, politicians, local shopkeepers … all people were welcome; the house was never empty.

He is a genuinely remarkable human being who never forgot his humble beginnings in regional Victoria. I do not suffer from the affliction known as 'starstruck' — maybe other than with Woody Allen when I asked him to marry me. Being able to relate to famous people in a grounded way is pivotal to the career I have enjoyed.

Back to the never-ending party at Molly's house. As the world's superstar musicians toured Melbourne, the post-show party was always on Highett Street. Stevie Nicks used the upstairs bathroom, adjacent to my bedroom, to powder her nose and nearly fell down the spiral staircase. One Sunday afternoon, we threw a quiet BBQ with Elton John, his mother, and his aunt.

Molly and Elton had a long-standing love/hate relationship. One argument between them was in Sydney during Elton's 1986 Tour de Force shows.

Elton and Molly, while drinking, could wind each other up ferociously. Molly upset Elton, and Elton was made to leave the venue. Dressed in a full 18th-century wig, à la Amadeus, Elton leapt into the waiting limo; Molly grabbed onto the door handle, begging him to return to do the show. Truly a sight to behold, and thankfully, before the dreaded social media could have made it anything more than the folklore it became.

Alongside Melodian, we started a dance label, 'Body Beat'.

Largely imported product of 12" tracks, it helped to serve the ever-growing number of nightclubs springing up across Australia. DJs came to my office on Fridays to pick up product. A female DJ from the Hilton Hotel surprised me with a question: 'Do you know a guy called Clive?' Yes, I replied, I used to be married to him. After she stopped laughing, she told me Clive was living with a woman who 'worked the rooms' at the Hilton, and he had no idea. Brilliant.

Kylie and Terry Blamey had relocated to London. All marketing choices were being made by PWL. Keen to repeat the success we had with Kylie, Gary and I signed Jason Donovan. I was eager to work with Guy Pearce, who appeared on the 'Locomotion' demo tape. He struck me as a refined intellect in the Neighbours group. But no amount of chasing him in the green room at Channel Ten would coerce him — he wasn't interested in a pop career.

Given his acting accolades, he made the correct choice.

It was a delight working with Jason and his manager, Richard East. His relationship with Kylie was well out in the open, especially after the Neighbours wedding sequence. It was decided a duet track should be released: 'Especially for You'.

I had a soft spot for Jason, a warm human being, and our paths would cross again years later in two separate stage stories.

My time living with Molly was coming to an end. Some days we became a bickering old married couple. I was turning into his moniker for me — Attila. It had suited Molly and me to cohabitate for a time, but now I needed a fresh start and moved to a flat near St Kilda Road.

My darling friend Molly — aka Lovey Luxor or Mouldy Mildew — didn't take the news I was leaving very well.

The upstairs bedroom I occupied had a waterbed. As I started to pack, Molly jumped upon the bed, tossing contents out of my suitcase. Some items ended up over the balcony in the pool. One was my autographed Bob Geldof book. Now I was mad. I gave up and was made to leave with what little I had.

I marched out the gate as dramatic as Bette Davis. Straight into my BMW, Molly was in hot pursuit. I commanded him to move away from the car.

He laughed.

A remorseful pleading broke the laughter. 'Oh, come on, lovey, come back inside'. NO. I put my petulant foot down — also literally on the pedal. I was faced with the possibility of killing the most important music icon in Australia or ceasing driving until he calmed down. My choice was obvious. This was certainly not the last daredevil move he would make; one years hence it nearly did kill him.

My new apartment was close to The Chevron nightclub where Molly DJ'd. To retaliate for leaving him, he got his revenge by turning up at 3 am, pressing my door buzzer until I let him in. God, I loved him.

Nothing would ever tear us apart. On his overseas music junkets, I would look after the house if Lynne Randell was not around.

One time coincided with Daryl Sims, the drummer from Indecent Obsession, celebrating his birthday. Everyone was in town, so we had a party for artists and friends. I may have mentioned this to Molly as he was running late to the airport; I don't quite remember … neither did he.

Well, the party might have gotten a bit out of hand. The band arranged a stripper as Daryl's 'gift'.

I had invited a few journalists — once a PR, always a PR …

The next front page of the Truth newspaper ran the headline 'Pop Bash Blonde strips to whip'. Molly returned from overseas, and I was summoned to Gudinski's office.

Poor Michael. Along with Warren Costello, during these 'differences of opinion', they became like parents in the conflict. You know the old saying, 'Wait till your father gets home!' My ears bled from how loud Molly yelled and no amount of sorry would appease him.

'Disrespectful!' 'My home!' 'You should know better!' 'I love you, but …' On and on it went.

I had a giggle to myself that I was being admonished for the lifestyle Molly lived by — namely partying 24/7. Gudinski looked at Molly and nodded his head in 'stern' agreement while rocking in his leather chair. Periodically, the real boss in the room would turn to me, out of Molly's view, and wink in solidarity at how ridiculous this had become.

In my own home once again, the adrenaline-fueled domestic tenure with Molly gave way to hosting Sunday afternoon parties. It became the hottest weekend invite in town.

I made a vow to myself on entering the music business that I would NOT sleep with musicians, a vow I kept until one pleasant Sunday afternoon, and his secret is safe with me.

I would go on to break that rule in earnest over a decade later!

The Indecent Obsession debut album was ready to launch.

I flew to Queensland for a photo shoot. We struck on the idea of filming in their natural habitat — the surf beaches of Queensland. Molly was fully on board with this idea — until he wasn't. The band was half OK with it and half uncomfortable. The look on guitarist Andrew Coyne's face on the album cover says it all.

The band employed an arrogant attorney named John Kenny, based in Brisbane. What is it about Queensland legal personnel that makes them believe themselves to be superior to the southern states? This has been my experience sadly more than once. Kenny was thrilled to be doing business with the Mushroom Group and stretched it out, thinking he was going to get legal brownie points for fucking over Michael Gudinski. What a rube. Simon Young can play legal racquetball with the best of them. Years later John Kenny tried to legally screw Michael Chugg, Kevin Jacobsen and me.

The Indecent Obsession album debuted in November '89. We were off and running with 'Say Goodbye' as a Top 10 single. The band appeared on a TV show also featuring musical comedy act The Doug Anthony All Stars. A bunch of smart-arses, university-type pseudo-intellectuals, attempting to be Monty Pythonesque. Not my cup of tea.

They attempted a demoralizing verbal joust with the Brisbane pop boys.

Andrew Coyne was going to punch Paul McDermott's lights out. This transpired in front of their manager, who was Paul's girlfriend — a petite blonde woman with a supercilious grin.

I would later learn this was Liz Koops. Our paths would cross again. Luckily, I wasn't goaded by the band into verbal retaliation with her that day.

'Tell Me Something' quickly followed as the second single. Gary was truly impressed with the band's performance and worked hard to garner interest for an international release. Frontier Touring came to our aid and created a 'double bill' tour with American teen queen Debbie Gibson.

'IO' as they became known, cut their teeth touring. They were a legitimate band playing venues that underage David Dixon shouldn't have been allowed entry to. This was no Milli Vanilli. They were a tight live unit. The tour with Debbie Gibson sold well. Jo Beth Taylor came on board as a backing vocalist for Indecent Obsession. She and Debbie hit it off and formed a real on-the-road gal-pal team.

There was a twinkle in David's eye every time he saw Debbie. It was clear something could, and should NOT, happen. Her mother was on the road as her manager and watched like a hawk.

There was interest from American record labels. Gary suggested we fly together on a swift-selling junket. First in line was MCA in Los Angeles, run by Al Teller. Next on the schedule were New York-based labels, which I preferred as appropriate for this band. My rationale was based on Atlantic signing Debbie Gibson and Epic having Wham!

The time in LA coincided with Gudinski being in town recording with Jimmy Barnes at Dave Stewart's studio in Encino. Toby Creswell flew in to hang out, providing an opportunity for another round in our elongated affair. We were staying at the Mondrian on Sunset Boulevard.

I was supremely happy.

Here was my California dream from 1974 writ large. Toby and I took a few days to drive out to 29 Palms and explore in the desert. In a red convertible sports car, my life was at a pinnacle. After my delusional first marriage, I now experienced joy in a relationship. Our fun and games amounted to the best sex I had ever had, moments I hold firmly in a metaphysical bottle.

Toby and I visited Jimmy and Jane Barnes in their Encino studio.

Gudinski was in full flight, so thrilled with how the tracks were progressing.

Toby and I had stayed on the down-low with our personal relationship, but now, entering the room after our Desert Dalliance, it was clear where we were at. Gudinski strode up to Toby and collared him.

Conjure Brando's Godfather: 'If you don't do right by her, you answer to me'. I blushed at Michael's genuine concern for my emotional welfare. A far cry from his questions when I joined the company and a welcome sign of the respect we had built between us.

A fortuitous reacquaintance happened on this trip.

Deborah Conway, whom I met in 1977 singing Linda Ronstadt into hairbrushes, was living in Los Angeles. Her band, Do-Ré-Mi, had hits including the controversial 'Man Overboard'.

Deborah had been enticed to London as a solo artist. Disenchanted with her record label, she left for LA. Her boyfriend was a friend of Toby's; we hung out.

DC and I really hit it off. I was keen to hear her songs. I espoused the virtues of signing with the Mushroom Group should she decide to return to Australia. It was only the beginning.

Focusing on the international future for Indecent Obsession, Gary and I met with Al Teller at MCA's 'Black Rock' built by Lew Wasserman.

Shoulders back, tits out. I am FABULOUS. This is the LA life I knew I was destined to live.

Al Teller was enthusiasm personified: 'We want your band, it will be huge, you don't need American management, you can do it yourself, Amanda, we will support your every move …'

My first experience of American corporate BS. They offered a huge amount of money as an advance. We left the meeting. Gary looked at me and said, in no uncertain terms, 'We are taking the deal'. I should have argued on instinct but was rendered speechless. I owned a third of the label; it was Gary, so I didn't argue. We flew to New York and met with attorney Paul Schindler from Grubman, Indursky & Schindler to iron out the deal. I regained my argumentative style and posited, as we were in New York, why not go ahead and meet with Atlantic and other labels? But it was Gary. And he always knew how to get his way around me.

Now Gary had Schindler on his side. A second opinion: 'take the deal'. I admired Paul and was pleased to work with him again decades later.

Debbie Gibson invited Jo Beth Taylor to her home in New York's Long Island to record. We spent a couple of days going over song selections before Gary joined us. Debbie was mostly a spoilt brat, and her mother was the atypical showbiz Mom. They personified 'nouveau riche' and flaunted details of neighbours, like Billy Joel, to impress us.

Gary and I had to head to London on other business. I would only be gone a matter of days. The last thing I said to Jo Beth was, 'DO NOT sign anything!'

I returned to find she had signed worldwide management and recording with Debbie's mom.

The champion Indecent Obsession had was Stuart Watson, who headed up International for MCA in London. Stuart was instrumental in breaking Britney Spears, the Backstreet Boys and Justin Timberlake worldwide. He was the first person in the world to hear 'Bohemian Rhapsody' — Freddie Mercury played it to him on the piano.

All-boy pop bands were a successful commodity in the late '80s. I use the word commodity deliberately. International tours take a lot of money, risk and hard graft. We were up against the new wave of Bros and New Kids on the Block amongst others.

A massive marketing campaign was put in place for UK, Europe, Asia and South Africa. The band were suitably impressed and knuckled down to get their live show perfected.

We had a saying: 'Tuesday, it must be Belgium'.

This is a common allegory amongst touring artists when every night is another city. The hectic pace would later become too much for David Dixon.

Japan became a huge market for the band. Fans clamoured as we exited airports, train stations and hotels. Indecent Obsession played stadium-sized shows with a Japanese act called Hikaru Genji, whose members performed on roller skates — it was both authentic and bizarre.

After the Osaka performance, we were taken to a nightclub. Some models, both Japanese and international, were invited to hang out with the band. The chances of both Michael and David meeting their future wives that night were likely one in a million, but it happened. Both Belinda from Brisbane (David) and Denise from the US (Michael) were working as models in Japan.

The biggest coup Stuart Watson pulled off was our success in South Africa. Indecent Obsession was the first international act to perform after Paul Simon's tour served to lift the cultural isolation rulings during apartheid.

Our teen band from Down Under was the first across that marvellous continent.

We had been out of Australia a long time. I feared our profile was on the wane. Molly suggested we take a journalist from Australia to witness how big the band had become internationally.

Tall poppy syndrome had set in, the phenomenon where any Australian artist — singer, writer, actor and dancer — who leaves for overseas is cut down to size. What a bloody joke. In that the world's contracted thus, to quote John Donne, that is fortunately no longer the case. Australia now applauds 'our' Nicole, Keith, Hugh, Cate, Naomi, Margot … for the accolades their talent brings to our distant shores.

Paul Stewart from the Sunday Herald Sun was a respected music journalist and member of the band Painters & Dockers, who'd been signed to

Mushroom. When the Dockers released the single 'Die Yuppie Die', I was the voice of the yuppie on the recording. Paul was a gas. We flew him to South Africa to witness the evolution of Indecent Obsession.

Despite the #1 records across Asia and South Africa, our dent in the UK market merely hit Top 40.

Enter Mushroom alumni — Ms Minogue and Mr Blamey. Indecent Obsession was granted the opening slot for Kylie's tour across the UK and Northern Ireland. Kylie's mother, Carol, was on the road with us. I was reminded what a wonderful family unit they were together.

Our tour journeyed in buses, and, for the most part, Kylie travelled separately. One day she joined us after a show. Somewhere salubrious like Sheffield, she jumped on the tour bus like the impossible princess she claimed to be …

Daryl Sims, our drummer, was a renowned sex fiend. Anything to do with sex and pornography — consenting adults only — floated his boat. He hung out at the back of the bus with porn publications, perusing pages with Kylie's drummer, John Creech. Why is it always the drummers?

Kylie was making friendly conversation with everyone when she made her way towards the back of the bus. I was filled with dread. She was going to spin out — not around — when she realized what Daryl was 'reading'.

To my amazement, quite the contrary occurred. Kylie sat beside Daryl, took the magazine and thumbed through the pages. Soon they were exchanging commentary on the publication's princesses:

'She is pretty', 'Oh, I love that thong', 'That position looks weird to me …'

Never judge a book by its cover.

The tour reminded me what an incredible performer Kylie had become. Guile personified and never a doubt this was the career format she would cherish the most — live performance.

Our last shows were in Belfast. We toured the ravaged city. The tanks and destroyed landscapes, while surreal, gave me pause and made me not want to return. I just didn't know why until 25 years later.

Next stop was Los Angeles for the Indecent Obsession American album release. I rented a fantastic apartment in West Hollywood previously owned by Maurice Chevalier. Occasionally I wish I had stayed there, as imagined in 1974. This was Laurel Canyon before I understood its cultural significance.

Indecent Obsession's single release 'Tell Me Something' cracked the US Top 40, but the album 'peaked' at #148 on Billboard. I was not close to delivering Gudinski his coveted #1 in America.

I spent endless days working in my apartment. It was Laurel Canyon, and I felt at home. A degree of irony hit me as another Australian band — INXS – were rocketing up the charts with 'Suicide Blonde' and the X album. I realized I should not have listened to Al Teller at MCA and secured American management. I had meetings with the Lippman brothers and would have happily handed the band's management to them. They inked a deal with UK act Bros, so it became a conflict of interest.

Michael, David and I had a bizarre meeting with the Bros boys at Barney's Beanery and walked away wondering how they managed to split one brain between them.

All too soon I moved back to Melbourne and bought a cat. I saw Clive the Ex occasionally, but nothing serious. LC and Rob got married and, as a bridesmaid, I was overweight and unhappy. LC was on a high: she secured her prince and was going to live her best life. Annual goals included a new Mercedes and Botox.

Deborah Conway moved to Melbourne and signed a deal with Mushroom Records for the 'known and unknown world's'. This amusing epithet appeared in a song she wrote for me 20 years later. Gudinski loved Deborah, and the recording of her debut solo album, String of Pearls, became a priority.

We rolled MAP Management into the new venture: MGM — Michael Gudinski Management. We represented Deborah Conway, Indecent Obsession and the man himself — Jimmy Barnes.

Deborah and I had a marvellously maleficent professional relationship. She was even more feisty than me and much more likely to get her way. I wanted to please her, as I thought the album was one of the greatest albums ever to be released by the Mushroom Group.

Now to that wrong turn …

I never had a 'run with the pack' mentality, but suddenly it consumed me. My friends were having babies; what about me? Did Clive and I really give it our best shot? Lingering doubts crept in. Was that the reason I was tempted again? The Elizabeth Taylor in me? The prediction LC made that I would be married five times?

I have always, without fail, chosen to see the best in people. Likely to the point of fault. I blindside myself to people's flaws and bad intent. This involves forfeiting what is best for me along the way. This predominant attitude remains to this day — if it doesn't work out, move on to something else.

Clive and I announced we were getting re-married.

My friend Andrew Lehmann photographed the event. Weather appeared inclement. My bridesmaid turned up wearing black — another omen. Clive's brother flew from London as his best man. This served as a solid reminder of the family I was marrying into — again.

A bouquet of flowers arrived. It was an old flame from Sydney saying, 'Don't do it, wait for me'. He neglected to include the word 'run', but I will always love him for the gesture.

There was no aisle this time, no jokes with Dad. It was the quickest service we could muster.

Then it was over.

Only ten months later did I truly understand why I went through this again.

I hit the road again with the band. No honeymoon, straight back to work.

I flew out to LA while Clive waited to join me.

Stuart Watson found a house for the band and their newlywed Den Mother, in Bel Air on Nicada Drive. The home was owned by John Deacon, bass player from Queen. John and his wife were so kind, allowing me to nest in their alternate home.

We were in pre-production recording the second Indecent Obsession album with Peter Wolf in Simi Valley. Gary introduced Peter as producer and co-writer. He had success with Starship ('We Built this City'), Wang Chung ('Everybody Have Fun Tonight') and Go West ('King of Wishful Thinking').

Our routine was akin to mom doing the school drop-off.

I would drive the band to Peter's studio, where they collaborated on songs and hung out. The house on Nicada Drive was inspirational as a space, enabling me to work 'remotely' with Deborah Conway. This was using 'dial-up'. For those of you who don't recall dial-up, it was the precursor to Wi-Fi/internet and used a telephone.

Deborah was putting the finishing touches on her album in Melbourne. She and her partner Willy planned to visit.

Clive arrived, and we took a few days off to 'honeymoon'.

The disconnect was already apparent. He was resentful of leaving Australia and disapproved of me working so hard. We drove south to Mexico, stopping in Ensenada.

At this point I was not a drinker. No frequent wine with dinner, no cocktail hour. Drinking was reserved for going out and party time. When in Mexico … a couple of massive margaritas later, I realized the merits of tequila.

We continued honeymooning, driving north to San Francisco. I had flashbacks to a year or so before — driving with Toby out to 29 Palms and how alive that made me feel. The comparison with my now dull companion and almost non-existent romance was startling. By the time we were in San Francisco, I felt ill, and it occurred to me I was pregnant. In Los Angeles, my doctor confirmed this joyous news. My fears were allayed: after years of uncertainty after my cancer scare, I was going to be a mother.

Clive returned to Australia, to his job and his beloved car.

It was that simple. His pregnant wife stayed in LA and pandered to the whims of her adolescent band members. Marital equilibrium alluded me.

I lay on the couch in Bel Air with headphones on, listening to Deborah's album and new demos for Indecent Obsession. As my first child grew inside me, I would place the headphones on my belly to get their 'opinion'. They — as I did not know their sex pre-birth — clearly preferred the String of Pearls album … she still does.

The Michael Gudinski Management company had grown, as had my belly. Ian 'Smithy' Smith came on to look after Jimmy Barnes, and we were one big happy family. Jimmy visited Dundas Lane and jokingly said, 'You're puttin' on some weight, darlin'!' Knowing full well I was pregnant, I was still mortified.

I forgave him.

Melodian Records was a much-loved point of focus for me. Molly was obsessed with Peter Andre. Jo Beth Taylor had had her '99 Reasons' and went off to marry tennis star Thomas Muster. Roxus was a stalwart of the Melbourne music scene, but chart hits evaded them.

And as I was on the cusp of giving birth, Indecent Obsession did a tour of South America without me.

I contemplated why we didn't expand the Melodian Records stable. Molly had a full schedule with Hey, Hey It's Saturday, the reboot of Countdown Revolution on ABC, writing for various tabloids, and his own life to lead. Michael Gudinski was touring the world's biggest acts under the Frontier banner with Chuggi. Gary was expanding Mushroom into international waters with plans for a London office. And I was about to have a baby. Everyone was busy.

Deborah's album was set for release in late October. The first single, 'It's Only the Beginning', was an instant hit. The video portrayed her à la

Katharine Hepburn, playing golf with her chum Kaarin Fairfax. Kaarin and I went to kindergarten together. She went on to marry Paul Kelly. Despite Deborah being artistically far away from Kylie Minogue, my creative instinct kicked in.

Elvie Hill's workroom whipped up a pair of red-and-white checked golfing pants for DC.

Michael Gudinski had no qualms about paying for Deborah's video until he saw the result. He tore strips off me. He presumed the imagery was going to portray his newest female star in a more permissive manner than playing golf in tweed trousers.

He needed to get to know Deborah Conway a whole lot better …

Festival Records scheduled the album release for October 25. I was due to give birth on November 10.

On the morning of Monday, October 28, I drove to Freemasons Maternity Hospital for my weekly checkup. Dr Peterson, the woman who saved me from cervical cancer, performed the perfunctory check and calmly mentioned, 'Well, you are two centimetres dilated. I think we are having a baby today'.

'I'm sorry, can you repeat that please?'

I asked to use her office phone and called Clive.

Calmly proffering instructions: 'Please go home, pack a bag for the hospital, you know socks and underwear, and meet me at the birthing suite'. Next call to my assistant: 'I won't be in today, I'm having a baby, cancel my lunch with Deborah, fax the charts to the hospital, I'll call you later'.

Clive arrived at the hospital, harried from the task of packing a bag. I opened the bag to find seven pairs of HIS socks and HIS underpants. Please God, don't let this child, whoever they become, inherit his lack of grey cells.

I hadn't been one of those women who creates a 'birth plan' or gets into the weeds on pain meds or down-dog positions. After six hours I stated very clearly to the midwife, 'GET ME THE DRUGS!'

The anaesthetist came from a nearby hospital. She inserted the epidural, and the world was instantly a better place.

At 7.12 pm a squidgy little girl appeared and thankfully did not inherit the nose I displayed at birth. She was perfect. I named her Olivia Elvie. A perfect alliteration to honor my mother and music powerhouse Olivia Newton-John.

There is a guy I know who wrote a song about this moment — it's called 'A Little Ray of Sunshine'. I didn't register its relevance then, and I wouldn't know until many years later how significant it was, but he sure was right. As Brian Cadd introduces his song on stage: 'It is the cleverest thing we humans do', create these little people who can grow into any manner of beings. For some of us happily, and for some — in his instance — not so much.

I left the hospital and went with Clive to start life as parents.

What could go wrong?

Many years later, in Paris, I met a woman who hailed from Melbourne. When I asked her why she left for Paris in her youth, she stated very plainly, 'I saw myself waking up one day living in Toorak, unhappily married, taking the kids to the same school I went to, driving a new Mercedes every year, and living in a house in Portsea, and I knew I didn't want that cookie-cutter life'. Hit the nail on the head. That was the life I had unwittingly created for myself, and so here I was … Day 1 at home in Toorak with a new baby — me crying, not the baby — and wondering where we would go from here.

I decorated the house in Laura Ashley wallpaper and hosted afternoon teas. Sue Gudinski was so sweet and brought me a beautiful lamp that sat beside Olivia's bed for many years. I thrived on making Olivia handmade vegetarian meals. I was growing into becoming the 'all round' woman — wife, mother, provider, feeder.

I loved cooking and had to question where I derived this enjoyment from, given my own mother couldn't boil an egg.

When Olivia had trouble sleeping, I put Joni Mitchell's Blue album on … 'A Case of You' lulled her to sleep while I dreamt of life in LA, in Joni's Laurel Canyon.

I moved back to Los Angeles four months later, baby in tow. We moved back into John Deacon's Bel Air house, and he helped me find a nanny for baby Olivia. She was a former Iranian princess. She had fled the regime and her tyrannical husband for a new life in America. I was beyond happy to provide her refuge. Olivia was turning into a cute, chubby baby and as a working, ostensibly single, mother, I felt peace.

Indecent Obsession's Indio album, recorded with Peter Wolf, was released worldwide. Touring progressed through Europe, where the band appeared at some wacky festivals and on TV shows. European pop music was diverse in the early '90s. They appeared with acts like Roxette and Army of Lovers. The next port of call was South Africa, which had become a watershed territory for us.

Irving Schlossberg was the head of our record company in South Africa. He went on record saying, 'Our country has never seen anything like the hysteria associated with Indecent Obsession. It's the closest thing to Beatlemania we have ever had. At their promotional concerts, it was the first time I have ever been able to introduce an international band to a South African audience'.

On our first trip we had been mindful of ensuring the record was promoted to both white and black radio stations, which remained as divided as oil and water in the early '90s. Irving told me when Paul Simon toured before us — he was the first international artist allowed into South Africa — his concert wasn't as successful as it should have been as he didn't have the support of the black nationalist groups. In collaboration with Stuart Watson and Irving, we agreed to hold a series of musical workshops on behalf of the South African Musicians' Alliance, who had ratified our touring and were in full support of the band. Overseeing the workshops as our MC and cultural guide was James Mange, the former ANC military commander imprisoned with Mandela on Robben Island, where he converted to Rastafari and became the first prisoner in South Africa to refuse to cut his hair. In jail, the dreadlocked James formed a reggae band called the Whiplashes.

Musicians attended workshops, and it became obvious there was a wealth of talent across this vast country. A small Jo'burg band named No Friends of Harry told us they had been disillusioned for a long time, as they couldn't take their music beyond their own borders. They credited us with opening the door to outside music. Progress was buoyed by the recent referendum to dismantle apartheid.

The next tour was the money maker. The lead track from the Indio album, 'Kiss Me', stayed at #1 in South Africa for 27 consecutive weeks.

Stuart Watson set us up with local promoter Mike Fuller. A numbskull character in a cheap suit. Stuart joined us in Cape Town to appreciate the success of our hard work. Concerts were in football stadiums everywhere from Jo'Burg to Port Elizabeth. Despite the apartheid restrictions having been lifted, Fuller only marketed and sold tickets to a Caucasian audience.

While tracking ticket sales, there was no way of ascertaining this hideous fact. I realized during the first show. I was infuriated. The promoter argued no 'black kids' could afford the tickets. I had Australian tour and production managers on the road — Jon Pope and Denis Sheahan.

Venues had wire fencing covered in tarpaulin to restrict viewing to paid ticket holders. Outside were hundreds of South African teenagers listening to the music. I grabbed Jon Pope and instructed his crew to rip the tarpaulin down. Fuck the racist promoter, fuck the ticket sales … we had to take a stand.

Was this how Michael Lang felt when he declared Woodstock a free festival in 1969?

A sense of civic duty and equality. I would not know that answer until much later.

With the band safely on stage, I roamed the outer perimeter, grinning from ear to ear, watching kids who would never have seen a touring pop group before.

Remember what I said about why I do what I do?

Boys and girls, black and white, jumping up and down with excitement was all the payday I needed.

We were treated like royalty by the record company and earned some well-deserved recreation at wineries in the Stellenbosch region. The crew scored some additional stimulants — 'Malawi Gold'. I was not a stoner, but this stuff was mind-blowing. David was very protective of his voice and got frustrated if we smoked on the tour bus. Szumowski built a plastic shield around him, which was both comedic and futile.

On a break we were invited to record in a lavish new studio built by the King of Bophuthatswana, himself a rock 'n' roller. 'Bop', as it was known, was made an independent principality in 1977 by the apartheid regime of South Africa and bordered Botswana. The self-declared king had spent $US5 million to build his version of Abbey Road. Our MCA manager arranged for a local choral band to record with us. The five hits Indecent Obsession had across South Africa were re-recorded with indigenous authenticity.

Recordings from those sessions are highlights from my career output.

I stood in the control room and wept at the beauty of the voices. Get a hold of a copy; do yourself the proverbial favor. I wished that Molly could have been there to witness this moment. The incredible journey from finding these young musical pups in Brisbane to that remote South African studio would have thrilled him — even without there being a full 48-piece orchestra in the mix.

As recording at BOP concluded, David came into my office. 'Dizzy Dixon', as he was known, looked like he had been crying. He poured his heart out that he could not continue touring; he wanted to quit the band and become a helicopter pilot. I began looking around the room for the hidden cameras; surely this was a joke? How could he not want to be in a band enjoying worldwide international success … look where we were sitting!

I was totally stunned. I could not decide whether to strangle him or show empathy.

I made him promise not to say anything to the rest of the band until the end of the tour.

Adding to the stress level: we nearly didn't get a payday from the tour.

I had a local lawyer handling our contracts. When it came time to depart South Africa, the lawyer said we were going to have trouble getting money out of the country.

The promoter's accountants were promising to wire the proceeds to us in Australia as soon as the tour was rectified. Gut instinct is everything, and I knew they were going to shaft us. We had a burly security guy who travelled with us throughout South Africa. This guy carried a gun. There were gun lockers at the entrance to nightclubs we entered. Fierce.

This had terrified me, but now I realized we could put it to use.

We met the promoters to finalize accounts. Denis and the security guy came with me, flanking me like I was Al Pacino in Scarface. I could have used some marching powder to give me additional courage. I took an empty suitcase and told the promoters we were not leaving until it was filled with our money. Like a Hollywood audition, I added, 'And hurry up getting to the bank or "Trigger Happy Terry" here is likely to get mad'.

I was trembling on the inside but blue steel outside.

It came time to face the music on the band's future. Gary Ashley was convinced David would come around. Stuart was as mad at David as I was but didn't skip a beat in maintaining his loyalty to the band project.

There was a band meeting where the terrible news was revealed. Dixon and Szumowski had a volatile relationship, but this betrayal was beyond compare, while Daryl tried to keep everyone together.

Molly took the news with a grain of salt, probably on the rim of a tequila glass. He was too busy consoling me because, like the true friend he was, he saw how much this affected me. I seriously thought I could have prevented it, but there was nothing I could do.

What pained me most was the thought of David throwing away his career when he was such a great singer.

Despite leaving the band, David's solo star was on the rise. He landed the lead role in Joseph and the Amazing Technicolor Dreamcoat and a part in Australian TV soap opera Home and Away.

For Joseph's opening night, publicist Bruce Pollack arranged live camels, with their coats painted in many colors, for a photo opportunity. Bruce is one of life's great people hands down.

It made a striking image, especially when a camel urinated all over David and Tina Arena!

Time came for my return to London. This generated a poignant argument between Clive and me in our second attempt at a happy marriage. He did not want to go back to his homeland. I vowed to make a happy home and asked if he would please try, for our daughter Olivia's sake.

For the second time, in a second country, I navigated life as a helicopter single parent. There was joy in my little toddler, despite her dreadful eating habits. Tinned sweetcorn and apples were all she agreed to consume. We developed a closeness in our 4th-floor walk-up. I shopped around for a home to buy and build our life together with Clive. My naivety got the better of me yet again; I thought London was our source of opportunity and happiness.

At MCA we conducted interviews for Indecent Obsession Mk2. Daryl and Michael had written a wealth of new material. We felt it was imperative to get a new album out quickly. Richard Hennessey arrived for his audition wearing more makeup than Divine and fancied himself as a George Michael type. I personally thought his voice was weak and he had no 'star quality'. But Stuart Watson believed he was a fit. Guitarist Graham Kearns, on the other hand, was a virtuoso, and after his time in IO, he went on to have a stellar career, including with George Michael.

David Dixon transferred from 'Joseph' in Australia to a touring run of the show in the UK. 'Home and Away' had put him on the pop star map, just like Kylie and Jason in Neighbours before him.

Clive, Olivia and I went to Scotland to see David Dixon and visit my Highland family. I convinced Gary Ashley to take advantage of David's media exposure and record a single called 'Faith, Love & Understanding' with Peter Vettese.

I was positive it would be a hit, but it missed the mark.

Mushroom never had their heart in it, so David and Belinda headed back to Australia. He was going to start his helicopter pilot career.

Life choice change was everywhere.

Clive flew back to Australia, this time with Olivia. It was the first cut in a festering wound of a marriage. This coincided with a visit to the London office by Gudinski. He bowled in to tell me it was my tenth anniversary with the company. I burst into tears and told him my marriage was over — never one for open displays of affection, the poor man didn't know what to do.

Indecent Obsession recorded their new album, Relativity, in Camden with Ian Richardson and Nick Coler. MCA positioned the band towards the dance market for Europe. Ian and Nick produced The KLF and were heavy-duty committed. The studio they used was underneath a drug lab. This could either turn out well or very badly. The drug of choice in this era was ecstasy.

I was in a frame of mind to disappear out of myself.

After an all-nighter at the band's house, I walked straight into actor Rowan Atkinson on the street. All I could see was his character, Mr Bean, in front of me. I thought I was still tripping.

Seal's debut album was a huge hit when I encountered Seal in the flesh.

We had tickets to the MTV Awards. I was rocking on way too much of everything by the time we got to the after-party. The euphoria manifested in a heightened desire to dance. I spotted Seal on the dance floor and made a beeline for him, using my best Countdown dance moves. I was locked and loaded and FABULOUS. While we danced, I started dry-humping Seal's leg on the dance floor. Oh God. Thankfully, there were no mobile phone selfies at this juncture of my sordid existence.

Christmas was approaching, and Gary asked me to put an office party together. This was the beginning of my passion for crazy event parties.

My favorite city, Paris, seemed logical. I didn't tell the staff where we were going. Gary was the only one in on the secret.

The Mushroom UK team was an excellent bunch of people. Amongst the Londoners were Aussie Mushroom recruits Nina Frykberg, Linda Williams and Colin Daniels. We partied all night and took a wicked photo of us all on the Champs-Élysées, printed later for posterity with the epithet, 'I wonder where we will all be next year?'

There was a rumble in the jungle at Mushroom UK. Peter Andre had a few hits, thanks largely to Nina Frykberg. Ash and Garbage were on the rise with Pat Carr and Korda Marshall, and Dannii Minogue was kicking goals with Terry Blamey — why stop at one Minogue when you can have two?

On a less positive note, the tension between Michael Gudinski and Gary Ashley was not good. There was always a 'my way or the highway' with MG. Fair enough, he had built the companies from scratch, but not — as he sometimes inferred — single-handedly. There was an innate contradiction in letting us all operate with unbridled independence and reining us in when he so chose.

The act that had not achieved huge chart success was David Dixon solo. Indecent Obsession was on a writing hiatus, and Deborah was doing exceedingly well touring Australia. It was time to go home.

Before I left London, I shared some parting words with Gary. I was heading into an abyss and needed advice on how to navigate it, both personally and professionally. On the topic of my career, he said something that has stuck with me and frequently reverberates:

'Stick to the things you know'.

CHAPTER 7: MENTAL MONOPOLY BOARD

It soon became clear that it was not only my second marriage at a crossroads but also my time with the Mushroom Group. Parting is such sweet sorrow, as the Bard said, but for Gudinski and me it was more a nod and a wink to a blind horse.

A part of me wishes I had stayed in that illustrious company. But knowing what I know now, I think I made the right choice. After thirteen wonderful years, it wasn't as if I would never cross paths with Michael Gudinski again. I left hoping we would find common ground again one day. My beloved boss didn't display open wrath at my departure, but I know it was deemed a kind of betrayal, as it had been with Michelle Higgins.

I wanted to pursue artist management — the 'things you know' that Gary had referred to in London. Gudinski had a friend, Isaac Apel, a lawyer who wanted to set up an entertainment management company.

We discussed a wish-list artist roster, an amalgam of his legal entertainment clients and my musical talent. We were 'IAM' Management — convenient letters for Isaac Apel and Amanda Michaelson. This was my marital surname I had adopted, second time around, to show a modicum of commitment. I quickly switched back, but not before the final countdown.

The 'IAM' roster of talent grew with the addition of actor/singer Michael Cormick, triple threat Kelley Abbey and more. From Isaac's legal side there was Brigitte Duclos, Rob Gell, Sam Newman and Eddie McGuire. The Nine Network's Footy Show was in its infancy. Sam was a bright character. His thought process could be discombobulated, but I always found him a lot of fun. Above all, he appreciated our work. It was fulfilling to be both seen and heard.

Eddie was not so appreciative. He and his partner Carla had become engaged on a romantic trip to Europe. I sent two gardenia bushes as a gift.

When Eddie came for a meeting, he did not offer a word of thanks. In fact, when Isaac briefly left the room, something strange happened.

The main discussion point of our meeting was sponsorship offers. Eddie had been silent on the topic as Isaac ran through ideas. When Isaac left the room, Eddie lunged at me verbally. With an index finger cocked like it was a Smith & Wesson rifle, he told me he would not take advice from a mere FEMALE associate manager … I smiled sweetly and stopped listening.

When Isaac re-entered the room, Eddie behaved as if only silence had transpired between us.

I hadn't gone through nearly two decades in business with zero misogynistic abuse to allow it to start now. I told Isaac he would have to look after McGuire by himself.

Despite not having a hit with his solo single, David Dixon was still keen on media work. He was invited to be part of a new TV show called Don't Forget Your Toothbrush. The host was Tim Ferguson, one of the Doug Anthony All Stars who had derided Indecent Obsession in the Channel Seven parking lot years before. David was far too cool to bring it up.

The toothbrush producer was the charming Peter Wynne. He invited David and me to the 40 Years of Television event at Studio 9. After the speeches came a surprise performance.

The curtain rose.

Billy Thorpe stunned us all, playing his guitar on 11.

After catching my breath, I thought of the transition from being a kid winning the Sunbury album featuring Billy Thorpe to this moment right now, in this room.

These moments in our lives should have a name, each personally identifiable only to us.

Serendipity? Kismet? Fate? Evolution?

Call it what you will, I sensed in this very moment not only the musical joys of my past but also somehow what were to be the musical joys of my future. An all-consuming cerebral cortex quiver, a knowing that can't quite be enunciated.

I watched Billy's performance transfixed and felt remarkably close to him, like we had met before or known each other in a past life.

It was inexplicable.

We did not meet that night, but it would not be long until we did.

I was playing tennis with my friend Tamara and an English journalist, Matt Preston. I told Tam I was going to leave the business partnership with Isaac. Riffing on names for my new management company, Matt hit the
    ball and offered, 'Firm Hand — you really are a firm hand'.

And there it was.

I stayed in touch with Michael Brereton, the lawyer I met through Gudinski. Unlike Isaac, this lawyer remained a friend. He helped me find an office with Ralph Carr Management. Brero' was diversifying into the world of theatre as a producer, along with his partners Mark Pennell, Tim Lawson and Jon Nicholls. Another piece of the six-degree puzzle, as I had worked for Jon doing PR in the 1980s. I needed an assistant and was lucky enough to get Lou Pennell, Mark's sister, to work with me. We built the roster to 36 artists, mainly 'triple threat' performers — actors, singers and dancers.

Michael Cormick landed the lead in Beauty and the Beast. We were in Sydney doing the deal with producer Kevin Jacobsen in the final days of casting. I had a soft spot for Kevin, a big galoot of a bloke who used Oscar-winning doses of self-deprecation to appear less sharp than he was. His older brother, Col Joye, had a more genuine manner.

Kevin was excited by a potential signing for the role of Gaston and asked my opinion on a recent graduate from WAAPA (West Australian Academy of Performing Arts) named Hugh Jackman. His audition had 'STAR' written all over it, no shadow of a doubt.

Kevin introduced me to members of the production team. He pointed towards the back of a guy in a floral shirt and whispered, 'That's Garry, on the phone as usual …'.

That day, I did not meet producer Garry McQuinn. It would be a few more years before I encountered the front of that floral shirt and its missing buttons.

Clive and I parted for the second and definitively last time. He left with vitriolic outbursts and his beloved car. He never understood Husbandry, and his passive-aggressive anger underscored his lack of character.

Olivia was just four yet strangely seemed relieved. My excitable daughter joined my sense of emotional relief, singing and dancing to Alanis Morissette's Jagged Little Pill. My parents were exemplary in helping fill the gap in child caring, both timewise and emotionally.

I may have been single, but I was hardly alone. David Dixon moved in while completing his helicopter pilot's degree. Olivia loved having him around. Orrong Road became an extension of the Sunday party house. Lots of friends made at Mushroom were still in my world, which was fantastic.

One of them played a brilliant trick on me.

The ludicrous gift of McVitty's ceramic koala had been hidden in a tree at our Red Hill property. We placed it far enough off a walking track that, when pointed out, it could fool little kids and drunken adults into believing it was real. One visit I discovered it had disappeared. I checked, and it hadn't fallen from the tree; it was a mystery.

After a time, ransom notes from the koala's captors started to appear in my mailbox. Newsprint cutouts of demands, along with Polaroid photos of the blindfolded koala. I was knocked out at how funny the prank was and had no idea who perpetrated the theatrical hijinks. Ransom grew serious at $20.

At one infamous party, my friend Hilary appeared, flanked by two gargantuan drag queens holding a hessian bag. Party-goers realized she was the Koala-Captor and fell about laughing.

Starting life as a single parent, I moved Firm Hand Management to my home office. A charming suite of rooms looked across tall trees, massively overgrown and shielding the light. I called an arborist who scheduled his son Damien to visit and quote to cut the bank of trees.

Remember the notion of intuition or premonition I mentioned?

As soon as this man mentioned his son's name, I got an inkling of a future connection. I could never have imagined the complexity that person would present in my already complex life.

Damien was 10 years younger than me, a wild-eyed bottle-blond stallion desperate to get out of his gate.

He climbed the offending trees outside my office with ease.

I sat at my desk, totally distracted, watching him ascend with no fear, his gorgeous body only a window away. I was having a dinner party that night.

I invited Damien to attend. As the evening progressed, the 'frisson' between Damien and me was palpable. My guests took their leave. He, on the other hand, never left. It was Lady Chatterley's lover writ large.

Flowers followed with love notes in the mail. Damien was a class act in the art of seduction. I was dubbed 'cougar'. Our relationship escalated quickly. Most importantly, Olivia was happy with a supportive male figure in her life again.

LC and I took turns taking our daughters to school. Here was the life I was so conflicted about anchoring into when Olivia was born. Toorak house – tick. Child in private school — tick. Happy marriage — well, no.

My career was in full swing, yet the other pieces felt somehow too prescriptive. Damien's 'joie de vivre' and 'otherness' from the Toorak gang helped set a balance, at least in my mind, if not in my more docile friends.

Damien's horticultural business was both ramshackle and booming. As he worked 24/7, I saw the manic come out in him. His staff would congregate on my patio deck to be assigned their gardening ventures. Never satisfied with one project at a time, Damien leased a restaurant in Richmond to develop.

Despite living together, we had a somewhat open relationship. I was aware he had a failed engagement prior to me and a girlfriend who hung around, hoping for the pickings I might leave on the bone, so to speak. The night of the restaurant opening, he seemed disoriented. I worried about his mental health for the first time.

Michael Brereton married his ballerina beauty, Sian, at their home. I spent a lovely afternoon chatting with Suzie Howie, joyfully reminding her she inspired me to become a publicist. Suzie saw Jon Nicholls and me speaking and pronounced to Jon, 'You should marry her; she is fabulous!' I had been anointed FABULOUS by a woman I admired so very much.

The open relationship with Damien was wearing thin; our age difference began impacting us. I was 36 and had been around the marital block a few times; he was 25 and wild.

My opinion of marriage was much the same as how you would describe a dead shark. Dead.

Then I attended a wedding. Not just any wedding, but the union of Hugh Jackman and Deborra-Lee Furness. As I approached the church, all I could see was a swathe of umbrellas. This was to shield the bride from paparazzi cameras.

I sat in the church between Kate Ceberano and Michael Cormick, both of whom were singing during the service.

I made some snide remark that marriage was overrated, romance was dead, fidelity is a myth … I may as well have been singing Tina Turner's 'What's Love Got to Do with It', such was my negativity. Until something happened.

The service commenced.

I listened deeply to the vows Hugh and Deb exchanged. The words spread as a soothing mist over everyone in the congregation. I was speechless and weeping at the depth of their love despite their age difference. It was a triumph that restored my faith in love. Michael Cormick and I attended a dinner at the newlyweds' apartment to watch the wedding video. I recognized myself in the congregation — openly blubbering. How embarrassing. At least we got a laugh out of it.

I had become pals with a casting director, Lou Mitchell.

One opening night, both of us tipsy, I suggested Lou accompany me to New York to see some new Broadway shows. 'I'm paying!'

Off we flew in style and went shopping in between performances.

I was there to see Rent. Written by Jonathan Larson, Rent had gestated from the New York Theatre Workshop to Broadway over a period of years. It was a groundbreaking piece of theatre whose author sadly did not live to see it open on Broadway or its phenomenal worldwide success. He died from an undiagnosed aortic dissection ten days before his 36th birthday and the day before Rent's first Off-Broadway preview performance.

It was the most revelatory night in the theatre I had ever experienced. The story of 20-somethings on the poverty line in NYC, with complex lyrics and music that brilliantly formed a bridge between musical theatre and rock.

We hung out with actress Lillias White, who was appearing in Cy Coleman's The Life. I was thrilled to meet her friend Billy Porter, who recorded 'Love Is on the Way' from The First Wives Club movie soundtrack. A superstar in the making with the voice of an angel. He would become the star of Kinky Boots, Pose, and Cabaret, the haute couture superstar he was destined to be.

Weeks later, I jetted off to Singapore to surprise David Dixon, who was starring in a reprisal of Joseph. Upon arrival, I felt queasy.

I put it down to jet lag and bad airline food.

In New York I ruminated with Lou about a life potentially parenting with Damien. Damien and I had pillow-talked about having a family.

I considered myself lucky to have had Olivia and didn't imagine I could become pregnant again. Damien was so wonderful with my daughter; I knew he would make a great dad.

Back from Singapore, a visit to my gynaecologist confirmed I was indeed pregnant. I was so happy. Damien and I giggled like kids, trying to work out when it had 'happened'.

Late summer, we had taken a houseboat in Eildon, figuring it must have been there. A journalist friend, Michael Idato, had joined us on board. We decided he was our lucky charm and nominated him as the impending godparent.

In between the 'boy or a girl' discussions came some darkness. We were unprepared, while also elated and trepidatious. I knew it was to be a lovely addition to Olivia's life, but Damien suddenly had darker moments.

I began to understand why some months later.

In New York, I caught up with Lori Silfen, a kick-ass lawyer who worked at Mushroom for a short time. She was a terrific lady, now working for New Line Cinema on a new film franchise — Austin Powers.

OMG, I had not laughed that much in years.

Revelling in our baby news, I told Damien I did not want to know the sex of the child. I wanted that moment of surprise in the birthing suite.

No ridiculous gender-reveal parties for us.

Dr Peterson, who had saved my life and delivered my daughter, was in charge for this next milestone. I told her I did not want to know the sex of the child ahead of delivery. She called, and Damien answered the phone. From his reaction, I knew I was having a boy. The little bun in my amazingly still functioning oven became known as 'The Shagadelic Baby' after the catchphrase from Austin Powers.

It became obvious upon his arrival he would be named — Austin.

I deviated much of my Firm Hand Management business into casting musical theatre. My offices were now in Flinders Street, alongside producer Jim McPherson. A much-welcome inclusion into my professional life at this point was a true gentleman: Chris Green, producer for Cameron Mackintosh, who employed me to consult in casting Rent.

We set out auditioning singers and actors — advertising in print and radio. Across Australia and New Zealand, we amassed 3,726 people to audition. When we arrived in Brisbane, I told Chris I was pregnant. A photo taken while we were interviewed about the show is the moment I told him my news. The happiness on my face says it all. Ironically, Rent was due to open in the week I was due to give birth.

The show's original casting director, Bernie Telsey, flew from New York for final auditions. His decision-making expertise was a joy to experience. Hearing stories of Jonathan Larson brought even more pride to our endeavours.

The Cameron Mackintosh office in Sydney was a visual feast.

A massive palm tree grew in the central space. At the end of a long day, Chris introduced me to Sir Cameron. I almost flailed into a curtsy, saved just in time by Chris explaining my role in casting Rent from a music industry perspective.

Sir Cameron shook my hand politely and said, 'Ah yes, the rock and roll chick from way back'. I found my voice and retorted, 'Well, not so much of the 'way back' if you don't mind, Sir'.

Damien seemed overwhelmed with work while determined to find us our own home. He did not want to live with the emotional spectre of my previous marriage. I agreed that the 'happy families' scenario there had tumultuously failed.

Many friends were wary of Damien. They just couldn't handle his flamboyance — so many madcap memories of his behavior.

The day he decided to fly out to Thailand and Europe with no luggage had me worried I would never see him again. I was only months into our pregnancy. His mother tried to console me; somehow, I knew there was another agenda.

I would find out what, or who, that 'agenda' was later in a very confronting manner.

On his safe but manic return, Damien sold his Richmond restaurant and found a cute cottage in Hawthorn he was determined we buy. He became more manic as the days progressed. I wanted to believe he was merely under a mountain of stress but instinctively knew he was in trouble. His staff called me to his office. He had devised a PVC pipe plant watering system inside the office. The employees looked on with relief, as if I had arrived to arrest the mayhem.

I was confronted with my beloved partner spiralling into a manic state that neither of us had any control over. He was elated at his watery experiment.

'This is the future of homegrown vegetable gardens!'

He babbled like a mad professor selling me on the concept: we just needed an investor. It would be a brilliant product once we registered the patent.

It was unclear which one of us was in more trouble.

Furniture was ruined, and bills remained unpaid. I called his father to come and help assess the situation. His parents unilaterally claimed, 'Oh, that's just Damien'. They had consistently excused his manic behavior as that of a rampant teenager.

Weeks later, proceeding with the purchase of the Hawthorn cottage, we met at the bank to sign the paperwork. I had not seen Damien for a few days, which was not unusual.

I knew emphatically this mania was not alcohol or drug induced. It is documented either substance can set off exaggerated episodes in what I now recognize as bipolar disorder. The wild blonde stallion I fell in love with arrived at the bank meeting, wearing no shoes or shirt and a dirty denim jacket. His eyes said it all.

Mental illness was scantily acknowledged at this point. I applaud the bank manager who, registering my pregnancy and panic, let the paperwork go through once we had both signed off on the mortgage.

I was terrified, not knowing how to approach the next piece of the conversation. My partner, the father of my unborn child, turned to me and with sincerity said,

'I am going away. You must not tell anyone. I have a cache of guns in the trunk of my car. The CIA reached out to me. They have asked me to go and fight for them in Angola. I may not be back before the baby is born… but I will try'.

It was heartbreaking. There was nothing I could possibly say. You cannot argue with mania.

Bipolar disorder chooses its own highs and lows. Damien was now in a state of high mania where many sufferers imagine themselves as in-demand figures, a kind of Christ-like complex. I watched him drive away. I was Alice falling down the rabbit hole. I took myself straight to the hospital, fearing I was having a breakdown.

Doctors placed me on a heart monitor and administered a relaxant while I made a personal vow. I spoke internally from my heart to my unborn child. Whatever would happen, I would look after him, my shag-a-delic baby, come what may. Losing control of my emotions was not an option. I had to support Damien's eventual diagnosis and recovery and mother my soon-to-be two children. These moments were difficult to navigate without the support of a sibling or best friend to confide in. I was alone in that hospital ward and knew I had to remain strong.

I was casting a spoof on Countdown, the TV show devised by Brian Mannix from the Uncanny X-Men. As if that little pocket rocket hadn't given me enough grief in the Mushroom days, now here I was casting his marginally funny show while heavily pregnant, with a partner gone AWOL.

Damien's accountant told me she had noticed a hefty sum withdrawn from our account and asked if I knew about it.

The next call informed me Damien had been picked up by the police and taken to the psych ward at the Alfred Hospital. He had tried to buy a car with the remainder of the cash he purloined from our account. When quizzed, he had no idea what he'd done with the rest of the money.

Finally, the words were spoken — bipolar disorder.

A doctor took me aside to explain the coming days. Damien had been put in the proverbial padded cell for his own protection. He was straight-jacketed for a short period. I was having an out-of-body experience: this cannot be happening to us, not now. I was only weeks away from having our baby. The full diagnosis was yet to be made, along with how long he would remain in care and the types of medication going forward.

I was thankful for the kindness of this doctor, and his concern shifted to our baby. What were the chances of him inheriting this illness? Male to male, the answer is one in seven. That is not a statistic I will ever forget. In a concerted effort to calm me, this wonderful doctor told me the signs to look out for once Austin reached adolescence — signs Damien's parents had ignored. Touching all the wood within my reach, I can safely say those concerns have never been an issue. Austin is a well-adjusted, highly intelligent young man.

My gynaecologist was apprised of the situation with Damien and monitoring me carefully. She asked me to choose either Friday the 9th or Monday the 12th for my son to be induced. How many souls come onto this earth with pre-ordained timelines according to doctor and hospital schedules?

My casting pal Lou asked if she could be present at Austin's birth. She was in two minds about having babies and wanted to gauge the experience.

We sat together, gossiping while my labor intensified. I barked at her while I was hooked up to a monitor that she could at least get me an icy pole!

Tim Lawson arrived with Olivia, one excited little girl awaiting her baby brother's arrival. She insisted, at age 7, she would stay for the birth. We placated her: 'Of course, you can'. Tim and I had a 'nod & wink'; when it was time, he would take Olivia to McDonald's.

The time came with Dr Clare's command, 'OK, let's push', just as the door flung open and Damien arrived. Thankfully, he was calm, not manic. I could identify the difference. My love held my hand, and with one easy push, our son arrived.

Clare made a joke about bringing a baseball mitt next time — Austin had arrived with such speed and ease. The nurse chortled as she laid our newborn upon my beating heart. They concurred: I was a natural at childbirth and should do it a few more times.

Somehow, I did not think so.

Austin was gorgeous. I was overwhelmed with love as I whispered into his baby ear that I would look after him every day. As opposed to Olivia's delivery and resulting spinal headache, I was calm. Hormonally charged and ready to be a superwoman at home. Amongst all its drama and indecision, isn't life wondrous?

Tim and Olivia arrived back from hamburger heaven. My daughter's protests at having missed the arrival disappeared when she held her tiny, squirmy brother. Damien took Olivia home, and Lou departed. Tim, ever prepared, brought out the champagne. I was shivering from the epidural and seemed to have lost my skill of savouring French champagne.

Tim took his leave; I was finally alone with my new baby boy.

My parents visited; my poor father was almost too weak to hold his new grandson. He had terminal prostate cancer. Amongst everything else life threw at me in these times, the reality of losing my dearest Dad was too much to bear.

My hospital suite was furnished with a double bed, and partners were encouraged to sleep over. Damien was zombie-like on medication.

I had a baby on each side of me.

Despite the ebb and flow of our relationship and the shock of Damien's mental diagnosis, I was the happiest I had been in a long time. Caring for others is my happy place. I had two beautiful children and a challenging partner — what could go wrong?

Finding a doctor to perform a circumcision in a non-Jewish hospital was not easy. On day three, the doctor arrived to do the deed.

I was immediately filled with dread. Not because of the procedure but because of the sight of this professional foreskin remover.

The doctor was an Indian gentleman of extremely short stature.

He was carrying a suitcase so large it could have housed a trombone.

My sense of humour had my mind reeling. A two days old baby penis requires tweezers, not a jackhammer!

I stifled my laughter while Damien slept unawares.

I listened intently through his explanation of the procedure. I handed Austin to the nurse and let the laughter blurt out.

The whole scene was reminiscent of Peter Sellers in The Party — entirely hysterical.

Half an hour later, Austin was handed back to me, neither crying nor laughing, seemingly totally unscathed by the experience.

The three of us made it home to Hawthorn, and, with Olivia, our family made four. Damien got rid of his business while his father and I sorted out his finances. He took on a sedate career while he mentally convalesced. He was still apt to disappear on occasion. But I was happy nesting and naively unconcerned.

Three weeks after Austin's arrival, Rent opened in Sydney. I was not going to miss opening night. Damien and I flew to Sydney with the baby. Austin was nicknamed 'The Qantas Baby' as he seemed to love flying. Sydney friends gathered at our hotel to wet the baby's head.

I had a fantastic evening and felt the weight of both my father's and Damien's illnesses lift off my shoulders. Chris Green and I revelled in the show's pending success.

As life goes, one minute you are on top of the world and the next you're flat on the ground. I received a frantic call from my mother that Dad was speaking gibberish.

While awaiting the ambulance, my beloved Dad sat in his favorite wingback chair. I could not speak. I could only stare numbly, terrified of what lay ahead. That moment felt like the last time we would spend alone — my last chance to speak frankly — yet I was rendered mute. The ambulance came.

I missed my chance.

The memory of this moment still plagues me: everything that remained unsaid, un-apologized for, made thankful for. The time was gone, as Mike Rutherford sang 'In the Living Years'.

The doctor told me point-blank the cancer had spread to his brain and the end was near.

Hector was permitted to return home. We organized an early Christmas gathering with family.

Days later, a different scenario played out at Christmas lunch with Damien's family. They were delighted to show off the baby. Emotionally drained from my own family experience, I turned in early with the kids. Damien partied on into the night with his friends. One girl amongst them gave me the evil eye.

I marked her as an ex-girlfriend and thought nothing more of it.

My father was taken to a palliative care hospice. I marked the weeks leaving my sleeping baby at home with Damien while visiting the hospital to read to my father.

On the morning of January 19 came a jolting call to rush to the hospital. On the ascent to my father's room, the sun was ferociously blazing through the floor-to-ceiling windows. I was forced to look up into the direct sunlight, appearing as if from the heavens. I squinted into the light, willing my father to hear me: 'It's OK, walk into the light — it is OK, you can go now'.

The end came. The sound of that final breath is not something anyone can describe unless you hear it for yourself. It is neither horrific nor ethereal, just final. It sounds like the word 'relief'.

I soldiered on back at work. I was full steam ahead opening a Sydney office for Firm Hand Management. I made a flying visit to London and was invited to attend previews for a musical co-produced by Jason Donovan's manager, Richard East. It was titled Mamma Mia.

I whispered to Richard: 'You have a MASSIVE hit on your hands'.

Enough said.

Along with a new baby came a new nanny. Hey Jude, she was a lifesaver. She kept our Hawthorn haven running like clockwork, despite my moods or Damien's absence.

Getting on with life, they say, is the remedy to death. We were essentially happy, the 'nuclear family'. Damien and Olivia were so good together it really warmed my heart.

Firm Hand Management had 34 clients and across many weeks we posted a 100 per cent employment rate. Professional success should have provided some antidote for how much I missed my father. But it did not.

Inside, I was not coping.

Damien and I took a trip with 6-month-old Austin — New York and London, then on to Venice. In New York, my adorable client Kelley Abbey joined us. We were sent by Kevin Jacobsen to the production 'Fame' in Hershey, Pennsylvania. The show went on to be a success in Australia with a dream cast. We saw many other new productions and were particularly moved by Hedwig and the Angry Inch off-Broadway.

In London I caught up with Hugh Jackman, who was starring in Oklahoma! for the National Theatre. After the show I drove him home, which he laughingly referred to as a luxury as he usually took the Tube. How times change.

We stayed in my Fulham house, where Damien had been a year before during his manic sojourn. This time he was medicated. The place felt ghosted with memories of Clive. We left Austin in the babysitter's hands and enjoyed romantic days in Venice. We owed each other some pause time after all the trials and trauma of losing my father, our son's arrival, and the constant elephant in the room of Damien's mental illness.

Our wandering urges were heightened by the trip and discussion turned to moving out of Melbourne. Nanny Jude held the fort with the kids while Damien and I flew to some place he claimed to be the new 'promised land' in Australia.

I had never heard of Byron Bay. Even in winter it is green and lush and full of opportunity for a gardening guru moving into permaculture. This was a way to consolidate our relationship and give the kids a truly organic life. We found a sprawling ranch house in Ewingsdale through local agent Glen Irwin. It ticked all of Damien's terroir boxes with two acres of land to cultivate, a swimming pool for me, and a view of the lighthouse.

I stared into the night sky and felt like I was home. Maybe in Byron Bay I could shake off the formulaic feeling of life? Was the strong spiritual feeling I experienced part of the area's heritage or a sign of things to come? Both.

Before we inked the deal, Glen suggested another house to view. It looked over the ocean, which appealed to me. Damien was convinced he needed acreage. We didn't even visit the property. Spoiler alert.

Primed for a new adventure, we drove north with kids, kit and caboodle. Damien developed the permaculture business while planting dozens of fruit trees. He was ahead of his time in recognizing lifestyle trends.

He delighted the children by bringing home scores of animals — goats and chickens — in the back of the car. The stench was another matter. Olivia's shrieks of glee at owning a goat were enough to take our minds off the odour.

Our love grew stronger in these idyllic surroundings. I cut back on work, renovated the house and came to terms with life without my father.

The millennium New Year's Eve was approaching. Talk about Y2K and how the world would change seemed ridiculous in this transmogrifying environment.

Byron Bay had started seeping into Melbourne society's psyche as the place to be and I was overjoyed to show off our new home to visiting friends.

I secured passes to the coveted Byron Beach Hotel soirée for the New Year's Eve event. Damien and I saw in the 2000s in our uninhibited way with a midnight swim in the warm ocean.

Byron Bay suited us at this juncture of our lives. I was able to maintain my business with one office in Sydney and effective communication systems. I flew to Sydney for meetings every other week. I would catch early morning flights from Lismore, able to call 'hold the plane!' if I was a few minutes late — that's how carefree everything was then.

Damien travelled to Melbourne quite often. Occasionally he would eschew his medication, which resulted in something as innocent as arriving home with more goats and chickens to the delight of the children.

I don't know which one of us had a bigger case of wanderlust. After only a year in Byron, we made plans to live in Bali for a few months. There was an advanced community of sustainable agriculturalists, and Damien was keen to explore opportunities. Olivia had her 9th birthday living in Sanur, homeschooled by me. We had a 'pembantu' for childcare, and Olivia loved riding on her motorbike. Austin learned to swim by launching himself into the pool willy-nilly. Other than stifling heat, we were all doing OK.

The heat inevitably won out, and I convinced my crazed partner to go to London for Christmas, with a promise of days in his beloved Thailand on the way. This was the trip that almost broke this camel's back. We drove to some godforsaken place outside Bangkok. The accommodation he parked us in could only be described as a 'hut'. Perched above a river, its murky water visible through the missing floorboards, the largest population belonged to mosquitos and fleas.

I did want to get out of Toorak, but not this far.

I didn't backpack in my youth, and if this was what it entailed, then thank God. We inevitably argued about the unsanitary conditions. I passed a sleepless night under a mosquito net, clutching my two children tightly. Damien's mania was back with a vengeance. I lay there simultaneously terrified that the floor could cave in underneath us and that my partner may have absconded for good.

He appeared in the morning looking like a jail escapee. Visions of previous manic episodes played out, and I insisted on a double dose of his medication for the remainder of the trip.

After exiting this hellhole, back on planet earth, we spent Christmas with my friend Nikki, or Snearky as I dubbed her, and her family in London.

The warmth of friendship enveloped me, and our kids formed one happy team, which they remain to this day.

The next stop was Paris for New Year's Eve.

After the disaster in Thailand, I was keen to show Damien how civilized European life could be. It was minus 6 degrees. I love the feeling of cold crisp winters and was eager to get out into the night air. A preferred state of being to jungle humidity in Thailand.

I wrapped the kids in layers of clothing, and out we ventured. Austin was strapped to my chest, a weighty 2-year-old, and Olivia was happily perched upon Damien's shoulders. We headed for the large space in front of the Trocadéro, looking back towards the Tour Eiffel. This was our first mistake, as the area was full of local gangs. The noise proved deafening from firecrackers and Molotov cocktails. The kids were terrified. The sounds, the cold and people shoving us every which way were just too much. I snapped into protective mother mode and got us out of there tout de suite!

It was clear we needed to ground ourselves back in Byron Bay. Our ideals of travel were worlds apart and caused additional friction to his state of mental health.

We returned to Byron Bay in silence.

We were no sooner unpacked than Damien took off to Melbourne. I settled the kids back into school life and attempted to find some mental solitude for myself.

Back in the bountiful beauty of Byron Bay, this should have been easy to attain, but walks on the beach did not suffice, and I was struggling to reconcile what the future would look like.

Damien stayed in Melbourne for an extended period. I missed him, but not the constant stress of watching his every move, gauging both his medication and emotional levels. A sense of calm evolved, with the children and I getting on with life together. Byron has history, as a healing place for women. I was about to need it in spades.

Damien told our Melbourne accountant he had become father to a son by his ex-girlfriend, information he then passed on to me.

Rendering me dumb or mute is no easy task. In hindsight this should not have been such a surprise. All the Melbourne visits, the previously open relationship, and the spiteful-looking girl two Christmases ago when I had just given birth to Austin.

I flew to Melbourne with the kids, not to find or reprimand Damien, just to get my head straight.

I packed up in Byron and moved back to Melbourne. I needed a support group of friends around me. Byron became just another place, like London and Toorak, where the ghosts of relationship disasters past won over my psyche.

Repetition seems to be a recurring theme in my life.

London Christmas

Olivia and Austin in Byron Bay 1999

Austin the Qantas baby

Casting RENT with Bernie Telsey, Chris Green and Lisa Malouf

GPO Casting RENT with Chris Green

Kelley Abbey in New York City

Mimi' Shephard and Michael Idato 1997

CHAPTER 8: THE CALL SHEET OF LIFE

I needed a home for the kids and me, somewhere safe.
My friend Tony learned that a penthouse in the Manchester Unity Building was for rent. Tony and Dom had an apartment a few floors below. This was heaven! A Collins Street address, a tower for my office and a massive balcony for parties.

Chris Green and I were full force with GPO Casting, while Firm Hand Management took a sidestep. We were working on Hair for originating producer Harry M. Miller and director Richard Wherrett. It was sadly to be Richard's last production.

I was thrilled to tell Harry the story of how I saw his production of Hair in Sydney, aged eleven, and the effect it had on me. Mister Miller knew he'd created a groundbreaking moment with Hair in the late 60s, but he had a much more evolved, and devolved, career after that one historical moment. The casting for this production was music industry-based, much like his production of Jesus Christ Superstar starring John Farnham and Kate Ceberano.

My music connections proved useful. Then Harry M. Miller surprised us by bringing in an industry heavyweight for additional advice.

He asked me, 'Do you know Michael Chugg?'

How much fun! Chuggi and I meeting again and riffing over ideas was a version of speaking our own language. I suggested emerging local and international artists to pull in a new audience for this essentially 1970s concept.

Amongst a mammoth list I suggested Alicia Keys and Pink … this was in 2001. Pink's debut album had been released the previous year. Harry yelled at me, 'I don't know who or what a PINK is; think again!'

Oh well, you can't please everyone.

Melbourne casting days coincided with my 40th birthday. In a way I was so glad to be busy because the idea of turning 40 did not appeal to me. Those milestones are, by nature, a time of reflection, and I wasn't ready for what I saw in the mirror: virtually three failed marriages, two marvellous, wonderful children, a mother I could no longer relate to without my father's mediation, living in an apartment I adored but a town I had grown out of, and no sense of what the future held.

Also, my hair was a mess.

Tony helped arrange a birthday soirée in my penthouse apartment, for which he held a key. I booked a caterer. Chris and I were flat out working on Hair. We invited a handful of friends, and that's all I knew. Tony took charge, and I trusted his judgement.

I got home to the penthouse to discover Tony had plastered the walls with photocopies of my 40 years, from childhood onwards. I was so touched.

Late into the evening, Damien appeared, uninvited. Like an old penny, as the saying goes. He was unmedicated and wanted to drop in to give me a gift.

I unwrapped what looked like a bedsheet. On it was spray-painted, in black childlike scrawling, one word: 'cunt'. Damien explained he thought it would be funny to fly the flag from the tower of the building to amuse people below.

I poured a round of stiff drinks. Damien left peacefully after seeing the flag flying. Tony immediately went and ripped it down. No photographic evidence of this moment exists, and for that I am grateful.

Richard Wherrett whittled his choices down to forty final auditions. He motioned to Chris and me, in confidence, that he wanted to run things a little unconventionally. He would ask actors to disrobe, down to their underwear, or all the way if they chose. This was a direct method of seeing how they would react to performing the required nude scene in the show. And he wanted us all to tag along.

Cool, this was art writ large, man!

I was fine with the idea and started assessing my lingerie drawer in a bubble above my head.

Not so enthused for participation, Chris suggested he would stay outside the room and monitor the actors' arrivals.

We arranged drapes to be hung across all the windows so no one outside in the production team could see the audition room. Chuggi and Harry Miller were outside, faces pressed up against the glass like schoolboys. Chugg tried a plaintive cry, 'Aw, come on, let me in, Princess', which was met with a firm (hand) no. God love him, it is probably the only time I said no to him in all the years we worked together.

Chuggi mentioned he had participated in an episode of a new documentary series for the ABC, Long Way to the Top; its title taken from the infamous AC/DC 1975 hit song whose video was shot along Swanston Street in Melbourne. This happened to be right outside the apartment I was living in, atop the Manchester Unity Building. Long Way was due to air in August 2001.

I decided to put my Orrong Road home on the market and say goodbye to another painful personal chapter in my life. Once sold, I could go on to figure out the next steps with the kids.

I loved city life in Melbourne, but hauling two kids across Collins Street to a car park each morning and the constant sound of sirens at night were mild deterrents. On the upside, one of the cutest things in this period was Austin riding his toy car all over the apartment. He would 'drive' his Little Tikes into the elevator. He would 'toot' the horn as his little legs peddled into the alleyway to David Jones' Food Hall. He examined the array of food to decide what was for dinner. He was 3 years old. 'Choppies…Sausages!' he would shout. David Jones customers looked on, wondering why the hell any mother would bring their kid all the way into the city in a Little Tikes car. I loved it.

These kids may have ended up with troubling and turbulent father figures, but they are both brilliantly interesting human beings.

Throughout August I watched the TV series Long Way to the Top.

Each week was a revelation of musical memory from Billy Thorpe and Sunbury to so much more. It made me happy and proud that I entered the music business and renewed my passion for it all over again. I could not imagine how much that passion would come to the forefront of my life in such a short time.

I had been able to marry that time in the music business to a new theatrical escapade led by Jon Nicholls, 'Always… Patsy Cline'. He looked to me for casting advice. The role was a very big sing and needed a powerhouse performance. There was only one choice: Deborah Conway.

Jon was unfamiliar with her work. I spent time waxing lyrical, playing her albums until he yelled, 'Stop!', and she had the role.

It was great to be back in DC's company, a woman I admired for her intellect as much as her musical ability.

High up in my magical tower, I received a late-night phone call from a journalist I knew in London. He hit me with some terrible news: a rumour that Jason Donovan had been found dead in Spain, and asked if I knew the circumstances. I was reeling with sadness and had not heard a word.

Who found him, I asked? There was no actual sighting of a body; it was still a rumour. Typically, the journalist was seeking a phone number for Kylie or Richard East, anyone to confirm or deny the story. I spent the next hour making phone calls. Finally exhausted, personally and without information, I turned my phone and the television off. I needed to get some sleep.

I thought about Terry, Jason's father. And his mother, Sue, who visited us on the set of many Kylie videos with Jason's stepsisters. I prayed it would not be true. Mañana.

During that night, the whole world changed forever.

Terrorists flew planes into the Twin Towers of the World Trade Centre in New York. We all witnessed images of people jumping from the towers to certain death. I froze at their horror. I was living twelve floors up in a city building with my two sleeping children. I muted the sound, it was all too confronting. I turned my phone on to some good news — a message from the journalist that Jason Donovan was well and truly alive.

The days following September 11 remain a blur. The panic was compounded daily by irresponsible media and an incomprehensible truth of global terrorism.

I moved with my kids to the Northern Beaches in Sydney. Whale Beach was a balm for the soul. I made the decision to live as a single mother, with a singular focus on my children's welfare and education.

The next project Chris and I undertook was casting Oliver! for director Sam Mendes. Chris joined IMG as an executive producer and we worked, as we always did, hand in glove, looking at music industry talent for certain roles.

One idea was Billy Thorpe for the role of Fagin. I set up a lunch with Chugg and Billy to pitch the idea.

I admit to having been excited meeting Billy over a languorous lunch. The excitement was bound in the influence the Sunbury album had on me. Add to that the bold feeling I had when I saw Thorpie perform at Channel Nine a few years before.

Billy arrived at lunch like a bolt of lightning. His presence, palpable energy and cheeky rockstar attitude built into one pocket rocket of a man. I adored him at first sight. We talked about theatre and Fagin as a character. It became clear he was not that keen to take on the role. We bonded over a steak and a glass of red wine. He was very disciplined in what he ate and drank, which made the way we inevitably lost him so much harder to understand.

Talk turned to the Long Way to the Top series that had finished airing on the ABC. The third episode was 'Billy Killed the Fish'; its protagonist regaled me with stories of his career. Poor Chugg, having heard it a thousand times as well as living through it, sat patiently while I was educated in the Thesis of Thorpe. Billy was pitching the series as a live event. We finished lunch, and I knew I would see my Aries brother again — and again.

We auditioned many people for Fagin, including Doc Neeson from The Angels. Harking back to Mushroom Records hey day I reminded him of our first meeting. He painfully inspected multiple hotel rooms before deciding the feng shui of the bed was suitable. He was the same kind of weird on the day of the audition, and sadly it was one of the least inspiring auditions I had ever seen.

Another masterstroke by Sam Mendes rocked Broadway and was destined for the Australian stage — Cabaret. Chris and I wove our unspoken magic in finding the right mix of talent. Cabaret was particularly difficult to cast, as the cast were musicians performing in character, not in the orchestra pit. It's hard to ask someone majoring in cello at the Sydney Conservatorium to put on a 1930s suspender belt and 'Death in Venice' makeup and be a tramp on stage. One performer I deeply admired got the AOK from Mister Mendes to play the role of Emcee, made famous by Joel Grey in the film with Liza Minnelli.

Toby Allen hailed from the pop group Human Nature. He was not only stunning looking but also a great actor who received deserved critical praise. We felt Tina Arena should play Sally Bowles.

Tina invited me to tea at her home, and we reminisced about our time on Lennox Street when she released the phenomenally successful Don't Ask album.

It was a magic moment watching her on opening night. It reminded me why I do what I do. I adore Tina's spunk and joie de vivre, and there is no doubt she is one of Australia's finest artists. We considered working on a project outside Paris in 2014, her beloved other home, but sadly it never came to fruition.

One weekend I took a cold call on my mobile. It was Damien.

I had no way of knowing what state of mental health he was in at the time. He begged forgiveness and asked to come to Sydney to see the kids. He always knew how to get around me. I agreed to a weekend visit. The scars of relationships and all the terrible things people do to each other manifest differently over time. I recall the verbally abusive things Clive said to me like it was yesterday. It doesn't go away.

In full transparency, I have never been physically abused by a partner.

I have no way of knowing how those scars measure up to verbal assault. I do know that working away from those memories and back to some semblance of self-respect is a long uphill battle. Undoubtedly, more of this was to come in my life.

Damien never set out to hurt me. The infidelity was part of his nature and never hidden; the abandonment was another matter. For that I was unsure I could forgive and forget.

A marvellous chapter of my professional life was about to begin.

Having varied career segments, it is impossible to pick a favorite, like you cannot choose your favorite child, or husband for that matter. Each chapter offers differing elements that make up your personal whole.

It was nearing the end of a turbulent year.

I had everything to look forward to for 2002. I was happily single and focused on my kids and my work.

Michael Chugg asked to meet at his office in William Street. It was a sprawling space with a handful of staff. Chuggi had gone out on his own after leaving Frontier and Michael Gudinski behind. This we had in common, and much more.

Chuggi's great trait is his ability to smell bullshit a mile away. He is impeccably honest, calls a spade a spade and is loyal to a fault. Being around him made me a better person. His laconic exterior hides a razor-sharp memory, like the proverbial elephant. He can recall exact audience numbers at festivals and events he promoted decades ago as well as accurately predict how many 'punters' would buy tickets when a show was put on sale. He never failed.

I was thrilled when Chuggi asked me to join Michael Chugg Entertainment (MCE) to co-produce Long Way to the Top with Billy Thorpe. Then and there in that first meeting, I typed out a piece of paper with a production fee figure on it. Chuggi signed it, we put it in a drawer, forgot about any further formality and got on with the show.

The 'Billy Killed the Fish' episode featured Chuggi, and he was recognized walking through airports. Fellow travellers would stop to ask for his autograph and stories about the 'good old days' of rock 'n' roll. He admitted Billy was onto something. Chuggi had enough on his touring plate without twenty daily calls from Billy Thorpe. That's where I came in and happily accepted the task.

Billy and I creatively locked horns on production style, artists to perform, songs to perform … a cornucopia of decisions that go into making up an event of this magnitude.

Chuggi brought Jacobsen Entertainment on as a partner. It was great being around Kevin again, albeit in a different capacity from when I pushed him to his limits as a bolshie artist manager.

Kevin's niece Amber, daughter of Col Joye, was the sharpest tool in the Jacobsen family shed. A brilliantly bright young woman, she went on to produce Dirty Dancing worldwide. Col Joye was the 1950s bookend to Billy Thorpe's 1970s closer for this musical joyride. I needed a director.

I talked to knowledgeable people, and one name kept recurring — Ted Robinson, an ABC legend who had worked on The Aunty Jack Show, The Big Gig, Live and Sweaty, amongst others. This was a tricky gig, as the director had to have first-class knowledge of music, stage production and visual elements. Ted filled all those criteria and more. He was a warm and funny individual who became the perfect foil between Billy and me. When our Aries hotheads needed a temperature check, Ted was our air conditioner.

Next was our choice of musical director. Amber suggested Jamie Rigg, who put a band together to augment the original artists on stage.

Add Eric Robinson on technical and stage management, Peter 'Sneaky' McFee as production manager, three individual tour managers and their assistants to wrangle the acts, and we were getting somewhere.

No sweat, we only had six months to get the show on the road.

Legal eagles finessed a deal with the ABC for naming rights, use of the logo and branding. We agreed on a budget to film and record the live event during the final shows in Sydney.

Grahame Grassby headed up ABC Enterprises. This was the biggest budget outlay he had ever signed off on. 'This tour better work', he warned us.

Like a dolphin rising out of the ocean, shrugging water while laughing cheekily, Billy Thorpe responded, 'Mate, you have no idea how big this is going to be'. He was right.

The filming would involve yet another team to manage.

Mark Opitz for audio recording along with Greg Clarke from Thorpe's studio and George Gorga. Add in a film unit put together by Ted with his GNWTV crew. The gorgeous Bruce Pollack was a must for PR, backed by individual state-by-state teams. Peter Simpson at Millmaine Entertainment adapted the logo and created the marketing plan. Ben Alcott had just started his own AV company and came on board to run the live camera feeds for each show. There were the Playbill Nebenzahl brothers for merchandising and far too many other departments to mention here. Safe to say there were 152 of us on the road once the time came.

In the midst of delightful professional chaos, I found time to recover some semblance of a personal life. In regular Melbourne trips to check on my octogenarian mother, Damien asked to see me again. He assured me he was on medication, studying for a business degree and no longer in a relationship.

He chose a French restaurant for a date, remembering escargot and Pinot Noir were one way to this girl's heart.

Damien seemed nervous, mumbling in secret to the maître d'. This complicated father of my son was like a jackrabbit at the table. He handed me a scroll of paper, which read, 'All my friends are getting married as the song goes, will you do me the honor of marrying me?' as he bowed down on one knee.

Christ on a baguette! This was the last thing I expected. Damien knew how I felt about marriage; he knew full well my history. Maybe he was playing to the fact I am more forgiving the second time around? No doubt.

Champagne appeared as restaurant guests broke into applause.

I suggested we digest our meal and discuss the ramifications of his proposal later, in private.

I wished a psychiatrist could appear to talk me down off the ledge, so to speak. My mind's eye visualized a scene in Annie Hall with Marshall McLuhan. A resounding 'What would Woody Allen do?' To see humour in all things, I revert to Woody Allen when terror strikes me. It would not be the last time.

I lay in our hotel four-poster bed, stroking Damien's hair as he slept like a child. He was Austin's father, 10 years younger than me. He loves me and wants to make me happy. What can go wrong?

Don't answer that.

I gave a perfunctory, 'I'll think about it'.

Weeks went by as I was flat out with Long Way to the Top production. Damien pushed, lovingly, for a trip to Thailand to tie the knot. Friends could help arrange the ceremony.

I told Chugg I would be gone for a few days. I did not mention I was eloping.

Once in Bangkok it was clear these friends had pulled out all the stops. I was the producer being produced! I was a bundle of nerves.

Oh, God. What am I doing? I never wanted another surname; I've got one I am perfectly happy with, thank you. Unlike many women I know who have married for 'the name', 'the title', 'the house', 'the car'… none of those apparent gains ever struck me as the raison d'être.

Well, here I was — 'third time lucky'?

That phrase, quoted by Elizabeth Barrett Browning in 1839, and Alexander Hislop's 'Proverbs of Scotland' in 1862, is a derivation from English law. It refers to anyone condemned to death: if they survived three hangings, they would be set free.

My friend, who was almost right, forgot to mention that part.

What if I did keep repeating myself and marry up to five times? Would you be set free then … along with a set of steak knives?

I was delirious as we set out for the ceremony in a stretch limousine. Damien told me the trip would take a couple of hours, so I prepared snacks for the drive — Tim Tams and a bottle of Mekhong whiskey. They go well together when speeding through the Thai jungle on the way to collect Buddhist monks from a monastery. What is the collective noun for a group of monks?

Apparently, 'an abominable sight of monks'.

Once we reached the monastery, our friends alighted from the limousine to negotiate which monk would join us on our journey into matrimony. A few whiskeys in, I was pleasantly calm and thought we were collecting just one monk.

I scooted over in the back seat of the limo. Then there were two monks, then three. There was a televised prize fight that afternoon, and the monastery did not have a television. The (abomination of) monks asked to join us on our trip to the waterfalls at Kanchanaburi, where there would be a TV.

The area was made famous with the building of the Bridge Over the River Kwai in 1943. Damien loved the region for the mystical nature of the waterfalls.

While the team negotiated how many monks we could accommodate in the limo, I reverted to 'dial a friend'. I descended deeper into a blind panic and needed to be talked down, or around. When in doubt, call a lawyer. I called Michael Brereton. He knew Damien and was always brotherly to me.

Even the limousine driver could hear Brereton yelling down the phone from Melbourne. 'Get a prenup, do NOT sign anything … I let you out of my sight for one minute!' And on it went.

Three monks and a bunch of red balloons filled the space left in the limo, which now had me riding on Damien's lap.

Once we arrived at the waterfall, Damien lovingly told me he was hiking to the top and would swim down once the ceremonial podium was set up. He knew in advance there was no point asking me to join that hike and swim … not my chosen method of arriving at my wedding.

This was a stark contrast to my first wedding: heels clunking on broken tiles down the aisle seemed as amusingly precarious as these next steps.

We had time. The monks watched the fight on TV, their prime reason for accompanying us. Our friends dressed the scene. Amidst blistering heat and humidity, I found a quiet spot in the jungle and changed into my bridal garb.

The whiskey flask was empty. I was having flashbacks to my first two weddings. No Elvie Hill couture in sight here — I dressed in Armani cotton and bright orange Thai wrap pants. Très chic for jungle nuptials. Any attempt at makeup slid off my face with uncontrollable sweat. There was thankfully no mother in sight screaming, 'Don't do it!' like the first two ceremonies. The serenity of the moment hit me as I took a few deep breaths of the heavy humid air.

Damien appeared fresh out of the water, like his own baptism.

Having euphemistically washed all his sins away, was he reborn to me? I should not have finished the whiskey. The symbolism of it became clear to me some years later.

The service started with our friends translating for the monks. We were in a public place, a throughway to levels of the waterfall. The heat was stifling.

I begged them to get on with our ritual vows. Humidity and hot weather are not my friends. There was heartfelt joy in us both that after so many travails, Damien and I ended up in this happy place. He was visibly moved to tears.

We must be doing the right thing.

My inbuilt niggling feeling long born of previous marital experience reared its head through the sweat and discomfort of the monk's stare.

Once again, considering other players in the frame, I summoned inner confidence. In childhood, when questioning my friend LC about where the furs and the jewels would emanate from, the more relevant question should have been 'What if it doesn't feel right?'....

After the monks indicated we could kiss, a photographer appeared. For once not summoned by me! He asked what we were doing; the publicist in me sallied forth and told him our long romantic story.

He took some shots, and the next morning, there we were on the front page of the Bangkok Times.

At least our friends and family would now understand why we disappeared for a few furtive days.

There would be no carrying over the threshold for me.

Back in Sydney and back to work.

My new husband was not even living under that threshold. Damien had gone to Melbourne to complete his business degree, and in a seriously bizarre twist — because there haven't been any yet, right? — he moved in with my mother. He would visit when he could. Part of me did not question this irregularity, as my days and nights were so filled with the children and producing the Long Way tour.

I did not give it a second thought.

There were weekly production meetings at Ted's office on the backlot of Fox Studios. We huddled around the large table and spread diagrams of stage designs and ideas out to each other. We finally nailed the setlist, and most of the artists are contracted. Billy wanted inflatables; the budget says no. There we were locking horns again. Billy wanted Marshall stacks for his set; the budget says no.

I made it a rule to sit down with each artist and explain the concept of the show and the overall logistics of the tour, asking what footage and photos they could deliver so Ted and I could build visual packages.

One of the first acts I had the pleasure of visiting was Glenn Shorrock. He invited me to his Double Bay home, where I was greeted by his effervescent wife, Jo.

Glenn asked if I had met Brian Cadd yet. I replied, no, I had not.

Ted, Billy and I were completely in sync and thrived on the exposition between us.

The kids regularly phoned Damien and Nanny Elvie and asked why they weren't with us. I worked long into the night and for the first time had a glass of wine with dinner. When deadline pressure started to hit, I occasionally finished the bottle, brainstorming more ideas for the execution of the shows.

I knew this was not a good idea, drinking alone, but it was 'occasionally'.

I considered myself lucky; I did not have an addictive personality. Maybe only towards music, and soon to be a certain musician.

On July 22, 2002, at 2 pm, a meeting took place that, unknowingly at the time, rocked my world.

It was a regular meeting for the LWTTT production team at GNWTV on the FOX Backlot. Teams around the conference table were trying to achieve answers; voices were at fever pitch. My phone rang, revealing an effusive Chugg, apologizing for being late. He mentioned he had someone with him; I did not catch who in particular … Just hurry up, I admonished him.

In most circumstances, Chugg was the only one who could make Billy Thorpe see fiscal sense.

Chuggi arrived while I was engaged in the team-shouting match, with my back turned. He and his mystery guest parked themselves in the corner.

I turned to see Brian Cadd smiling at me.

I became a true believer in love at first sight.

We looked at each other and have both acknowledged, after the fact, that 'something' transpired between us. A feeling. A knowing. More than a look. The inexplicable 'je ne sais pas' you cannot replicate to anyone in words.

The meeting concluded. My diary reflected this as the appointed time I was meeting Brian to introduce the project. We sat for our first meeting on the old leather couch in Ted Robinson's entry hall. I waxed lyrical about buying Brian's eponymous album in '72, at which point he was probably trying to figure out how old I was. I established that the woman I had been dealing with on his contract was his girlfriend, Linda, and they lived on the Gold Coast. That explained the hideous floral polyester shirt he was wearing.

Jamie Rigg, Ted Robinson and I had — including and excluding Billy — gone over the setlist a thousand times trying to hone it down to acceptable timing.

Some of the bands had not played together in decades. Not only were they re-acquainting themselves but also ensuring they had the musical chops for the gigs.

There was one delicate exception.

Stevie Wright from the Easybeats was to perform his masterwork — 'Evie Parts 1, 2 & 3'. Stevie had suffered the ravages of time, drugs and alcohol, prompting us to keep his appearance private for now. Billy arranged for the original Aztecs to rehearse at his studio. We added Stevie into that safe rehearsal space. Time was miraculously erased. Billy enveloped Stevie in his arms; old friends reunited. Ted and I united in tears at the scene, both acknowledging how much it meant to Stevie. None of his trademark handstands were expected this time; just being on the stage would be a triumph.

Ted and his crew melded quietly into the studio background to capture these moments on film for a 'Behind the Scenes' DVD.

Video packages to introduce each act were by the most recognizable voice in Aussie radio, Trevor Smith. Some clips were highlighted by well-known actors. This surprised audiences and gave a feeling we were all in it together.

Billy was widely loved and counted amongst his friends Jack Thompson, Bryan Brown, Sam Neill and Olivia Newton-John. Jack's descriptive words on Billy's performance being akin to 'being tied to the front of a Mack Truck' were priceless and hilarious.

I cannot count the number of setlist iterations there were before rehearsal in Perth. We were still seventeen minutes too long. This is when I needed Chugg's authoritarian true grit to step in. I asked him to break the news to artists whose songs had been cut. He earned the nickname 'Toe Cutter'.

Luckily, everyone took it in good spirits, but the show still ran for more than two and a half hours!

Our brilliant director, Ted, knew there would be one-upmanship and onstage antics as these rock & roll warriors reunited.

Chuggi would turn to me and say, 'Don't sit so-and-so together because he fucked that guy's girlfriend in '72 …' What happens on the road, stays on the road.

Almost always.

Perth was a resounding success with an ecstatic audience, giving an indication of what coming months would reveal in these sold-out shows.

Billy came straight off stage and enveloped me in his brotherly hug — a scene thankfully captured by photographer Peter Carrette. In that moment all my adolescent premonitions about music and its place in my world were solidified.

If you can generate happiness in other people and, as importantly, in return become fulfilled by the work you create, then how else could anyone choose to live their lives?

I really needed a nanny I could depend on, as I was on the road 24/7. An agency introduced a guy called Tim, and, apart from not wanting to stereotype a nanny as having to be female, I thought it was a good idea for the kids to have some male energy around, as Damien was still living in Melbourne.

Despite our Thai marriage, he felt as far removed as he had ever been.

As the tour wound on, Brian Cadd and I exchanged nightly pleasantries in venue corridors. I cannot say for sure it was with or without 'frisson'. Then we played Adelaide.

The dancers were sweeties, and when I would bemoan feeling old, they took me on board like some middle-aged Barbie doll … adorning me in braided plaits and glitter eyeshadow. After every show, our tribe — artists, band and road crew — would take over our hotel bars. Billy Thorpe and Col Joye worked up management and bar staff, remaining open longer than normal hours.

Billy referred to our tour as 'a two-hour show which got in the way of a 22-hour long party'.

Brilliant. And true.

We congregated in the bar of the Adelaide Hilton. Billy generously bought champagne. I was in a particularly jolly mood after being Barbie-dolled-up. As the girls and I danced, I felt 20 again — transported back to nightclubs in Melbourne. The work pressure of previous months peeled away.

Twirling around in my best Countdown dancer moves, I turned to see Brian Cadd in front of me. He put my face between his hands and drew me to him, kissing me flush on the mouth.

All I could think to say was, 'What ARE you doing?'

His sweet reply was, 'I have wanted to do that for the longest time, and now I have. I adore you'.

The moment lasted until a foreign power appeared and broke the moment's intensity. Like in Star Wars movies when Darth Vader enters the scene — with a swish of his cape and a sharp, mechanic intake of breath. Our Vader was Billy Thorpe.

Darth Billy came marching over and physically pushed Brian away from me, admonishing him loudly. 'GET OFF HER! What do you think you are doing?"

He told Brian in no uncertain terms to 'bugger off' and 'go to bed'. And he did.

The dancers giggled at the scene unfolding. We finished the champagne, with Billy growling at me: 'Don't go there!'

He offered no reason why or why not; just don't.

I never felt the David Dixon tour sorrow of 'It's Tuesday, it must be Belgium …' I loved life on the road and the ease in my role of helping keep the juggernaut afloat.

The only regret was missing Olivia and Austin in an era well before FaceTime and Zoom.

Damien suggested a conjugal visit and came to Canberra.

It felt awkward having him amongst this musical family of mine. He was on his best behavior, showing off, gilding the lily too much for my liking. In the bar he played up to Jo Shorrock. She enjoyed the attention, given her husband paid her scant regard. Brian sat in a corner, and we exchanged knowing glances.

The next morning, with rock stars making their way to the next venue, I waved them all adieu. I caught Brian's eye and knew we shared a disproportionate amount of unspoken 'where do we go from here' thoughts. That was going to last for a while.

Even though the show was running like a well-oiled and, thankfully, sold-out machine, there was a lot of work to do putting the recording together for the live DVD and CD release. The ABC were thrilled with the success of the show, so Chugg and I started discussing with ABC Enterprises the idea of recreating the same formula for Countdown.

My experience as a Countdown dancer surely stood me in good stead. Molly and I felt very strongly that his role in propelling Australian music onto the world stage had to be documented in more than artwork for the Archibald and a gong from the Queen. I had a very clear vision of how Countdown as a live event should be created.

Brian and Russell Morris were inseparable on tour, a lifelong friendship stemming from the '60s. A little-known music history fact — Brian sang, from the back of an Ampex tape box, the megalomaniac voiceover at the end of 'The Real Thing'. That's not what melded them together but does explain their joint love of the ridiculous. After a show in Sydney, a few people came back to my room for drinks, an extension of the closed bar, a lot of talk about how fabulous we were and how great the tour had become. As the invitees wound down, Brian and Russell were the last to leave.

Except Brian came back.

Life leads you in all sorts of directions. To reiterate what George Michael said, 'Turn a different corner and we would not have met'.

Brian and I turned a corner that night, but there were a lot more hurdles to navigate before ending in the same corner. Our primary concern was our current relationships, notwithstanding that mine was rather more complex than his.

He was at the tail end of an affair that had broken up his marriage of 20 years. This gargantuan woman with 'big hair' was referred to as L2. Both she and his wife were named Linda. I had experienced only a few conversations with her, and, as later experience would attest, I wish it had ended there.

The tour was in A1 shape prior to filming shows in Sydney that would become our prize-winning DVD/CD set. Ted Robinson and his GNWTV team were akin to having Noah navigate the Ark. Our production carried as many demented animals on board as the biblical story goes, that's for sure.

Ted knew the public service nuances of the ABC as importantly as he understood the musicians' requirements at a gut level.

The TV production bumped into the Sydney Entertainment Centre ahead of the first-night shoot. Chuggi arrived as we did a pre-show rehearsal. Sighting the boom crane in the middle of the venue, he went off his rocker.

He came backstage, snapping at Ted and me like a wounded hyena.

'The audience are going to go mad; there will be so many complaints, what are we thinking?!' Chuggi does have a wonderful sense of the theatrical — vis-à-vis the Toe Cutter nomenclature. Ted and I stifled our laughter. Chuggi knew that we had a B-roll team filming all the backstage antics, which in turn ended up as the docu-rockumentary 'Behind the Scenes'. This moment was captured in all its glory with Ted retorting to Chuggi's complaints with a tacit,

'Michael, you gotta get out more'.

A golden moment in rock history.

The multi-camera shoot was a triumph, and many a long night was spent editing the wealth of footage. We rushed the release to keep momentum up ahead of the second phase of touring in early January.

A post-tour awards night was deemed appropriate. Michael's son Nick Chugg became the event ringleader. We manufactured awards in the shape of a golden sausage roll. This was an ode to the AC/DC mock title 'It's a long way to the shop if you want a sausage roll'. Over 20 years later that 'nod' to the sausage roll gag became a major advertising campaign for Mitsubishi.

Brian and I had managed a few discreet liaisons over the remaining part of the tour. Nevertheless, the knowledge that we would soon be parted at the tour's end weighed heavily on us.

As he was accompanied by 'L2', I kept my distance. I reverted to my 'happy place' — dancing the night away like it was 20 years ago. Brian's watchful eyes burnt a hole in my soul; the unknowing of what would come next was almost too much to bear. So, just dance. And dance I did.

The final 'Long Way' performance was in Melbourne, and everyone was enthusiastically exhausted. After Brian performed, we would tuck ourselves out of view into a side of the venue and enjoy the 'fruits of our labour' away from prying eyes. On this final night he whispered, 'I love you darling; we will make this work'.

It was impossible to count the number of 'hangers-on' at the after-party at the Melbourne Hilton. But true to his Tour Captain form, Billy kept the bar open until the bitter end. The next morning, Chuggi, Marcia Hines and I made our way back to Sydney in exhausted silence. Marcia is one of the kindest souls I have ever had the joy of knowing. On that flight, hungover and emotionally spent as I was, there were times I wanted to turn and off-load all my woes to her. But discretion prevailed.

The four walls of my Northern Beaches home were closing in on me. I found a beautiful house in Paddington to rent. Brian managed a trip to Sydney, and we secured the house we planned to cohabit together. Our love was sealed on this trip in a moment that remains enormously poignant in my life, my loves, the trial and tribulations. In that moment of wonderment, it felt like nothing could stop us; no fears or disagreements could ever overshadow this love we felt for each other.

The future looked bright.

CHAPTER 9: MY INTERPRETATION

There are accidents in life. And there is also fate. Each is open to an individual's interpretation. So here is my interpretation.

There are infinite types of spirituality in this world. We pray with only ourselves in silence or we worship in a congregation. I was not raised with any religious affiliation, but I also don't consider myself secular or without 'belief'.

I believe there is something else out there, beyond us on this planet. Where we go after death, if our souls move to another plane or person, I do not know. But I feel strongly I have been 'here' before. Manifested in this life as a very fortunate human being born in the 1960s, my sense and sensibility tells me I have lived in a previous era, also in female form, around the 1800s – in France. It is a metaphysical interpretation, why or how I know this to be true. If we take our feelings and gut instinct as 50 per cent of our purpose and drive to strive forward, then I know what I know.

Similarly, on occasion I have 'felt' the spiritual presence of other souls from the past. Years onward in our farmhouse in Daylesford, I sensed several previous tenants in the space — only with affection and no fear. They were happy we were there.

As my father lay dying, I could only talk to him internally to feel I was reaching him. I watched him slip away and while the bereavement overtook me, I never felt it would be the last time I would sense him near me.

Again at our farm, I spotted a paper square in the damp garden bed. I was inexplicably drawn to it. Turning it over, it was a photograph of my father and I. Taken in 1972, we were walking the grounds the property on the Mornington Peninsula he had longed to buy. I had no possible way of explaining how the single photograph appeared there. No boxes had been unpacked outside. It was simply inexplicable.

Overcome with grief at seeing his image and joy at recovering the photo I didn't even know was lost, I took it as an absolute sign that I was meant to inhabit this place.

I have spent a lot of time wondering why we are placed where we fall on this earth. Not just by birth, but in the seemingly endless movements many of us make around the planet.

Some of us choose to stay in one place — either out of contentment or fear of the unknown. Others take a rollercoaster journey around the Earth — out of curiosity or longing for the unknown. What in fact is 'heritage'?

Why do some of us feel more inclined towards one culture than another?

In my case, I am born of Scottish, Italian and second-generation Australian/Welsh bloodlines. I am in my physical being like my Scottish grandmother, yet I feel the European-ness of my paternal side more acutely.

I feel confident my travelling journey will never be over, until the ultimate physical 'over' takes me. As tiring and emotionally exhausting moving can make me, I know I will never be still in one place.

In this lifetime.

Even tour exhaustion could not stop me planning another journey.

I owed the kids a holiday after all my absence.

We ventured to Hotel Versace Gold Coast, Brian conveniently close by. This was the first time he met my kids, and my mother. All went well until my mother caught me crying after Brian left.

I had to spill the beans on what was emotionally taking place.

Paddington became the centre of my universe — close to the office, closer to Billy and future projects that would evolve with our professional passion.

We were a team.

One day, Billy appeared with a bottle of Cristal champagne to celebrate our 'Long Way' success. I was close to telling him about the situation with Brian, but something stopped me. The moment between Billy and I was more important — spellbinding, timely and life-affirming. I know I told him in those moments how much I loved him and our firm friendship.

Our future was filled with as much effervescence as the bubbles in the Cristal we devoured — laughing and planning great projects ahead.

My heart felt I was giving up on Damien's promises of a unified marriage. He came to Sydney and walked through my Paddington house like it was going to be his own. I knew it could, and would not. Yet, there was no confrontation; I just wanted Damien to enjoy his visit with the kids.

At the height of Brian's solo-stardom, his first wife gave birth to twins. His time with those twin boys was marred by both his performance schedule and his imminent move to Los Angeles, into the arms of another woman he formed a relationship with — L1. She would then bear him two children over the ensuing years. Brian's regard for fatherhood and its implied commitment never really improved. The mark of a highly selfish individual, for better or for worse.

Here he was, in his mid-50s, contemplating a new start with small children. How would he face his four semi-adult children and tell them he was now taking on other children, after his abandonment of them? It was a lot less about my two and creating a family with me than it was his guilt at having left his own. I would not recognize this as his truth until much later — for now, in my opinion, it was the relationship deal-breaker.

We talked through this speed hump and met in Melbourne. I did not recognize it then but the 'child' speed bump was about to turn a corner in a way I could never have contemplated.

At Capers Supper Club, Brian introduced me to his daughter, Jessica. She was 19 years old. Sullen, uncommunicative, incapable of conversation — I knew I was meeting a difficult girl — to say the least. After the show, Brian excused her as 'shy'. We enjoyed a post-show evening together and it was clear Jessica understood the move about to be made. I did everything I could in that first evening to make her feel comfortable with me.

Time was nigh to come clean with our respective partners. Brian had a TV performance scheduled in Melbourne. I planned to tell Damien our checkered history had come to an end. I was trepidatious how to break the news. Part of me wondered why I should be considerate, given everything Damien had put me through. The truth was we had a beautiful son together and for the most part our lives had been well intentioned. If I had known the mental health issues that would mar our existence, when I first saw him climbing a tree outside my window, would I have continued?

Yes, without doubt. My desire to look after a partner in all ways: physical, spiritual, mental — in sickness and in health –has I believe been informed by my growing up an only child and wanting to care for someone without reservation.

What if I had known this would in my future repeat itself, again?

I went to consult my oldest friend for guidance. LC and Rob, in their Toorak 'mansion in the clouds', seemed happy to see me. In the kitchen, alone, I explained to LC what was about to unfold. Rob entered and I reiterated I was about to tell Damien the truth. I was shaking with emotional uncertainty. Rob was the publisher of a music gossip rag. He asked, I believed jokingly, if he could tell his entertainment writer the news about Brian and me.

There was no news to tell yet. The fine line between friendship and betrayal was about to be crossed.

Damien and I met up and I confessed the reality of our situation.

I remain grateful that he took our marital downfall with such dignity. There were no arguments, no unpleasant transactions over assets. He became, in essence, despite his mental challenges, the gentleman he was always meant to be.

Betrayal is a funny beast. In some people it induces them to rail against the protagonist, in others to withdraw completely. Given Damien's history, I considered myself lucky he became the latter.

Back in my Paddington haven, summer was in full swing. Breathing in the heady jasmine in the air, I had no idea my credibility was about to crash wide open. The first call came from Billy. He was apoplectic, between laughing and yelling: 'Please tell me it's not true … What are you thinking? … How could you not tell me? … I told you NOT to go there'.

STOP. What are you talking about?

Billy explained he had read a story in BEAT magazine that Brian Cadd and I were an item.

Shit.

What did I say about the boundary between friendship and betrayal? Above all, my darling surrogate brother Billy was happy if I was happy but saw the humour in the scenario. Didn't we all?

I begged Billy not to spread the word until I could make a beeline for the office and tell Chuggi in person. Michael did not proffer any words of wisdom — approval, denial or otherwise — just a snort of 'good luck, Princess'.

In the New Year, Brian arrived in Paddington to commence our new life together. His daughter Jessica was with him. I should have recognized then they were an incontrovertible package. Olivia was thrilled to have an 'older sister', Austin was busy learning to ride his bike. I learned from Brian that Jessica's favorite color was mauve. Despite my detestation of this ambivalent palette, I decorated her bedroom accordingly. However, much I tried, she remained sullen and uncommunicative.

In one moment, the golden daughter was not the centre of attention. Brian had to have a procedure to check for nodules on his throat. This is the dreaded curse of all singers. He arrived home from the successful surgery unable to physically speak. Most women are infused with caring 'spirit'. I looked after him like a wartime nurse. Our love was so new; his wellbeing was on the top of my list — always. I had not spoken to his broader family at this stage. One evening his mother rang. As Brian was unable to physically speak, I took the call for him. Jean was sweet and welcoming but the reason for the call was grave. Brian's sister-in-law had passed away from cancer. Despite not knowing any of these new family players, I felt a massive sense of empathy for Brian's brother John.

Brian and I were about to hit the road on the second Long Way tour. We revealed ourselves to our peers. The first person we bumped into was Max Merritt. He laughed and offered me a 'good luck'.

Brian and I were in nirvana — on the road making music, making love, making memories with our now communal friends.

Our age difference was 15 years. In this early blush of love, it did not register as a looming impediment. Brian was lucky he had found in me a woman less Germaine Greer in the kitchen and more Marilyn Monroe in the sack. It suited his somewhat antiquated view of relationship dynamics.

The tour's only hitch was we were over budget. We had to cut down artist and production numbers. Between Chugg and Jacobsen, it was decided to drop Kevin Borich, Lonnie Lee, Stevie Wright and Pig Morgan, the original keyboardist for Sunbury Aztecs. We offered them a 10 per cent cancellation fee which was above what they would have been contractually obliged to receive.

Halfway through the tour we heard from lawyers threatening to sue for wrongful dismissal. Much to my amazement the lawyer was John Kenny — latterly the lawyer for Indecent Obsession who made the Melodian Records deal elongated to say the least.

Ugh. Brisbane lawyers. Only a taste of what was to come.

At the end of the tour, Brian and I returned home to Paddington. This was the first of many homes together where I devotedly threw myself into making a domestic paradise. I loved to cook, and the house had a fantastic kitchen where we all spread out and pitched in. All except Jessica. This girl was not interested in integration on any level.

Paul Clarke at the ABC, who devised the original LWTTT series, approached Brian and me to take part in his music documentary Love Is in the Air.

How apt, we thought. His intent was to shoot us individually regarding both our careers. We met at a café in Paddington and confessed our new blissful domestic togetherness to him. For every new person we told we took on some added pride in our liaison. Brian was fond of describing it as we had both been on all the rides and now this was our final 'go round'. After three previously failed — and excruciatingly short — marriages, I felt I had finally found someone on my wavelength. We were 15 years apart in age but still wanted all the fun that life had to offer. Out of all our similarities a kind of reckless abandon for 'joie de vivre' was dominant.

Maybe taking from original Bohemians in the 1930s, we never worried about tomorrow like our parents had done.

I knew that I knew better than this, having been trained under my father's watchful fiscal eye, but I initially trusted Brian and saw in him a partner who would keep me safe. I would find out soon enough that first impressions — particularly of one's circumstances — can be deceptive. Brian was in fact a bankrupt and I would go on to spend years and huge amounts of my own money to rectify his financial downfall.

Within months, Brian suggested we move to Melbourne.

I was reluctant as my professional life with Chuggi and Billy, and other casting opportunities, was based in Sydney. A pattern was emerging — Clive and leaving London; Damien and Byron Bay; now again, Brian and Melbourne.

He wanted to make an album with his old crew — including Ernie Rose and Tony Naylor, preferably at the old Armstrong Studios in South Melbourne.

I revelled, watching my new partner writing and collaborating on his first album in years.

Quietly Rusting took its title from a line by James Taylor. The song itself is an ode to the death of relationships while people still maintain a domestic status quo — a state of being he was watching several of his musical comrades endure.

So, move again I did. I found a sprawling Brady Bunch house in Brighton. While Brian settled into recording, and my kids settled into new schools, his son Nick arrived from LA. Nick was 18 and a wonderful bright spark. He had a happy-go-lucky vibe. Along with Brian's eldest twin son, Jason, we were now domestically The Brady Bunch. Five out of our six kids under the one roof. Then the dogs arrived.

I have never been a dog person, but Jessica wanted dogs, and what Jessica wanted, she got — a phrase oft repeated by her brothers across many years.

Our love story became media fodder — colorful spreads featuring us playing happy families, offers to film an Osbournes-like family tell-all TV show … all while we were trying to find our feet as a couple.

Privately I loathed being back in Melbourne. It felt cut off from my professional reality.

Diligently working at being an outstanding partner and as a new couple, we threw lots of wild parties. This became a hallmark of our relationship — always the couple with the open door, hosting teardown knockout events.

A fancy-dress party featured Brian and I dressed as God and his Angel with the theme — 'Come as you are not'. Brian's tour manager came dressed as a nun and spent the night rolling everyone's joints. I can't count how many people came dressed as a 'little ray of sunshine'. My friend Serge photographed the revelry.

Another visitor was Brian's LA pal, Ruth McCartney, stepsister of Beatle Sir Paul McCartney. Effervescent with a capital E, she was a great storyteller with a sharp wit. Her stories of childhood with Paul at the height of Beatles fame were fascinating. During an evening of inebriated conversation, Ruth mentioned David Cassidy.

I stopped in my tracks.

It appeared I was in the presence of someone who knew him, David Cassidy. Learning I was a Cassidy tragic, Ruth turned to Brian and said, 'Haven't you told her?'

The truth sprung forth: Ruth had previously been in a relation-friendship with David and was still in touch with him. All the years of Tiger Beat fanzines, kissing his image on posters came flooding back. After swallowing a double vodka, I pleaded with her:

'One thing … please tell me one thing about him'.

Ruth ruminated. 'Well, I don't know, I guess … two Coke cans' — demonstrating with her hands spread six inches apart.

Oh, my Giddy Aunt. I certainly knew why Brian had not told me that story.

By a magnificent twist of fate, David Cassidy came to Australia for a promotional trip soon after. The promotion was with TV1. My friend Michael 'Mimi' Shephard was the orchestrator of this trip. He knew an introduction was a deal breaker to our long friendship!

On a humid Melbourne afternoon, I finally stood in front of the adolescent love of my life. The reality of time passed was evident in the amount of Botox and hair-dye that replaced the innocent cherubic Partridge Family idol.

We hugged and posed for photos while I stumbled for words.

A moment not dissimilar to meeting Woody Allen was unfolding. I just forgot to ask David Cassidy to marry me. Damn.

After a year under the same roof, Jessica moved to the Gold Coast to her first fiancé. Nick took an apprenticeship with Holden, Jason moved on from his first marriage, and we kept on with our respective careers. Everything was golden. Olivia had occasional weekends with Clive; Austin had less frequent visits with Damien. I made it clear to Damien that it had to be 'all or nothing' as Austin grew older and wiser. Damien gifted me a voucher for an art gallery. I nearly threw the paper gift in the trash, but something stopped me.

Olivia and I ventured to the art gallery one sunny Sunday.

At the counter she spotted a real estate brochure and said, 'Mummy, this house looks like you'. I picked it up and instantly fell in love. A heart-shaped fire surrounded by painted flames made this c1863 old miner's tavern scream just our kind of kooky.

The gallery owner was selling his country home and offered it to us for a weekend visit. Brian and I were sold on the quirky little farm outside Daylesford that became our true heart home for thirteen wonderful years.

The place that became known as 'Sandon Ridge' had previously been owned by the author John Marsden. A mudbrick cottage was where he wrote many of his prize-winning children's books. It passed on inspiration for Brian writing his own autobiography. It also became a painting studio for me, a pastime I had not enjoyed since the tower in Manchester Unity.

Many hours were spent in the garden, Austin learned to chop wood, our pal Murf became our own Chauncey the Gardener. Brian surveyed us all with encouragement while opening another bottle of wine.

My beloved partner toured in support of his new album, and I was thrilled he had written a song about me.

'You're the Reason' is a rollicking romp about my work/life balance featuring guitar master Ross Hannaford from Daddy Cool. The line 'I pray they leave enough of you for those who need you too' echoed the reality of the fast-paced lives we were both living.

Having gone from two children to six, albeit emerging adults, was challenging but thrilling. Having grown up an only child I had always longed for a big noisy family. I just didn't bank on how complicated it would become. Brian's younger twin son Kristian had struggled with drug addiction for some years. In taking on this menagerie of complex personalities I knew I had to take the good with the bad.

I nurtured Brian through the pain of watching his son disintegrate into drug-addled oblivion as much as I kept my own two small children unaware of the circumstances.

Researching drug rehabs was emotionally heartbreaking and financially costly. Unbeknown to me, it would not be the last time I had to do this.

I kept busy producing the Australian Idol Live Tour for Chugg Entertainment. One of its judges, Ian 'Dicko' Dickson, was an English A&R guy working at BMG in Australia.

We hit it off straight away. Let the madness begin. We designed the show from scratch, and Dicko became 'judge-as-narrator'. The first year of Idol was a stellar lineup including Guy Sebastian and Shannon Noll.

Then there was Courtney Act. An amazing drag artist who didn't make it into the final Top 12. For the tour I insisted we put her on as 'Lucky 13'. Drag was in its infancy when it came to being portrayed in the general media. Its cultural depth was well known in certain circles, especially in Sydney with Carlotta and the Academy Award winning film Priscilla, Queen of the Desert.

What a showstopping moment Courtney created in Idol Live. Everyone on the production crew felt we were opening young people's eyes and hearts to diversity in the community. Natural acceptance of 'diversity' took so long to emerge. Shane/Courtney has gone on to have a brilliant international career, including in RuPaul's Drag Race.

Olivia and Austin came on tour. I employed a raucous rotund nanny, Sarah. I don't know who was more starstruck over Guy Sebastian — Olivia or Sarah. Austin blissfully sat in my office playing with his 'Beyblades'. He remains as unaffected by show business today in adulthood.

Our reasons for living in Melbourne ran dry along with any enthusiasm for my old hometown.

Jessica was planning her wedding on the Gold Coast. And after completing a mechanic apprenticeship, Nick returned to Los Angeles.

We made plans to head back to Sydney but before that, Brian had one more tour in WA with Glenn Shorrock. In Perth, they took a break to play golf one afternoon prior to an evening show. Glenn whacked a ball that looked like it was going to hit Brian square on the head. Brian ducked. Taking the fall violently, he ripped the cartilage in his right knee. That night, Brian was wheeled onto the stage in a wheelchair, pumped up with period painkiller Mersyndol, administered by the box office lady. She was clearly unsure what dosage to administer to a male rock star who had never experienced period pain.

Brian performed the show in some out-of-body experience, which he later explained as being on stage with The Rolling Stones circa 1962!

On his return, I took one look and called a doctor who, in turn, called an ambulance. Brian was headed for full knee reconstruction surgery. Unfortunately, this was the first of many accidents to befall Brian and have long-lasting physical and mental effects.

I made a trip to Europe. While casting musical theatre, I had been professionally tracking an ex-pat Australian couple who set up business in London with Janet Holmes à Court. The venture was called Back Row Productions and, along with auteur Dein Perry, the company launched Tap Dogs to the world.

Liz Koops and Garry McQuinn were a couple personally and professionally. Garry was a NIDA graduate and one of the happiest, most open-hearted people I had ever met. Our initial paths crossed at the Jacobsen offices during casting of Beauty and the Beast. The next time we were to meet was at a rehearsal for the opening of Tap Dogs in Sydney. I suggested to Chuggi we work with Back Row to bring their productions to Australia.

My first meeting with Liz Koops, at lunch in London, was the only time in the years to come that I spoke more than she did. I even got the last word. I spent the time singing her praises and pitching Michael Chugg Entertainment as a perfect venture partner in Oz.

I ventured to Sydney to find the next in a long line of homes. It may be a cerebral glitch, or itch, that makes me adapt to frequently moving. I imagine it is the joy of the unknown that keeps me moving, some resolute belief that everything will always turn out OK in the end, or I can move, again.

That's my interpretation.

Our new home enveloped us in a world of friendship that remains sacred to me. Our street was a dead-end enclave overlooking the water. One afternoon, our neighbour was sweeping the footpath. I peered down from my balcony and heard a friendly 'Hallooo', spoken in Scottish brogue. Lorraine and I instantly bonded. Coincidentally, the next neighbour was also of Scottish descent. Brian and I met 'wee Irene', as she became known, at the annual street party.

Irene approached Brian and me and said in a hearty Scots welcome, 'Well, Heellloo Lil, hello Ray … so lovely to meet you'.

Perplexed, Brian and I moved onto other conversations. Later we learned she thought our names were Lil and Ray as Brian's car registration plate was 'LILRAY' — a gift I bought him as a nod to his most famous song, 'A Little Ray of Sunshine'.

That age-old wonder — does where we land geographically ultimately determine many of life's outcomes for us and those around us? Absolutely, it does.

We spent New Year's Eve watching fireworks from the yacht of our new friends, Liz and Garry, with Chuggi as we entered a new business, starting with Tap Dogs. Chuggi and I felt confident with these like-minded individuals and knew that more good times were ahead.

Our new life in Sydney felt like a truer beginning. Being in Sydney had many upsides. For Brian, he was in proximity to Glenn Shorrock. We had many a well-lubricated evening at his home in Double Bay. Brian and Glenn performed shows together, morphing into a full-blown tour and album — 'Sharky and The Caddman'.

We took a holiday in Byron Bay and rented a house owned by local artist Colin Heaney. I was transfixed by the beauty of his ceramics and artistic design. Brian and I stood on the balcony with an unexpected 'homecoming' feeling. We commented how sharp the feeling was, gazing at the moonlit ocean, reducing us to joyful tears. Soon enough those tears would be repeated, in both happy and sad circumstances.

Colin Heaney was contemplating selling this house. We lapped up the holiday weeks and moved back to our busy lives in Sydney.

Brian began touring with his comrade Russell Morris. They created a bundle of laughs in two hours of hits. I loved watching their friendship, on and off stage. They played self-deprecating roles, brilliantly taking the mickey out of each other. Much of it was unscripted and night after night new one-liners would appear and leave the audience in stitches of laughter. Russell was a lot more fun to be around than moody Glenn Shorrock. It irked me that Glenn acted with a level of superiority over Brian. Having made a huge success with the Little River Band in America, while Brian's career in the States had been as a songwriter, seemed to warrant Glenn behaving the way he did. Being protective of Brian, both personally and professionally, this did not sit well with me. I never brought it to a head.

One afternoon Russell, Brian and I were having lunch together. Somehow the topic of WW2 came up. Russell spoke fondly of his mother. Talk turned to how much our mothers had endured because of the war. Little could we have known how much — and how closely. The conversation wove on to reveal that Russell's mother's first love and my mother's first husband had both been soldiers together on an island called Ambon. Off the northern-most coastline of Australia, this island was overrun by the Japanese. Multiple soldiers were lined up and beheaded on that island.

It became clear the two men betrothed to our mothers had perished together. The harsh reality that neither Russell nor I would have existed had either of those men survived became abundantly clear. We went on to report the story to our mothers.

For Brian's part, he understood that he would not have encountered his friend or wife save that fateful wartime day.

Chuggi and I went back into show development mode, working with Slim Dusty's widow Joy McKean, our Back Row pals Liz and Garry, Matthew Bourne's Swan Lake, Tap Dogs and another little idea …

In all facets of show business there are 'light bulb' moments. The chill-up-the-spine moments when an idea becomes a tangible future success. Much like my first day at Mushroom Records with Divine, my excitement level pirouetted into space when Liz Koops casually said, 'What do you think about Priscilla, Queen of the Desert being a musical?'

The film, released in 1994, was a worldwide hit and earned costume designers Lizzy Gardiner and Tim Chappel an Academy Award. The film's executive producer, Michael Hamlyn, was a friend of Liz and Garry's in London and the rest, as they say, is history.

Chugg Entertainment had grown enormously in the preceding years, adding CEO Matthew Lazarus-Hall. Rock 'n' roll was becoming corporatized with smaller companies being consumed by global behemoths. Chugg remained fiercely independent and ran his own race with expert guidance from Business Manager Jacqui Crouch.

Chuggi's investment in theatre was a leap of faith as it certainly wasn't one of his personal cultural touchstones.

A brief example was opening night of Swan Lake in Sydney at the Capitol Theatre. Chuggi was not known for sitting still for too long, certainly not for the entire duration of a play or a musical. There was, however, political protocol on this night as the Governor-General was present. We ran through the chain of command for entry into the theatre as we all stood anxiously backstage awaiting the GG's arrival. The stage manager would announce the audience to be upstanding right before the line of dignitaries and producers would take their seats. Disregarding previous instructions, Chuggi emerged first from behind the backstage curtain waving at the audience as he made his way to his seat. The Governor-General's entourage meekly followed behind this Emperor in his new clothes. Brilliant. When it came to speeches at the after-party, Chuggi was nowhere to be found. I motioned to Garry to get on with the previously arranged salutations and Matthew Bourne's speech, without my fearless leader.

An hour later he meekly appeared — what goes on the road stays on the road. One of the hundreds of 'Sorry, Princess' dog-eyed apologies I received over the years, which made me forgive him and love the Boss even more.

Development on Priscilla went into full swing. I was the casting director as well as overseeing Chugg's producorial investor role. In my previous incarnation as an agent with Firm Hand, I had been in awe of director Simon Phillips. All actors and agents wanted to work with Simon's brilliant directorial intellect. Getting to know him on Priscilla was a real thrill. Up close he wasn't professionally terrifying, just genuinely gifted and giving.

While Brian was away on tour we were robbed.

I awoke on a Sunday morning to find the downstairs ransacked. Austin's room and ours were on the upper level. Austin, in his six-year-old naivety, said to me, 'Mummy, I saw a man walking past my room last night'. That was enough for me, too close for comfort. Brian and I lamented our lost computers and video cameras containing precious family footage. A kooky old ships chandlery corner house in Balmain East took Brian's fancy.

This was it, I told myself with courage and determination, we would not move again while we had school-aged children. How naïve I was to my own foibles and my partner's lack of fiscal responsibility.

There was a lot going on in the Chugg empire. We moved offices to a building in Elizabeth Street — rife with hookers and hustlers outside the front door.

I stumbled across an idea to work with David Hasselhoff.

Connect the dots — from Indecent Obsession in wetsuits to my love of musicals and back around to recording artists … it was a natural progression. Hasselhoff had entertainingly helped bring down the Wall in East Berlin in 1989 singing 'Looking for Freedom'. I recalled having seen The Hoff on Broadway doing Jekyll & Hyde during the same magical trip I discovered Rent. I reached out to his management and suggested we develop a show I loosely titled 'From Baywatch to Broadway'.

I was taking Olivia to LA for her 16th birthday, so I planned to meet up with The Hoff. We lunched at The Ivy. I instantly knew we were a perfect match. Both of us had notified paparazzi about the meeting without informing each other — always a PR now with an equally PR savvy client!

Next stop, Las Vegas. Liz and Garry were 'eloping'. Garry asked me to be his 'Breast Man'. Shades of the role reversal Deborra-Lee Furness managed in her wedding with Hugh Jackman. I was honored and Olivia was the flower girl addition. True to Vegas folklore it was an Elvis chapel. Elvis appeared and took an immediate shine to my Olivia, my sweet 16 Olivia. He swept her up and planted a huge kiss on her, quite enough to put her off men for a while.

As the girls fussed with final preparations, the groom and I attended to paperwork. I watched Garry's pen hover over the page, poised with reserved reflection. My instinct kicked in to verbalize my thoughts. My mind spun back to the Thai jungle driving to my own precarious nuptials. The time when I 'dialed a friend' and called my lawyer. Now I was here as Garry's friend — should I speak up? 'Don't do it', I could say. But I did not.

As Kylie Minogue said, you've got to be certain. We made our way into the chapel. Elvis started with his 'hunk of burning love' off-key vocals. Garry and I turned to see Liz enter in a frock that could only be described as a meringue on steroids. My inside voice felt the marriage was already doomed.

In New York, Chuggi and I met up with Brian and Billy Thorpe.

The CMC Awards were being held at Madison Square Garden and Keith Urban was performing. The Australian Consulate put on a soirée before the event. Chuggi's business partner was one of Keith's earliest mentors, Rob Potts. Rob was a genial chap who loved a drink and a laugh and was always terrific fun to be around. He had impeccable taste in music and led us to a young Taylor Swift some years later. Rob took us aside and whispered discreetly, 'Do NOT look shocked when Keith arrives –he has fallen in love, they want to keep it private'.

As his words lingered in the air we turned to see Keith with Nicole Kidman. The idea of these two successful Aussies forming an alliance was magnificent, however much they seemed from different worlds.

Hasselhoff was in New York, so we flew production manager Peter 'Sneaky' McFee in to work on show ideas. Hoff and I had chosen Scott Faris to direct. We met in The Hoff's suite at Trump Hotel on Central Park. This was the one and only time I stepped foot in a Trump establishment. As far back as 2006, it was impossible to imagine within a decade the havoc that hotel's namesake would wreak on American politics.

Chuggi came up with the brilliant idea of recording Aussie classic 'Jump in my Car'– the perfect ode to Hoff's time as Knight Rider. Everything was targeted towards establishing The Hoff in Australia ahead of the debut of 'Baywatch to Broadway'.

Next stop, Miami. Chuggi and I met financial backer, Jack Utsick. We had our ducks in a row — projections on theatrical enterprises for the following three years. The linchpin was Hasselhoff. We knew that would float Jack's boat. He lived in the penthouse of Miami's tallest apartment tower. As the elevator doors opened into the apartment, we were greeted with two life-size blow-up dolls simulating sex. One of the moments in life you can never 'un-see'.

Jack came leaping out from behind the door, laughing like an insane asylum inmate at his 'joke'. This meeting was clearly taking place on planet Mars.

We proceeded with 10 per cent of Jack's attention. He was desperate to reveal footage from a film he funded starring Paris Hilton, and Jack's teenage daughter. Titled Bottoms Up it was released straight to DVD. Taking a cigarette break we ventured out onto the balcony. Thirty floors up, looking out across the never-ending Atlantic Ocean, I felt vertigo and feared Jack's mania might cause him to push one of us, you know, as a 'joke'.

We couldn't get out of there fast enough.

Funding secured, the 'Don't Hassel the Hoff' project kicked off. We created a media campaign with Pepsi and shot a clip for 'Jump in my Car'. In retrospect, the clip today would be deemed sexist and predatory. Three nubile young ladies meet up with Hoff in a dark alleyway and one by one go for a ride in his car. Outrageous by today's standards but tongue-in-cheek when we made it.

The trip coincided with the ARIA Awards. I secured Hoff a guest spot. His star turn ended up being front page news when a starstruck Missy Higgins jumped Hoff like she was riding him in a rodeo — kissing him with such voracity she cut his lip open. Pure PR Gold.

Months later, 'Baywatch to Broadway' literally fell off a cliff.

I received a discombobulated phone call from the Hoff. He was in Cabo, Mexico, clearly drunk out of his mind. He told me he had left his wife, Pamela. I was less concerned about this information than I was that he was drinking again. He wished me a Merry Christmas and assured me he would be OK. The next day he fell badly and broke some bones. There was no way we were going into pre-production with our show now, for many reasons.

Having success with Tap Dogs and Swan Lake, and our expected hit with The Hoff, I convinced Chuggi to let me secure rights for other productions from the UK. The hottest new TV phenomenon was Little Britain. They were touring across England, so off I went.

In Sheffield it was arranged for me to meet David Walliams and Matt Lucas after the show. From the opening sketch I was hooked. At interval I went backstage to say hello to Peter McFee, who was working on the production. The management scuttled me into a dressing room, saying David and Matt wanted to meet right there and then.

In they came, dressed in character prior to the opening of Act 2. It was extremely difficult to keep a straight face with them dressed in character — Matt as Bubbles de Vere. I constructed my selling pitch and went for it.

Lesson One: don't ever try to make jokes to real comedians. They were both delightful and, after a few minutes of polite banter, asked what I thought of the show. I did the comic knee-slap gesture, tossing my head back in a raucous laugh for added effect. I chortled, 'Guys, the show is SO pant-wetting-ly funny I have already gone through a packet of Depends pads!' Silence. Nothing.

I am ruined. I will never get this tour.

We made offers but were outbid by Michael Coppel. He never makes jokes.

As a kid, Chuggi loved science fiction and particularly War of the Worlds. Jeff Wayne wrote the stage production and remounted it for an anniversary tour. I caught the show in lovely Brighton by the Sea. I went to the pebbly beach and fondly remembered sitting there with my father in 1974.

In moments like this I wondered what he would have thought of my career path. It made me miss him so much more not being able to share the triumphs and tribulations.

I thought War of the Worlds was mediocre at best. It tried to be a full-blown stage musical, à la Les Misérables, while using limited screen graphics to portray the alien landscape. I was however interested in the idea of working with orchestras, having started that journey with Billy Thorpe for his musical opus Tangier.

I got home in time for Billy Thorpe's surprise 60th birthday at the 18 Footers in Double Bay. His wife Lynn got the A-team together. Thorpie really had no idea. It was so much fun seeing Billy, of all people, get caught out!

He got his own back, surprising me when Brian and my kids did the same for my 45th birthday. I walked into a party none the wiser to see Billy and Lynn, Chugg, Toby Creswell, Ted Robinson and others all there for me.

I was thrilled.

My world took an interesting turn during this time.

I was asked to audition as judge on a new TV series for the Seven Network. Based on the UK series Duets, it was re-titled It Takes Two. The premise was twelve established vocal performers would take on a person, renowned in their field, and teach them to sing. Simply the same format as Dancing with the Stars, just vocal rhythm instead of toe-tapping. We, the four judges, would assess both 'teacher' and 'student's' ability in a ten-week season — once a week, live to air.

The producer for the series was Julie Ward, whom I had met at Foxtel in 1996. She signed David Dixon and Hugh Jackman as two of the network's first flagship artists. We had an instant rapport and I was pleased to meet her again. Her husband, Jamie Rigg, had been the musical director for LWTTT. I had done a series of backstage interviews on LWTTT and felt comfortable in that setting.

I approached the audition with an open heart and mind. There in the room was James Valentine, a member of the Models, a Mushroom band in the '80s. 'Quite a departure for you', he quipped. He had become a successful ABC radio jock and looked like he was going to challenge me to a verbal duel during our audition. I ate the attitude, and our chemistry did the trick.

The next day I was enjoying cocktails with Liz above the Lyric Theatre, where Priscilla was opening in a matter of months. The producers of the TV show walked past a one of them nodded with a thumbs up that I had got the role.

Raising two children, helicopter-step-parenting four others, managing my mother's move to Sydney, and Brian's recording career, was already a handful. That wonderful modernism about women and 'having it all' … I loved it.

I never saw the glass ceiling, even when it looked like falling in on me. I sure as hell didn't worry about the ton of bricks in emotional weight. Brian and I were solid. I learned a lot about his ego over our years traversed together — emotionally and geographically. I figured he would be happy for me. But his narcissism, from both a male and celebrity perspective, treated my new enterprise with a level of disdain.

Flying to Melbourne for the live-to-air show meant checking in on my mother each week. She made the difficult decision to sell the family home, so we spent hours packing up 43 years of 'life'. Elvie was keen to be in Sydney near to us.

The emotional dichotomy of 'performing' on TV one night and packing up my childhood home the next was bizarre. One thought rang through — if only Evie Hayes could see me now. The woman who had been Australia's most famous TV judge, who told my parents not to waste their money on my singing lessons. And here I was fulfilling a role she performed proudly for years, after the years I spent working with some of Australia's most successful recording artists.

The three seasons of It Takes Two were a lesson in music industry camaraderie, much like Long Way to the Top. I found it amusing to be described as the 'Simon Cowell of Australia', inferring I was the nasty judge. There was no doubt, week after week, I did not hold back on any act if I thought their performance was lacking. One week I described swimmer Daniel Kowalski as 'looking about as excited as shopping in Aisle 7 of Woolies'. Once or twice my producers told me it wasn't 'attractive' for a woman to be so bold. I reminded them why they employed me in the first place — my nickname as dubbed by Molly Meldrum was 'Attila the Hen' after all.

Marina Prior and I were the perfect female foils for each other. Her reputation is squeaky clean. Off camera, Marina gave as good as she got. I adored her.

In Season One a young Home and Away actor named Mark Furze appeared. He reminded me so much of David Dixon when he started out. I had a lot of faith in him as a performer and took on management of his band. In the long run he didn't have the discipline to make it and returned to live in regional NSW.

After each performance, we judges had thirty seconds to decide on points to score the artists. Somehow, I ended up being the mathematical tally person, ironic given I had virtually failed Year 10 math.

The Seven Network crew were stellar. Much to my surprise, an old ABC face appeared. Ilter Cimilli was an original cameraman on Countdown, back when I danced on the show under Molly Meldrum's direction. Team spirit is everything with live broadcast; it was a great lesson for what was to come in the mid 2007 once I went back to the other side of the camera.

In the few years since Long Way to the Top, Billy Thorpe had been touring and working ferociously on his 'Tangier' project. When his wife Lynn turned 50, they had a life-changing trip to Morocco. Billy became consumed by the culture and the music. Just like Spinal Tap, he was always on 11, darling Billy. He would summon me to his studio in Surry Hills to listen to the latest takes for his gestating opus. It was Pink Floyd meets Brian Eno with a dash of ELO thrown in. We would sit for hours listening and plotting. Would it be a stage show or a film? 'BOTH!' yelled Billy.

'Shut up and let me think', I would retort. That was the magic in our friendship — we could tell each other to shut up and still be smiling.

Billy's trusty engineer Greg Clarke was always in the studio. He had a kind of dark side I never understood, somehow mired in suspicion. He would occasionally talk about Billy's studio as having 'something wrong with it'. Not in a cosmic energy type of way, but a legitimate toxic issue with the building.

Other than Tangier, Billy was working on his third book.

His first authorship netted two literary award-winning autobiographies titled Sex and Thugs and Rock 'n' Roll and Most People I Know. His third was almost finished. Billy typed it all himself into his computer.

This was just before regular use of thumb drives. One evening, Billy left his Surry Hills studio but forgetting something, he doubled back in his car. He parked out front and quickly bolted upstairs. On return, his car had been ransacked, his briefcase stolen and with it the computer containing the only copy of his third book. He was both heartbroken and understandably furious at himself. No amount of police reporting would ever recover the end of the intended trilogy.

Billy had become a board member for Support Act — the music industry charity helping its members through hard times. Brian had started a lunch group called The Debonairs which donated proceeds to Support Act. It grew from one Melbourne branch to what culminated in more than 2,000 members nationwide.

In taking on the Support Act board membership, Billy became all too aware of the dire straits many technicians and roadies were left in when they could no longer perform demands of the rock 'n' roll road.

One case hit him hardest — that of his old mate Lobby Loyde. Lobby had been a member of the Aztecs and was now in last stages of lung cancer. Just like when he lobbed the thought-grenade that became Long Way to the Top, Thorpie hit Chuggi and I square between the eyes to put on a benefit concert for Lobby. Agent Frank Stivala secured the Palace venue in St Kilda. Billy and Chuggi pulled out all the performance favors and we put on a show.

Jimmy Barnes flew back from Europe, and Angry Anderson put Rose Tattoo back together, featuring Lobby who managed to play a few numbers. Paul Stewart re-formed Painters & Dockers, a band Lobby had produced and managed — and for which I was the vocal Yuppie on the track 'Die Yuppie Die'!

Jack Thompson and I forged a bond that night — he was a consummate MC and a true gentleman with an intellectual energy that positively vibrated. Far from being the first nude centrefold in Cleo, he was still a very sexy individual.

During afternoon rehearsal, Billy turned to me off stage and said, 'If we don't get Tangier up and running soon, you'll be doing one of these for me'.

I laughed it off. How ridiculous. Billy Thorpe was invincible and would outlive us all.

God, I wish I had listened.

Despite living in Sydney, we would visit Melbourne often to go to the Sandon Ridge farm. On the weekends Brian was not performing, we would take a flight on a Friday afternoon. We kept a car at Melbourne airport and could be at the farm by early evening. This arrival was often met with the stench of animals that had taken willing occupancy during elongated absences. Austin liked to imagine them running amok, as in the film Ratatouille.

Relaxation spread across a sublime evening by the heart-shaped fire. Austin would fall asleep on a beanbag by the fire. I carried him into his pre-heated bed and relished those moments us parents have of gazing at our cherub-like offspring before they all-too-soon grow and fly the nest.

We were in final stages for Priscilla's worldwide opening in Sydney.

The excitement was palpable as production departments ran the mile to the finish line. All cast and producers navigated PR angles with aplomb, under the guidance of Judith Johnson. Having worked with many theatrical PR dynamos in my time, I was honored to be in the presence of Miss Johnson. Her career spanned 30 years — shows as varied as Whoopi Goldberg to the Bee Gees. The team gathered to finalize seating arrangements for opening night when word came that Judith had passed away in her sleep.

We were all speechless. Assembled and trying to rouse the team with a 'show must go on' demeanour, I went to the staff kitchen and reached for a bottle of gin Judith had placed there. 'For emergencies only', she always said. I defined this moment an emotional emergency and we all took a tot in her honor.

Seating people for opening nights may not sound difficult but it is akin to being a spy in the cold war trying to figure out which side you are on. A puzzle like snakes and ladders, you must be cognizant who is side by side but also behind and in front … politics, industry, history, who screwed who — metaphorically and literally.

For my own part I wedged myself between Michael Chugg and Barry Humphries. With Chuggi to the right of me I could ensure he didn't get up and wander.

Barry, to the left, as my date.

My life partner was absent on tour. For many years Brian made a joke of this, telling people he begged his agents to play 'anywhere there was electricity' when there was an Opening Night. Like many performers before and since, this was a habit borne of the fact he couldn't navigate not being the centre of attention. I dismissed it and enjoyed the moments I was privileged to enjoy for myself.

One of those was sitting with Barry Humphries that evening. A man of style and elegance, I recalled our first meeting in my mother's atelier on Collins Street in 1976 — a mere 30 years earlier. His then wife, Diane Millstead, was dressed by Elvie Hill at the time. Out of memory lane and back in our seats, Barry loved the show.

As the second act went into full swing, he kept grabbing the flesh above my knee. Gripping it with glee he whispered in my ear, 'It's marvellous, darling!' This was heard as one word out of his elasticated mouth. 'MARVELLOUS, I love it, it will run for years'.

My shrieks of delight were in part professional triumph –remembering his quote for the press release — and part agonizing pain from his grip on my leg.

I wore the bruises for days afterwards as a badge of honor.

Post-opening night, Brian attended a matinee of Priscilla. Billy Thorpe and his family came along with Chuggi and his partner Chutimon — visiting Australia for the first time from Thailand. At interval we crowded into the Green Room lounge. Billy approached me and whispered, 'So are they all blokes in dresses or are there any girls in there?' For a guy who matured in Kings Cross in the late '60s, surrounded by drag queens, I was dismayed by his naivety.

I had to ask twice if he was pulling my leg.

Chuggi looked restless — after all, this was his second time seeing the show. Then he pointed out this was his girlfriend's first time in a big theatre.

I looked at her and realized the sound and lights were ringing around in her head like an acid trip with Timothy Leary. Off we went for Act 2. Still thinking about Ma'am Chugg, I had a moment's panic about an upcoming scene. For those of you who know the film and the show, you know what I mean. The character of Cynthia is an Asian woman of some 'ill repute', a mail-order bride to Bob. The cultural characterization of a woman in this instance is not at all flattering. We were in our seats, so it was a strap-yourself-in and see what comes. As we exited the theatre after the grand finale, Ma'am came out laughing heartily and said, 'Oh, the scene with ping-pong balls was so funny!' Phew.

Billy Thorpe was fulltime on Tangier arrangements and keen on the idea of touring in 'acoustic' mode. He created a streamlined simplistic set with a storyline/Q&A monologue idea. He was so ahead of his time. We did a deal with Mushroom Records. I was back in touch with Warren Costello and the Mushroom team. Billy booked a show at The Basement in Sydney. We booked a video crew to film the show — as much for his own edification as to on-sell the show idea to agents.

Billy would visit me at the Priscilla offices for development meetings on the Tangier project. By February he had got as far as he could with the recording process. We were formulating a budget to go to Morocco and record with the national orchestra. From his time in Morocco, Billy had made some influential friends; we had letters out to The King and his envoy, asking for cultural and financial assistance.

Late February was our last meeting.

I walked Billy out of the building and gave him a huge hug.

I reassured him that Tangier was as much a priority for me as he himself was. Despite the demands of working on Priscilla's early success, we WOULD make it to Morocco and fulfil his dreams of releasing this magnificent musical opus.

I remember thinking he looked pale as we held each other's gaze for the longest time.

Brian and I flew to Melbourne for a 50th birthday party. We arrived late as my mobile phone rang. The caller ID was Billy. I didn't pick up as we rushed in; I would call him later.

Halfway through the evening, bored by the event, I went outside to call Billy. He didn't pick up. I now know he and Lynn were enjoying a quiet night watching a movie.

Brian and I were staying at a friend's home in Brighton.

We snuck in after the party and quietly went to bed without waking the household.

After midnight my phone started to ring. It was Norm Sweeney, Billy's tour manager. I swore at the phone, thinking Sweeney and Billy must have been out on the tear or at a gig somewhere. So again, I didn't pick up. The phone kept on ringing every few minutes.

Giving in, I answered, admonishing Norm. 'What the hell are you guys up to?'

The next words just rung around my head in a vicelike grip until I could repeat the words to Brian as he shook me.

'Billy is dead'.

It was nearing 2 am by the time I shut my eyes for an hour.

I booked us on the 6 am flight back to Sydney and tried in vain to reach Chugg on any phone number I had at my disposal.

I desperately wanted to give Chuggi the news before the media got hold of him. It was Richard Wilkins who broke the news to him. By the time we landed in Sydney, Matthew Lazarus-Hall was at the airport to drive me to Lynn and the girls. Lynn was literally catatonic. We left her to rest while the arrangements started to be made. The family authorized me to speak to the hospital and commence funeral arrangements.

Billy had been taken by ambulance to St Vincent's Hospital but had been pronounced dead on arrival from a massive heart attack. Lynn would later tell me he was perfectly fine all evening. Shortly after they turned in, he grabbed his chest and fell to the ground. Back in the confronting daylight of arrangements, a medical officer called from the hospital to ask permission to donate Billy's eyes while there was still time to — as they so casually called it — 'harvest' them. I could not stomach the thought: not his eyes, and his daughters completely agreed.

I got to the office late afternoon to find Chugg fielding phone calls of condolence. Mark Pope arrived as we pondered over where to conduct a memorial service. By early evening I told Chuggi I felt a strong compulsion to go and be with Billy. I couldn't bear the thought of him 'alone'.

St Vincent's Hospital staff led me to a chapel-like room outside the morgue. Like waiting for him to enter the stage, I waited one last time for my beloved brotherly friend to arrive. They warned me about the sight of a dead body. I was now being the one to reassure the staff I had experienced 'deceased' before — with my father.

Nothing would stop me being there to hold his hand. It's entirely evident – upon death, the soul and essence of the person has completely disappeared.

My Interpretation.

I held Billy's hand, imagining it playing across his twelve-string acoustic the sound of 'Since You've Been Gone'. I quietly wept words of apology to him: 'I'm sorry, I'm sorry'.

Why was I sorry?

That I hadn't seen his off-color pallor at our last meeting as a sign? That he would never see the realization of 'Tangier'? His hand was cold as I held it in some vain attempt at warming him up. His fists were not clenched, a sign that he did not experience any excruciating pain when the heart attack hit him. The hospital provided a nun who consoled me after they took Billy away. I was weeping but quite passive, in tune with the sombre room setting which was designed to comfort the living as they grieved the cold dead in the morgue next door.

She spoke words of religious dogma about life and death and God ...

I couldn't help feeling Billy was watching from the corner, chortling, 'What a lot of claptrap!' As he wrote in 'Since You've Been Gone':

'Forget your dogmas, your religions and your creeds ...

Forget your mantras and your oms ...

There are no methods to this crazy life we lead ...

No secret paths to walk upon'

Around 10pm, the nun accompanied me to a taxi. The air was hot and humid from a day I had not physically experienced. I took a big deep breath. It felt like I was trying to take one final breath for Billy. I looked back at the hospital entrance and recalled what I had heard Richard Wilkins tell me earlier in the day.

That very morning, after Billy's lifeless body had been wheeled into the hospital morgue, Jimmy Barnes was being wheeled out to go home after heart surgery. The coincidence was not lost on me; I vowed to call Jimmy the next day.

I am around the age now that Billy was when he died.

I am overweight and I drink too much but I am not ready to go yet.

I know Billy wasn't either. His stubborn nature, like mine, most likely caused him to not seek medical help when he could have. He had had a turn at Jack Thompson's homestead outside Coffs Harbour the previous December but dismissed it on his return to Sydney.

Cleaning out the studio after his passing, Greg Clarke, Norm Sweeney and I found a plethora of empty aspirin packets. Was that long last look before we said goodbye a warning I missed?

I have maintained a morbid-like fear of not picking up what might be last phone calls with people I care so deeply about.

One of those calls I thankfully didn't miss some 15 years later was with one of my Michaels.

The kids had waited up for me, knowing what a shocking blow this was to their mother. I had not forgotten about Brian's own grieving. It came home to us both now. He and Billy had been mates for 40 years, especially during their mutual years in Los Angeles. We hugged each other with a true sense of purpose that night.

The following days were filled with private funeral plans and arrangements for the memorial. I called Olivia Newton-John and John Farrar who both agreed to come out from LA. Billy's wide group of friends all agreed to deliver eulogy speeches: Jack Thompson, Sam Neill and Bryan Brown. And Michael Chugg officiated.

I asked a favor of my dear friend, director Ted Robinson. Ted had himself suffered terrible grief at the loss of his daughter years earlier. Billy and I had attended that funeral together and marvelled at the life-celebration tone of the confetti cannon as the coffin was taken out. I asked Ted to repeat the confetti performance at the end of the memorial at the Sydney Entertainment Centre. When we met to plan this, Ted picked me up in his arms and held me with such courage and kindness. I will never forget it. We had lost a comrade, yet he recognized how deep in shock I was in that moment.

By securing the Entertainment Centre we ensured it would be the last stage for Billy Thorpe. His actual last performance had been at the San Remo in Victoria, not exactly salubrious — with all due respect to regional venues.

The only cross words exchanged between us as a team in those painful days were when Mark Pope stupidly suggested ways for Billy's coffin to be ushered out through the front of the venue. I profusely disagreed and exclaimed there was no way Billy Thorpe was going out from front of house with the audience!

He was the star. He would go out from the stage door, into an old 1940s funky hearse — with an honor guard of hundreds of invited industry guests.

The event was free to fans and public alike. More than three thousand people gaped in awe. The event began and a huge velvet drape covering the coffin revealed that Billy was already on stage. Sweeney dressed the stage with a selection of Billy's guitars, treating each of them with reverence. Poor Norm, he himself was ill with cancer — like Lobby Loyde; neither of them could have expected to outlive Billy.

It was a fitting public send-off followed by a family and friends funeral the next day.

During the wake, in the venue's foyer, I walked around in a daze. Molly Meldrum had been sitting behind me during the memorial and was so loving and kind. On the flipside, Michael Gudinski strutted around the wake like he owned it and completely ignored me. Not a word. Gudinski's arrogance, or EGO, is well documented but his inability that day to put our professional distance aside was disturbing.

Billy would have been furious.

Word must have got back to MG because later that year, at Brian's Hall of Fame induction, Gudinski came to me and apologized.

The funeral was a calm oasis of close friends bidding a quiet goodbye and paying close attention to Billy's grieving girls — his wife Lynn and two daughters. Warren 'Pig' Morgan spoke of experiencing a squawking cockatoo that morning on the balcony of his hotel room, positive it was Billy in spirit.

We all liked to think so. A communal interpretation.

Stuart Spence, my photographer mate, gifted me a copy of the amazing shot he took of Billy at The Sebel Townhouse for his gold jacket series. Billy, shirtless with the jacket tossed at his feet, stands defiant in a boxing pose, his 'fighting the world and I am going to win' look on his face. The photo adorns my office, and I say good morning to brother Billy every day.

I am still seeking inspiration from whatever plane he now inhabits.

A month had gone by since Billy's passing and the media were still spreading 'how did Thorpie die' rumors.

One journalist, Jason Walker, decided to write a book, unauthorized and wildly inaccurate. Gil Matthews, drummer from the Aztecs, threw himself into the limelight by bandying around stories of Billy's long-term ill-health and financial woes. It was nothing more than an utter betrayal and hurt a lot of us deeply.

As the rumour mill spun, I began to realize I had not grieved Billy's death.

Brian was on tour, I was spiralling and knew I had to get some answers.

I picked Austin up from school and we went to Byron Bay.

I called a woman I had met back in 1997, Joan, a psychic medium. She communicates with those we need to reach in spirit. I drove straight to Joan's home and spent the next hours with her. I had not seen her for some years and certainly not since I had been working with Billy. She picked up on my sense of grief, not hard as I was red-eyed and clearly distraught. It was like all the pent-up grief was oozing out of me in that one moment.

After a while she said, 'Is it Billy love? Billy Thorpe?'

For an hour, Billy 'came through' to her. She said things there is no possible way she could ever have known in total intimate detail. For example: 'He wants to talk about the motorbike … the girl on the back of the motorbike'. And he was laughing. This referred to the first time he ever saw Lynn on the day they met. He saw her on a motorbike in Melbourne and told his cab driver to follow the bike.

I smiled, I wept, I looked to the heavens in gratitude that Billy was indeed out there somewhere. This was grief counselling in redemption form and just what I needed. He came through to me and I will never forget it. In that intense grief it was as if he had guided me to Joan so I would know he was OK. Even in death, he somehow validated 'My Interpretation'.

Rest assured that his ethereal self was intact, I vowed to get on with Tangier and ensure its release.

CHAPTER 10: CARRYING A TORCH

On my return, Brian was less than impressed I had taken off without telling him. I tried to make him understand that the grieving process had been impossible to work through with him, for several reasons. As he and Billy were long-standing professional colleagues, there was a dynamic for him entirely different from my own. As witnessed the first night Brian ventured to reveal his feelings in Adelaide, Billy had not exactly been approving. Brian held a level of jealousy at me dedicating my time and expertise to other people and projects.
I had to fathom this devastating departure on my own.

Brian was not one to outwardly display his emotions. I wanted to wail and scream at the injustice of Billy's untimely passing with someone who could commiserate on the same emotional plane. Not to be with my partner.

His emotional coldness had also occurred when his father passed away. I was amazed at how removed he seemed inside the experience. At this time, more than ever, I needed him to take me in his arms and tell me he would make everything OK, but he couldn't. By his own admission, Brian did not contain a shred of empathy. Whatever the circumstances, when I cried, he would run and hide. Many people excuse this as symptomatic of 'Aussie men of a certain era'. Bullshit. It is, at its core, a narcissistic mechanism, being unable to see that someone else close to you needs support.

Artists are not renowned for putting others before themselves. This is intrinsically where Brian and I differed as human beings. I am always thinking of everyone else before myself, in the long term, to my own detriment.

Brian, first and foremost as a performer, thinks selfishly because his ID is ego-driven. Narcissism would rear its ugly head again.

I knew I had to find purpose in my work without all the momentum Billy Thorpe created in my life. I would always remain carrying a torch for him.

My first show 'back in the saddle' after Billy died was on 7-7-07 …

Al Gore, after his term as Vice President of the United States and a sadly missed opportunity to be the next President, began many climate awareness initiatives. Topics we are still ruminating over today in endless political talk-fests. His documentary An Inconvenient Truth was an Oscar-winning feature film with a sequel in 2017. Producer Kevin Wall and VP Gore set about creating seven global events on the same day to highlight climate issues. Chugg Entertainment was chosen as the Australian production team, and, along with Joe Segreto's IMC and Mark Pope, we got to work.

Sydney Cricket Ground confirmed as the venue and a stellar group of artists contracted. We sweated over the production bible and conference calls that ensued with Kevin's team in Los Angeles.

Eric Robinson was head of production and frankly found some of the planet-saving targets for the show's footprint laughable. But on we pressed.

There were video messages from Hollywood stars to insert into programming. To complement these, I created a hit list of local celebrities to deliver on-stage messaging. These included David Wenham, Toni Collette and Hamish & Andy.

Joe Segreto scored a coup in managing to get Prince William and Prince Harry to record a message of support. The footage arrived from London by download the night before and was guarded like the Crown jewels.

Show day came, and 50,000 strong audience teemed into the venue. As we were about to go to air, live around the world, Joe's phone rang. He motioned to us all to be silent — waving his arms around like Rudolph Valentino in The Sheikh. His caller was none other than Al Gore.

Sydney was globally the first show of the day, and VP Gore was calling to wish us luck … a sobering moment before the madness engulfed us all.

Crowded House had re-formed as the headline act.

We tore through a remarkable day with all performances on time and international message-markers played out. The hardest thing to wrangle was Michael Chugg, who spent the day wired for sound — literally — as a camera crew from the ABC trailed him for a TV special. At least I knew where he was, unlike various opening nights I have mentioned.

Once Crowded House took to the stage, it felt like we were golden and could take a moment to enjoy watching their performance. Peter Garrett and I stood on the side of the stage peering through the scaffold stage design.

Then … the lights went out.

Literally.

The production had been run all day on bio-diesel fuel, part of the ecological footprint design. Think of it like your car running out of petrol when you are twenty minutes from home. All production staff ran to the back of the stage as the band came off — unsure of next steps. I yelled down the walkie-talkie for Chugg to appear. He bowled towards the stage screaming blue bloody murder at Eric Robinson, Head of Production, as if it was solely Eric's fault.

Eric, in his benign way, shrugged off Chuggi's abuse and went about securing what light sources could remain by generator and assessing how long it would buy us for time.

Joe and I guided Chuggi to the stage, prompting an announcement — literally making light of it (pun intended) and cajoling the crowd with 'the show must go on'. The venue's safety lights went up on the crowd. There was enough last generator ambient light back of stage to make it safe for the band to continue, and back on they went.

As Neil Finn sang 'take the weather with you', all the headliners joined Crowded House on stage in a moment of solidarity and poignant messaging. Neil ended the event with a mindful message to the audience on the ground and all over the world:

'We have all entered the arena now, so there is no going back — over to you, world!'

The newspaper front pages next morning heralded the moment as pre-planned to lend more weight to the global climate crisis message. Yeah, OK, the PR chick in me says I will go along with the hype, but it was far from the truth: a happy accident.

During the second season of It Takes Two, I regained my positive attitude to life.

I thought about Billy Thorpe every day. It was impossible not to dream and wonder, given the years we had spent planning for Tangier. As they say, life must go on. Lynn and the girls were recovering from the shock of their loss. Lynn re-partnered through a bizarre twist of fate with the man she had dated before meeting Billy.

I had children and a partner to take care of, and a mother now starting her new life in Sydney.

Brian was booked to perform in Byron Bay on Father's Day, so we took a family trip. We rented a beachfront villa. Jess and fiancé Kyle came from the Gold Coast and talked excitedly about their marriage plans. He was a solid, intelligent guy. She had chosen a wedding gown which hung in their closet like a beacon! I advised her it was bad luck to show the groom the dress beforehand. She never took well to advice; I was met with the tightly closed mouth and angry stare, which I had come to know so well.

We drove past Colin Heaney's home, hoping it may have been for sale. As we despondently drove away, a house on the ocean side had a sale sign on it. The agent was one I had dealt with previously, so I made a quick call to Glen.

The first rule of real estate is 'don't act too keen'.

We entered the bland '80s front door as Brian yelled at the top of his lungs, 'SOLD'. Oh God, here we go again. The view was mesmerizing.

The agent floored me when he queried, 'You don't remember whose house this is, do you?'

Why would I?

He cast my mind back to when Damien and I scouted properties around Byron Bay. Damien had the need for acreage to go into permaculture. Glen had recommended places in 'town' and mentioned another that he was selling. He was at the time going through a divorce, and his family home was on the market. Without even looking at it, then, it was out of my price range.

Back in 1999, the sellers of the home I bought went on to buy Glen's home. That couple were now divorcing and selling this home, which was the one we were standing in!

Full circle.

Glen joked that if I bought this house, he wanted a caveat in the sale agreement that if Brian and I 'divorced', it was not his fault. How could I have imagined something so good could turn so bad - in real life and real estate.

The house did now feel cursed, which I tried to translate into a cost reduction. With my real estate experience, I knew there was no doubt it was a good buy. But in my heart of hearts, I wanted to stay in Sydney. It was easy for Brian as work entailed getting on a plane, from anywhere to everywhere. But leap we did.

I sold the ship's chandlery in Balmain while we treated Byron as a holiday home.

In our first Christmas in Byron Bay, it was all ho-ho-ho.

I have never been a fan of the Christmas spirit. This festive malaise I attributed to being an only child with limited extended family. During this holiday, Jessica appeared alone, telling us she was breaking off her engagement. She was distraught, and I nurtured her with advice about life choices. For the first time, I felt vaguely close to her, that she was grateful for my wisdom. She met someone, an affair had begun and that was that. The cursed wedding dress was never mentioned.

I had been canvassing for Brian to become a Hall of Fame inductee. My colleague Mark Pope was onside as an advocate. The ARIA Hall of Fame indeed chose Brian as a recipient along with Frank Ifield, Hoodoo Gurus, Marcia Hines, Jo Jo Zep & The Falcons, Radio Birdman and Nick Cave. Never has a more diversified group been awarded.

We had a magnificent suit made for the occasion. It was emblazoned with embroidery inspired by the 'Nudie Suits' that were famous in LA in the '60s. He looked magnificent, and my heart swelled with pride. The event was held at the Regent Ballroom in Melbourne. Our family table comprised Brian's mother and sister, Jessica, Olivia and Austin, and Brian's brothers John and Alan.

Prior to the induction, introduced by Jimmy Barnes, a short film of Brian's career was played. There was black and white footage that set a pall over the evening. It was a newsreel piece featuring his mother looking like she had a three-day moustache growth. She went into a dead faint seeing herself so represented on the big screen. To quell her upset, mother Jean launched into the white wine with gay abandon while Brian made his speech. He spoke from the heart, and thanking me as the love of his life was a happy moment.

Here was fabulous. The love of a magical man, a family celebration and a career I was proud to embrace.

Brian had written music for surf film Morning of the Earth in the early 1970s. I hit upon the idea of resurrecting the film with live musical performance.

My friend Gaynor Crawford was close with the films creator — Alby Falzon. Introductions were made over a long lunch in Coffs Harbour. Alby struck me as an ethereal spiritual master.

Chuggi immediately saw merit in the idea.

Other than Brian, the show needed new talent to re-create the soundtrack. The original soundtrack was developed by G. Wayne Thomas for Warner Music. He agreed to be part of the show and off we went. I added Lior, Old Man River, and the sublime Mike Rudd. In rehearsals, it became clear that G. Wayne could no longer sing a note. It was agonizingly obvious to us all, except for G. Wayne.

With Alby's permission, I edited the film to work around the musical layout. As the movie was non-linear and not narrated, it worked a treat. I inserted interviews with original surfers from the film and the result was, well, cosmic. The show sold out in cities around the East Coast where the surfing community still struck a chord.

At The Palais, show girls I had gone to school with, part of the 'surfy gang', approached me. They loved the show and queried how I ended up with Brian Cadd. Those adolescent years of being the chubby Brighton girl who didn't quite fit into their gang immediately dissipated, and I was made whole.

And fabulous.

The final series of It Takes Two commenced.

James Valentine and I would fly down and back together from Sydney each week, and he was a lot of fun to hang out with. I formed a friendship with the series producers during this time, and we enjoyed great times together in the ensuing years — both in Australia and overseas.

Unfortunately, Matthew Lazarus-Hall took my appearance on TV less enthusiastically and tried to create negativity between Chugg and me.

We had a heart-to-heart. Chugg Entertainment didn't want to pursue more theatre projects, reserving capital for headliner tours. Fair enough, it was the mandate of the empire that Michael had successfully built since 2001.

Brian and I were keen to get out of Sydney, so my full-time position at Chugg Entertainment came to a mutually agreed end. There was an understanding that the door would always remain open for new ideas and collaborations.

Our house, looking over the ocean in Byron Bay, beckoned. We ventured up for the Christmas holiday and told the kids we were not going back to Sydney. There was a huge sense of relief in this move, whether it was the atmosphere or the time we were all in, I'm not sure. Austin rode his bike to and from primary school. Olivia moved into Byron Bay High.

Socially, Brian and I did our usual routine of hosting parties and making new friends on a regular basis.

Brian's adult children were always welcomed into our homes, despite the rocky start we had in Brighton. Jason had entered a second marriage with a pole-dancer whose intellect was akin to a mosquito. At the nuptial party, he came to me begging for valium. Doomed with a capital D. Jessica eloped with Joe in Las Vegas. His intellect was a notch above the pole-dancer. Brian was very upset, robbed of the opportunity to walk his daughter down the aisle. I felt desperately sorry for him and suggested we throw a big party on their return from the States.

Nick in Los Angeles had fallen in love with a firebrand named Alex. I immediately adored her. She was open and kind, opinionated and strong. We hosted everyone in Byron Bay, yet the tension was palpable. The boys always acknowledged that their father's affections were unevenly skewed towards his daughter. I admired them for it. For now, Brian had what he always wanted — his brood all together.

The summer of 2009 saw some of the worst firestorms Victoria had ever seen. There was an immediate call to action by the music community to raise funds for people who had lost everything, and to applaud the first responders.

The event, known as Sound Relief, was put together in six short weeks. It was also the first collaboration between the Michaels, Chugg and Gudinski on a public scale in years. The production was developed by Chugg Entertainment, Gudinski's Frontier, Joe Segreto at IMC and Mark Pope. All hands were on deck. It was decided to run two shows simultaneously in Melbourne and Sydney, at the MCG and SCG. The broadcast was being run by Foxtel's Channel V under the command of the gritty Shaun James. With close to 100,000 people at each venue, they got a double dose of talent as each city's production was beamed to the other. This formed a changeover time in production terms for each band.

In a reverse headline, Coldplay opened the Sydney show. This was the only logistical possibility as they had their own show that night at another Sydney venue. They crushed the opening performing 'You're the Voice' with John Farnham. Here, I was face-to-face with another of my childhood idols. As John prepared to take the stage, I smiled sweetly and told him to take the chewing gum out of his mouth in case of camera closeups. Glenn Wheatley was shocked when I told his star client what to do.

Next up was a young girl from Pennsylvania that promoter Rob Potts had convinced us to take a punt on. She was doing her first promotional trip to Australia at age 19, and her name was Taylor Swift. She took to the stage with an acoustic guitar that over-shadowed her diminutive stature.

We granted time to perform four songs. After the first two, she put the guitar down, ripped off her black outfit and revealed a glittering gold dress. Star power. The next time I saw this remarkable artist was fifteen years later at Wembley Stadium playing to over eighty thousand people.

During rehearsal, I had been walking across SCG grounds with Chris Martin when he spotted Olivia Newton John. He stopped in his tracks and asked if I would introduce him. It was such a sweet moment to see him as a fan. Olivia was hanging with Barry Gibb, and we took some great shots of them all together.

When I had called Olivia to ask her to participate, she suggested calling Barry to come too. You don't say no to Olivia or to Barry Gibb. It was magical having them together. During those songs, Toni Collette and I stood together on the side of the stage, singing into imaginary hairbrushes to 'Guilty' and 'You Should be Dancing'. Molly Meldrum was beside me, making the moment special as I danced again — for and with him.

The event raised millions of dollars for the Red Cross and earned us all an ARIA Award for the five times platinum DVD sales and a Helpmann Award for Best Live Event.

After the intensity of Sound Relief, I returned to our Byron cocoon and the soothing sound of the waves and smell of the ocean breeze.

Billy Thorpe had been gone from us for 2 years, but in those intervening years, Chuggi and I worked diligently to bring his Tangier project to life. The job of dismantling his studio in Surry Hills had fallen largely on Greg Clarke and Norm Sweeney.

I would stop by when in Sydney and try not only to reconcile that Billy was truly gone, but also how to honor his legacy with the final opus that defeated him.

I had known Mark Pope only briefly during my Mushroom years. He had a great set of ears, but also a reputation that preceded him — for excess in all the major music industry ways. I was not fond of the boys' club ethos that was so dominant in '80s culture. I never felt weighed down by the glass ceiling, but there were some men in the industry who had been chauvinistic douchebags.

I got to learn that Mark's heart was in the right place. He was in awe of Billy as an artist and never got to know him. Mark held a strong sense of duty to the music industry, as do most of us who strive to bring music to audiences to create a better world. That sentiment may sound far-reaching, but the reality of our day-to-day labors in producing and curating music is to make people fundamentally happy.

I needed a record producer who understood orchestras. We had scant recorded material from Billy's time in Morocco. Charts had to be written, and a veritable spider's web of tracks disseminated. Mark introduced me to Daniel Denholm. I liked him instantly. A goofy guy and brilliant where soundscapes were concerned.

Chuggi and I set off to get a deal with Sony Music to enable finishing this Tangier opus-in-waiting.

Denis Handlin was not going to be beaten to the punch by Michael Gudinski and threw the cheque book at us straight away. Gudinski's Mushroom Music had the publishing, so he was already in the box seat.

I introduced Billy's widow to a charming journalist, Dino Scatena, and together they created a fantastic picture book of Thorpe memorabilia.

During his time living in LA, Billy had been in a band with Mick Fleetwood called The Zoo … how appropriate. I got in touch with Mick and asked him to contribute drums and percussion to Tangier. Daniel and I flew to Mick's studio in Hawaii and had a marvellous few days talking only about Billy.

In some moments, I felt Billy was in the room.

Additional collaborations were similarly fitting tributes to Billy. Jack Thompson recorded the spoken word voiceover for 'A River Knows' in one take. His uber-masculine voice sent shivers up my spine as I watched him in awe. Being back in Jack's presence was a joy, and our mutual love for our long-lost friend was both spoken and unspoken.

There was one track Billy never intended to be a part of Tangier.

'Since You've Been Gone' was written on the passing of his mother, only a few years shy of his own demise. It was a hit song and essential in sentiment. The vocal chorus for the song was performed by Brian Cadd, Ian Moss, Melinda Schneider and Vanessa Amorosi. Mark Pope arranged for them to perform the track at the ARIA Hall of Fame event in 2010.

There was one aspect of Mark's input into the Tangier project that infuriated me. I mentioned the good ol' boys' club that dominated the record industry. Mark got in Denis Handlin's ear and convinced Sony to let him create the marketing campaign and video for the title track. His first ludicrous suggestion was more than $60,000 in advertising in cinemas. He argued that seeing and hearing the 30-second TVC on a big screen would sell the album. The money went virtually nowhere and made no impact. The second and most upsetting outcome was the video. Mark employed 'Influencer' filmmakers who flew to Morocco to shoot the clip. Noah Taylor was in London shooting what became the hugely successful Game of Thrones series. As a huge Billy Thorpe fan, he agreed to be the principal character in the clip. The song 'Tangier' is about midnight in Tangier. The whole clip was shot in daylight. Billy would have hit the roof. I kept my mouth shut as Mark played the video to Jack Thompson and others, seeking approval and adulation. I only ever told Mark many years later what a complete cock-up I felt he made of the project's release.

Chuggi had for some time wanted to write an autobiography, so we started scouting co-writers. His story was imperative to tell for the Australian music industry archives, and, on recommendation from several people, journalist Iain Shedden rose to the challenge. 'Sheddy' was a laconic Scotsman with a passionate musical knowledge. I first met him as a drummer in The Saints with lead singer Chris Bailey.

Iain spent a lot of time with Chuggi and Maam at their home in Phuket to write in a sense of solitude. I met with four or five publishers to make sure the right company was on board for the release. They needed to know who they were dealing with — Chugg, not me.

A publishing deal was made while word spread around the industry that Chuggi was penning a 'tell all'. Several people began quaking in their boots. Especially the other Michael.

Gudinski summoned his lawyers and put a hold on publication until he could sign off on comments mentioning his name. There was a bizarre meeting between the two parties and the relevant legal teams. It felt especially strange to me, given my relationship with both Michaels. There was no sitting in the middle on this topic; I was firmly on Michael Chugg's team.

It was hardly Knights of the Round Table. Gudinski took exception to a few paragraphs; it was agreed to omit them. No one, especially Chuggi, wanted to destroy reputations or friendships.

The book took its title from a random comment Chuggi had made on stage.

During a Guns N' Roses tour, there was an issue with crowd control. Angst was rising as the band was delayed going on, almost a given in anything to do with Axl Rose. Chuggi took to the stage in his other guise as MC/audience wrangler and, urging calm, yelled: 'Hey, you in the black T-shirt, sit down!' Close your eyes and imagine a Guns N' Roses audience: 99 per cent of them are wearing black T-shirts.

For the marketing campaign, Chuggi re-lived the barking order as a radio ad, which was hilarious, especially for everyone who knew him.

I loved working with 'Sheddy', and we spoke frequently about other book ideas. He was keen to write with Olivia Newton-John. I made several calls to Olivia, assuring her Iain would do a great job, but she declined all offers.

One terribly sad day, Iain Shedden was gone from a massive heart attack. Life's cruel flick of the switch once again. The shock and horror of losing Billy Thorpe came flooding back.

Austin was thriving at TSS boarding school. We were hardly a family who embraced sport as a hobby, but Austin took to early-morning rowing with great aplomb.

As a mother, inwardly I was struggling. I missed my son enormously, and Olivia had moved in with a girlfriend after high school graduation. With Brian on tour, it was an empty nest. I felt lonely and isolated. Byron Bay was an idyllic place to live, no doubt. It was still relatively undiscovered by celebrity glitterati. Our regional town grew with seasonal tourists, both domestic and international, but a morning walk on the beach was not a fashion catwalk 'see & be seen' … not yet.

I dreamt of spending time in another place, another experience. The wanderlust took hold again. Byron Bay never felt like somewhere to settle, especially with our still active professional minds and spirit.

As the saying goes, Paris is always a good idea.

I was turning 50, so Brian and I concocted a fantastical birthday celebration. I decided six months at a Parisian international school would encourage Austin to think globally for college and beyond.

Our apartment was on Avenue Kléber, right under the Arc de Triomphe. Our arrival was in the depth of winter, and a beautiful fireplace warmed us. Brian had a grand piano and wrote with gusto. Birthday invitees were told to arrive in Paris ready to party — all else remained a big surprise.

Austin had mid-term break, so we decided to explore Egypt. I was keen to show Brian and Austin the sights, sounds and smells of that amazing country.

I decided upon Mena House, under the shadows of the pyramids in Giza, ahead of a tour up the Nile.

Arriving on Thursday evening, our chaperone spoke of some 'possible unrest'. He recommended not venturing out before Friday midday prayers. There was no stopping us. When you wake up and the first sight is the pyramids of Giza, you walk across the road and venture up the hill.

You simply sit and gaze.

I took photos of Brian and Austin and noticed the area was extremely quiet.

Momentarily, the sound of gunshots rang through the air.

Hotel staff explained a major political coup was taking place, and we were instructed to remain within the hotel grounds. There was no internet, phone, transport ... nothing.

Another day passed with no comprehension of whether we would be able to tour. The impressive front of the hotel featured armoured tanks rolling past. Austin was intrigued and ventured forward. I pulled him back as more gunshots were heard.

News reached us that President Mubarak had opened the jail in Giza and paid the inmates to quell the riots against his political ambitions.

The Arab Spring, as it became known, was in full swing.

Our group met with tour representatives, explaining we would be evacuated out of Cairo to Jordan. As soon as they secured a private plane!

There was a plethora of hoity-toity Americans getting up in arms that their tour schedule had been cancelled because of some foreign political problem that had nothing to do with them ... and they wanted to see the Valley of the Kings!

The ignorance of some people is truly astounding. Money or no money – dumb is dumb. Egyptian nationals were outside our gate being shot and killed for their beliefs while 'Missy from Omaha' was worried her nail varnish wouldn't last the trip.

The major airport had been closed while thousands of people were trying to flee. Internet service was recovered, letting our respective families know we were safe. I was able to upload photos of Brian and Austin aside the pyramids to music journalist Kathy McCabe. Brian wrote a piece on our firsthand experience — a front-page story.

Yet again ... once a PR, always a PR.

The next day, in a rickety bus with blacked-out windows, we wound our way to supposed 'freedom'. Outside the gates of the unaffected Five Star Mena House Hotel, the reality of the past few days became apparent. Burnt-out buildings and cars took the place of our turned-down beds and private swimming pools.

A hitch with the getaway plane meant we had to spend a night in a Cairo hotel. There were hundreds of evacuees littering the lobby, unable to secure rooms, waiting for any way to escape. While the whole scenario had now lost its allure and reality struck us, we were very aware how lucky we were to be guided by a reputable American company.

Brian's anxiety level became insane.

I was stoic and brave and kept my boys safe under Mumma's wing. After a few hours' sleep we made for the subsidiary airport and boarded a plane bound for Jordan. 'Missy from Omaha' had finally shut up. After 24 torturous hours not knowing our fate, we were all on our way to Jordan and our respective homelands.

I called Molly to tell him what had transpired. He laughed at the absurdity of it all and said, 'Trust you, Lovey, to create an insurrection wherever you go!'

Paris felt like the centre of the universe on our return.

Birthday plans hit full swing, and 36 friends from all over the world RSVP'd to the madness. We arranged four days of events, culminating in my birthday evening at Hôtel de Crillon — the oldest hotel in Paris.

We opened with a wine & cheese afternoon at our apartment, followed by a private cruise on the Seine. Champagne and crayon drawing in the Tuileries, drinks at Harry's American Bar, a scavenger hunt in groups around Paris, and a private dinner at the waxworks Le Musée Grévin along with a magician. Untold fun and games for everyone who joined us from Sydney, Byron, Melbourne, London and New York.

Kathy Lette, having broken her ankle, was on crutches; that didn't stop her from dancing the night away in the Crillon Ballroom while her husband, Geoffrey Robertson, looked on. Chuggi made his MC speech, followed by Brian introducing a video of people who couldn't be there to celebrate my half century.

Deborah Conway wrote a dedicated lyric to her song 'String of Pearls' for me as a gift.

'A long time ago when Mushroom was my label for the known and unknown world

I had a manager; she was a woman amongst girls

We were inseparable, except when the pub was too grungy for her to come on the road

Or when Indecent Obsession called

Or Jo Beth Taylor found 99 more reasons to moan

Now you know I've had a few managers in my day

And they don't always say what they mean

Or indeed mean what they say

But Commander Pelman was never backward in coming forward

She demanded three chords and the truth or darlin' she'd tell you she was bored

Sometimes you tore the enemy apart
Sometimes you charmed them right off their feet
Sometimes you left them with nowhere to hide
But a string of pearls always made you cry
I remember that about you … always made you cry
Sometimes we were the best of friends
And sometimes we were Godzilla vs King Kong
It was crazy high times; it was definitely full on
Whether we were hanging in Melbourne at Dundas Lane, Memphis, New York or LA …
Gudinski was always picking up the bills
Remember that house in LA we swanned around in, with the pool and jacuzzi owned by Queen's Brian May … oh, yeah
Sometimes you tore the enemy apart
Sometimes you charmed them right off of their feet
Sometimes you left them with nowhere to hide
But a string of pearls always made you cry
Always made you cry
So thanks for the hard work, and thanks for the lessons learned
You and I only know too well there are lots of ways out there of getting burnt
We got some runs on the board: Pearls, Epic and Always Patsy Cline
I want to thank you for going to bat for me
Amanda, Happy 50th!
You are a woman in your prime
Sometimes you tore the enemy apart, and sometimes the enemy was me
Sometimes you left them with nowhere to hide
But string of pearls always made you cry, you soft-centred thing.
Happy Birthday Amanda

My birthday adventure is still talked about amongst the friends who were there. We really showed everyone a fabulous time, people who knew Paris and those new to its magic. I was floating on air, in love with Brian and surrounded by friends.

There was one nagging disappointment.

From the moment Brian and I cohabitated, he hoped his disparate family would be reunited, and I was 100 per cent supportive. We were both apparently oblivious to the fact none of his children thought that way — at all. All the family milestones I imagined we would share were lost on them.

My expectations for marking birthdays or shared events were not in their moral playbook.

If I ever mentioned a missed moment, it was shot down by Brian as blatant criticism of his children. ADULT children.

My etiquette expectation level was never going to be met. There were no other issues we had as a couple that got close to percolating trouble between us, other than this. My 50th was the boiling point. None of his children sent a message or gift. This marked the onset of hurt from that day, which never left me.

We returned to Australia after our glorious time living 'la vie en rose' in Paris.

Byron Bay is a world away from Paris and was still a small, idyllic Aussie coastal town. No Hemsworth's, no Maserati's or farm-to-table produce.

Brian rushed to see his daughter on the Gold Coast; I was not invited.

He returned home with puzzling news: Jessica had decreed she 'never wanted to see me again'. There was no reason or explanation. I could not hide my shock or disappointment at such an abrupt decision with no underlying rationale. I wrote her a long, heartfelt letter. No response.

I learned the term for this is 'ghosting'.

Another painful shock came when journalist Alan Howe called to tell us that Molly Meldrum had fallen off a ladder at home. The accident is well documented, but there is an important backstory to Molly being saved. For many years, he had an incomparable right-hand person in Yael Cohn. One of nature's true force fields, Yael would never let anything harm Molly. They had professional bickering; everyone did with Molly at some point in life. I certainly knew what she had gone through! On some occasions in the early days, she would call for my counsel.

On the fateful day he fell, Yael had been working installing Christmas decorations. Molly was a maniac for Christmas festivities. She left for home but called Molly's maintenance man to remind Molly of an appointment the next day. Molly had climbed a precarious ladder to continue stringing lights, and he fell. That call meant Joe discovered Molly's fall, and while he administered first aid, Yael called the ambulance.

Fate and accidents.

Brian and I spent the night in silence, waiting for news. It was a similar scenario to the awful call when Billy Thorpe was pronounced dead. Undoubtedly Molly Meldrum has an angel watching over him. After a long recovery, he came back fighting fit with no loss to his sense of humour or zest for life.

In the New Year, we took Morning of the Earth back on the road. A new promoter took the show on, but there was something unsettling in business terms about him from the onset. We sold out shows and powered on. When people were not getting paid, I called a halt. I refused to let everyone take the stage one night prior to a performance. The financial backer called me, desperate to assure me of payment on completion of the Opera House shows in Sydney. As Brian and I were due to fly to Paris the next day, we took it on face value. I lost a lot of trust in people over those next few days when we arrived in Europe to realize the huge loss we had sustained.

I read a story by Paul Cashmere about 'Honky Château' outside Paris being for sale. This piqued my interest as a remarkable business venture, combining our love of music and my real estate acumen.

The 18th-century Château was named by Elton John when he recorded his 1972 album there, closely followed by David Bowie, The Grateful Dead, Fleetwood Mac and the Bee Gees.

This 1740 architectural masterpiece had fallen to ruin. Its owner was forced to sell to pay family death duties. Through an American realtor we arranged to view the estate. I could only hope Brian wouldn't repeat his 'SOLD!' real estate faux pas when we entered its hallowed halls.

On arrival, it was clear these halls were anything but hallowed.

The magnificent 30 rooms, swimming pool, garden folly (built by Pink Floyd) and recording studios were almost beyond repair. Years of vagrants taking residence was apparent. Yet the ghosts of Frédéric Chopin and his lover George Sand resonated off the walls where they had laid in their lovers' tryst. The marble bathroom installed for Elton John was still in place. The blue-painted bedroom walls for Bowie also remained.

Standing in the broad stairway where the Bee Gees echoed their 'Stayin' Alive' refrain was history itself. How could we not become the custodians of this musical legacy? How many obstacles would we face?

The property was a mere 40 minutes from central Paris.

Our idea was to make it a music history destination for tourism and outdoor concerts/podcasts. We built the business case and took it to investors.

First came the knockbacks. British American businessman and philanthropist Len Blavatnik, never backward in coming forward, spoke of fond memories of the place but said he was 'not interested in old bricks & mortar'. I knew I had to keep trying. Within a few weeks we were sitting in the

Parisian bar at Hotel Costes celebrating Honky Château's rebirth with active investors.

My relationship with Brian had been defined by throwing caution to the wind, and it seemed nothing would stop us now. Shades of author Peter Mayle's 'A Year in Provence' started to emerge. We were thrilled with the possibilities.

Back in Australia, life continued as normal while we contemplated years ahead in France. I would dream of Château Hérouvilles' grounds seeing finer days after so many decades laid fallow. The 1970s recording studio heyday followed the Château's military poignant purpose. It had been utilized by the French resistance during WW2 as a war plane lookout. Even further back in local history, Vincent van Gogh, buried nearby in Auvers-sur-Oise, was known to have painted the Château and surrounding fields.

What could go wrong?

David Bowie was terrified by ghostly visions at the Château during the recording of Low, which in turn horrified Brian. He never let me refer to the apparitions I would occasionally see at our farm. I couldn't imagine how he was going to cope with Chopin's ghost.

Even with additional investors and more due diligence, the costs mounted inexorably. The project lost momentum. After two bidding wars, we lost our French restoration dream. We visited Hérouville years later once it was purchased by French sound engineers. They had done a little work in terms of studio renewal, but much of its beauty still languished.

Never say never.

The end of 2012 had an auspicious date on the ancient Mayan calendar — December 21, 2012, marked the end of a 5000-year epoch and the beginning of another. It had in some circles a doomsday overtone as a potential 'end of the world'. We chose to celebrate it as a new beginning, throwing a party at our Byron Bay home. The invitation asked everyone to dress in what they would wear if it were the end of the world. As people rolled in before sunset, the outfits varied from the sublime to the ridiculous.

Brian and I dressed as Napoleon and Josephine. Jo and Glenn Shorrock were staying with us and had arranged a funny trick for everyone later in the night.

John and Delvene Cornell arrived wearing pyjamas. Try standing next to the stunning beauty that is Delvene in a negligee — not me! Our Balmain buddy Paul Young won best costume with a full Mayan indigenous tribal outfit.

One guest arrived walking in slow motion.

As he came towards me, I thought he looked like John 'Strop' Cornell. I did a double take as John was already in the room, in his pyjamas!

This snail-paced enigma swept me away and whispered, 'Sssshhh, it's Hoges, don't say anything. Pretend I'm Caddy's long-lost roadie — Stormy'.

Brilliant. Paul Hogan was totally unrecognizable — glasses, wig, false teeth and stocking-like armbands that appeared to be tattoos. The only possible giveaway would have been his wife, Linda Kozlowski, standing next to him. As an actress, she was too smart for that. She slinked around the room, cat-like, dressed as Olivia Newton-John in Grease.

I guided Paul Hogan up to Glenn Shorrock and said, 'Glenn, look who is here, your old roadie Stormy!' Keen to get in on this interesting guest, radio legend Trevor Smith sidled up. He was taken in and muttered a vague acknowledgement of ol' mate Stormy. 'Oh, yeah, Stormy ...'.

It was a brilliant 'fooled you' gag.

Next was Brian. He was harder to fool, and as the giggles set in amongst those of us now in on the joke, Hoges revealed himself — taking out his false teeth and removing the wig.

As midnight approached, Brian changed out of his Napoleonic outfit and into more casual 'Shaman' attire. He had written a marvellous speech and gathered our tribe by the swimming pool to listen to his brilliant oratory. Shorrock then appeared as Superman, renamed 'Super Droop'. Before Glenn could deliver the rehearsed punchline, a drunken guest pushed him into our pool, and the joke was lost. Everyone looked on aghast, hoping Glenn wasn't drowning. I briefly imagined a Brian Jones scenario as the next day's headline. His sweet, attentive wife Jo rinsed him off and gathered him up for a cool change, and the party went on until dawn.

From a professional standpoint, we decided to move — once again — to Melbourne. I found a townhouse in Windsor. Renovation number 'I've-lost-count' was about to get underway.

Some people thought we were crazy to leave Byron Bay; I knew we were doing the right thing. Brian's son Jason questioned me about the decision one day at the farm. I suggested he and his father spend more time together.

I was pleased when he thanked me for making so many selfless decisions with his father foremost in mind.

Life's revolving door was renovating, navigating Brian's latest album release and touring, our whirlwind social life at the farm, all wedged in between family duties with our two elderly mothers and my errant daughter.

Olivia's erratic behavior became more apparent on our return to Melbourne. Living alone in some desultory Melbourne suburb, she rang hysterically to say that she had been robbed. I ventured to her apartment and was horrified — first, at the police-rendered black ink markings over walls and furniture. Second, at the state of the place — smashed windows, broken door locks and walls kicked in.

My daughter was in the foetal position; fear in her eyes signalled drugs were involved. All her valuable possessions had been stolen. Her car had been kicked in on one side. I took her home. We secured an apartment not far from her grandmother, and she vowed to clean up her act.

I reconnected with Gary Ashley, who was living in London, managing A&R for Van Morrison. I had an idea to write a musical around Van's remarkable canon of work — in the vein of Once by Glen Hansard. Olivia needed to get out of Melbourne, so I proposed a move to London together — I could work on my proposal and get Olivia set up in a flat and a job. It was a great bonding time. I felt so confident for her on this next step in her life. She was positive and upbeat and made friends easily in her new city.

Being back around Gary Ashley was a true full circle. It felt like we had both lived several lifetimes of stories since the Mushroom days, more amusing in the re-telling.

I asked Garry McQuinn to take on the production with me.

Along with two Gary's — one with one R, the other with two — we met to plan our strategy for Mister Morrison — not yet Sir Van. Garry rallied Glynis Hall as producing partner, we collectively found Rachel O'Riordan as director, and Glenn Patterson as writer.

Over many months we devised a theatrical experience, not a jukebox and not linear in its storytelling, but unique.

I presented the show storyboard to Gary Ashley — ahead of Van's management team in Belfast. He was bowled over with excitement and called, yelling, 'They love it!'

We flew to Belfast. Glenn Patterson and I spent thrilling hours creating storylines and images for the show. I was in professional heaven.

Rachel was an intuitive director; I knew Van Morrison would love her Irish energy. She brought her husband, Richard Dormer, to drinks one night. I scored cool-parent brownie points with Austin by obtaining an autographed photo of Richard starring in his role of Lord Beric in Game of Thrones.

The collected works of Van Morrison are, in my mind, one of the top ten music catalogues of this century. Diverse, poetic, spiritual and folklore all rolled into one canon. This was never intended as a jukebox outing.

Time in Belfast coincided with Van performing at his old school in Orangefield.

I had seen Van perform a few months prior. He seemed withdrawn from the audience and the experience. At these events in Belfast, he was the opposite. Here was adorable Van, not the 'cantankerous bastard' people had chosen to label him.

At the first show I was seated beside Van's old school headmaster.

Moments before the show began, Headmaster Malone squeezed my knee and regaled me with stories of young Van's bad attitude from decades long past. Not quite as brutal as Barry Humphries's knee-squeeze at Priscilla's opening night. Listening to stories of juvenile Van Morrison scallywag was riveting. The show was magnificent musicianship in its finest form. This served to reinforce my belief in our theatrical endeavour.

Halfway through the show, Van the Man performed 'Precious Time'.

In the first chorus I thought I was hearing things. Did he just sing, 'Love Amanda till the day I die' instead of the actual lyric, 'Love her madly till the day I die'? I knew what I heard. Cheekily, and hoping no one would see, I quickly pressed record on my iPhone. And yes, there it was again. I have it on record. I took it as a good sign.

Gary Ashley was unable to be in London when the Duets album needed to be delivered to Sony Music for their 'listen through'. Gary entrusted me to deliver and support the album, as I had worked with him so many decades earlier in similar endeavours.

The Sony hierarchy, headed by Rob Stringer, entered the room. I had mapped out the order of songs I would play for them — under strict instructions from Gary not to leave the disc with them. Spending so much time engrossed in Van's canon, I was glad to endorse Duets and could speak with musical authority on its author.

Unfortunately, after six months of development, the theatrical production fell apart. Van withdrew from the project. A letter came from Van's lawyer, Peter Paterno. The conundrum in this was that Paterno was a good friend of Gary Ashley's and surely knew we meant well in wanting to develop this work in full consultation with Van and his advisors. Gary confided to me that Van had consulted with his buddy Ray Davies on his experience creating Sunny Afternoon, which made it to the West End.

I could not understand what led to Van's negativity.

Never say never.

The London International Live Music Conference (ILMC) was honoring Michael Chugg. I attended to see him rightfully lauded. We always had a great time together wherever we met up around the world. Amongst the delegates, I said hello to my 'older' boss, Ed Bicknell from Dire Straits.

The swell of the Savoy Ballroom overtook us all. Chuggi and I took our seats, noticing a weird hissing sound emanating from the kitchen doors far behind us. It was like a large bee swarm approaching.

I turned to see David Hasselhoff trying to attract our attention. How marvellous! He was a surprise guest. He had straightened up and was doing well after his stint playing Roger De Bris in The Producers. I adore The Hoff and hope we find a way to work together again one day.

After the ILMC event concluded, Chuggi and I exited the Savoy Hotel.

I had my head down ordering an Uber. I heard Chuggi's clarion call, 'G'day mate!' He had met a London colleague.

I looked up to realize I was face-to-face with Tom Jones.

He took my hands gently in his and said, 'Hello, I'm Tom', kissing me on one rapidly blushing cheek. This move, executed with an air of old-world elegance, was flabbergasting. Full. Body. Tingle.

Action: quick brain scan for conversation. He maintained his suave Cheshire cat grin. Internal dialogue: Amanda, don't get distracted. Speak. I asked how he was enjoying his judging role on The Voice. I mentioned something about my association with Kylie Minogue. I asked him to say hello to her for me. I prattled on about being a judge on a similar TV show in Australia. Thankfully, I was rescued by Chugg, who grabbed my elbow and pulled me to conversational safety.

Full disclosure: inside the makeshift conversation, all I really wanted to do was reach for Tom Jones' crotch. His masculine animal magnetism was breathtaking. I had had a Bridget Jones internal dialogue through an external experience. Bridget would have never washed her cheek or hand again.

While I was wooing Van Morrison and being snogged by Tom Jones, Brian was on the road with Glenn Shorrock.

They created a retro album, The Story of Sharky & The Caddman. It was recorded 'live in studio'. I loved helping Brian create his artistic visions, but sometimes there was a disconnect.

This was where the fine line between marriage and professional careers came into play.

The 'Sharky & The Caddman' tour had a cast of musical characters, amongst them Sam See as musical director. Sam had worked with Brian in the 1980s. I always referred to Sam as 'my favorite' — beguiled by his immense wit and love of all things French. Politically and personally aware, he referred to himself as 'Le Grenouille' — the frog. He built that show for Brian and Glenn and kept them in musical check night after night.

There is a diverse dynamic difference between artists I have witnessed over the years. Some are on top of their game — waking every day to think about how they can improve their artistry. Others wake slowly and wonder what someone else is going to do for them to advance their stardom. The audience can never discern the difference in these characters.

Believe me, it is profound. This phenomenon is not a generational thing. I tend to think the artists who think, create and fend for themselves are much more accomplished overall. Many elements are in play — zodiac, personality predilection towards empathy or narcissism.

My husband was the latter. His mantra was always 'I can only do as good as I can do'.

Molly Meldrum had been working on an autobiography for decades. The long-suffering journalist Jeff Jenkins had been guiding him through the prose for many years. I had an image of Jeff like the jailed character in Life of Brian, constantly being dragged back into Molly's home to write another storyline. Many years before, Molly's production credit on The Ferrets' debut album was 'Willie Ever finish', a pseudonym that appeared to be appropriate.

Finally, Molly's book was being published, and there was, of course, a celebration.

ARIA's Hall of Fame chose to induct Molly that year, the first non-artist to receive the accolade. He titled the book The Never, Um, Ever Ending Story. The release had been delayed for many reasons, but the most humorous was the choice of the cover image. Molly refused to have his photo on the cover. The publishers were adamant. He wanted an incredibly naïve painting of his dog Ziggy on the cover. Just another one of Molly's foibles that was designed to frustrate, delay or annoy — or perhaps all three. The publisher called me, asking me to intervene, knowing I had a way with my old friend. That I did.

Fearing the worst with the deadline looming, the publisher had printed a limited quantity of the books with the Ziggy cover. When it was all over — including the shouting — they bequeathed me a copy of the book with that ridiculous cover. I treasure it as much as I do the creatively insane person who devised the idea.

I got a call from my Long Way to the Top colleague Ben Alcott, who had built a company in digital media. A division of the Commonwealth Bank — Comm Sec — created a mentorship campaign, and I was asked to be one of three 'examples' as a mentor to Kylie Minogue.

I agreed on the basis that any use of Kylie's name or image had to be run past her management. Unfortunately, this was no longer Terry Blamey, who, after his decades-long brilliant stewardship of the good ship Kylie, was no longer in charge.

The print campaign was splashed across bus stops and outdoor media across the country. I got word from inside Gudinski's circle that it particularly irked him. Several of the life-sized posters appeared on his chauffeur-driven route from home to office.

MG's version of revisionist history, that he alone signed Kylie Minogue, is not something that angers or upsets me; when I hear or see it in any context, it makes me laugh. I channel Gary Ashley knowing the truth of the time. As Gary told Stuart Coupe for his book on Gudinski, 'Did Michael Gudinski sign Kylie? — 'No'. 'Did Amanda Pelman sign Kylie? — 'Yes'. 'Did Michael try to stop us? — 'no'. As uber manager John Watson said in the same book, 'The other way to look at it is that Gudinski is the man who employed the woman who signed Kylie Minogue'.

In May, Australia entered the Eurovision Song Contest for the first time with Guy Sebastian as our entrant. Paul Clarke, who created the Long Way to the Top series for the ABC, asked me to chair the judging panel for the event. Given the time difference between Australia and Europe when the show went live to air, the judges all had to be on deck by 4am. Richard Wilkins may have been used to these early-morning calls, but Danielle Spencer, Mrs Russell Crowe, and I were caffeine-deprived and/or hungover.

Over those drawn-out days we judges never agreed on individual voting choices for the contestants, country by country. Long live La Difference!

We were all so proud when Guy came fifth. Honestly, his performance was way above those odds. It felt like a cultural cringe vote.

The high of that professional experience was countered by a personal dilemma. My daughter had not learned a lesson from the home robbery and, in fact, went further off the rails.

I asked Olivia to come home for a family night. She arrived buoyant and without noticeable trace of drugged behavior. I was grateful for a family evening without conflict. Doubt prevailed, so I double-locked the front door to avoid her disappearing.

I planned to have a calm conversation with her about drug rehab choices in the morning. I awoke early to doorbell alerts and two police cars in the driveway. I was greeted with two police officers accusing me of wrongful detention of my adult daughter. I was too stunned to respond; in that same moment Olivia strode out of her bedroom and waltzed out the front door.

She thanked the officers while spouting vitriol and strode off, giving me the proverbial finger. Who was this person? The Jekyll & Hyde moment so many families have had to endure over the ages: fragile mental health, addiction, psychological abuse … it doesn't matter which variation you experience. No one can explain it until you go through it.

I collapsed into shock and the hideous reality that I may never see my daughter again. I had been so wrong. That lovely family evening was only designed to pilfer our pockets, take what cash and goods she could find and run off for the next score.

Weeks later, another dreadful police presence appeared at dawn on my doorstep. I feared the worst. I was almost relieved when they explained Olivia had had a major car accident. She's fallen asleep at the wheel and was in the hospital. She refused to see me. One police officer was kind enough to suggest this was out of shame rather than spite.

I went to sign off on the car wreck to discover she had been living out of the car. I retrieved her belongings and took them home. The sadness was compounded by how many framed family photos she had with her. After getting out of the hospital, she came home for a few days before going into rehab. The price of private rehabilitation is high in so many ways — financially, psychologically on the family, and in loss of pride and purpose for the addict.

I didn't want my mother's impression of Olivia to be destroyed.

I invented a story that Olivia had moved to Byron Bay. My damaged daughter would handwrite on Byron postcards, and a local friend would post the cards to my savvy 97-year-old mother. Thus, we got through six months. I created this façade to protect both my mother and daughter.

Austin would frequently accompany me to see his sister. This was extremely difficult for all of us. Brian only came with me once.

Overall, Brian was not wired for emotional support.

We decided to sell up in country Victoria and had our last Christmas at Sandon Ridge. By a happy coincidence, all of Brian's siblings, families and mother were able to join us.

It coincided with a happy event for Brian. His daughter gave birth to a daughter. As phone calls were coming in with progress of the birth, I was left in the dark and outside the conversation. It was beyond hurtful. Jessica's, and Brian's, position of not including me in her life had never been resolved.

My mother turned 98. Far from sitting quietly in the fading twilight of the nursing home, my mother instead appeared valiantly on the front page of The Age newspaper. We had recently been introduced to a fashion historian, Tom McEvoy, who was beguiled by Elvie Hill and her place in Australian fashion history. I arranged for Tom to meet Elvie. Watching the memories Tom evoked in my mother was magnificent. She lit up like a glow-worm and the result was a fashion retrospective. Olivia had made it out of rehab and was on the way to recovery and a happier life. She was a model in the retrospective parades and made her grandmother proud.

CHAPTER 11: BROKEN ARROW

Brian and I made yet another rash life decision. We planned a move to the United States.

He commenced writing an album to complete in Nashville.

Ex-pat Australian producer Mark Moffatt in Nashville was earmarked to work on the project that was to become Silver City.

I bought a house in Santa Fe, New Mexico … under the stars. Anything for adventure and to make Brian happy. My lifelong belief to go with the flow and change if the flow ebbs prevails. Life is an ever-changing river of directions. People, places, thoughts and feelings. No fear. Just movement.

Our beautiful Tesuque ranch was secured, so we stopped for lunch at The Cowgirl in downtown Santa Fe. Happenstance saw us sharing a table with a man who emanated charisma somewhere between Truman Capote and Doris Day.

It started with the legs: for a gentleman in his 70s — or maybe 80s, it was hard to tell — Ira had exquisite pins. This was topped by his paint-splattered bespoke shirt and cowboy hat. We chatted like we had known each other forever. This divine human being was Ira Yeager, a renowned painter with homes and ateliers in California and Santa Fe.

Ira and I became inseparable. We re-imagined ourselves in 1940s Paris with me as Gertrude Stein and him as Picasso.

Ira's husband, George, was many years older than Ira but equally as refined and elegant. Together, they had built a home in Corfu decades earlier. George's book, Under Calypso's Thrall, was a magnificent lesson in retirement renovation — well before Peter Mayle and after our dreams of Hérouville had faded. Over the years I visited them in Calistoga, at Ira's exhibitions in San Francisco, and always when in Santa Fe.

How many men have commiserated with women: 'I'm so sorry that I've hurt you'?

Life hands us lemons, you make lemonade — that's what most women do, with an unswerving belief all will be well.

In 14 years together, Brian and I had never uttered the word 'marriage'. It was not an overarching issue for me. Having performed the ritual thrice, I was not compelled to do it again, other than wondering about LC's prophecy.

It was the fact he never asked me, hinted at it, or wrapped me in that kind of 'you're my forever wedded bliss' blanket that irked me. Occasionally.

One of the few times surrounded the events of my 50th birthday. A friend attending the events suggested to me that Brian had discussed our potential marriage.

She unwittingly led me to believe he may propose at the party at the Crillon. Getting dressed for the event that night, I was alone in our magnificent hotel room. Already a dream come true. There didn't need to be any grander celebration of our love for each other than that. But in that room, believing he may have been going to 'pop the question', I was filled with nervous dread. What was to say it wouldn't turn out as woeful an experience as the other three times? Why would I want to diminish the love we already felt for each other?

In that moment, all I could ponder was what would I say when the moment came. I could hardly say, 'No' in front of friends in a Parisian wonderland.

I faced the moment unsure of how it would pan out. I needn't have worried.

Now here in Santa Fe, establishing our lives together in America, obtaining green cards required legitimate marriage. A pasty-faced, ill-humored attorney told us this in no uncertain terms. We sat in our Tesuque mountains hacienda as the attorney said, 'Make this easy on yourselves and get married for God's sake'.

Brian turned, looked at me and simply said, 'Well, do you want to?'.

We decided to keep it a secret, the elopement you're having when you are not actually eloping. A calendar ordained that the very date Brian first kissed me, at the Adelaide Hilton, was a date we could make this work. So, the Adelaide Hilton was chosen as the venue, a willing celebrant was seconded into our secret.

Now for the cast of characters. There had to be witnesses, but we could not deal with a whole family scenario for a myriad of reasons.

Our hoax was disguised in a lie that Brian was booked to perform at the Barossa Food & Wine Festival. His old tour manager, Murf, and my friend Gerry were invited to 'tag along'. Convincing Austin without raising suspicion was slightly more difficult, but we swung it. He truly represented the best of us as a family, as disparate and messed up as it really was internally.

We flew to Adelaide together. I was behind in my producerial planning. The others waited for baggage. I peeled off to call a limousine service for post-ceremony and I still had to book a restaurant! What is it with bridezillas who spend months planning one day's worth of events? We gathered room keys and suggested meeting in our suite prior to the 'gig' that Brian was 'performing'.

Our celebrant was hip to the deceit. I remained unsure if she was more excited by the intrigue or the responsibility of marrying a musical idol.

In preparation, Brian and I giggled like children, hiding the pre-arranged decorations so no one would suspect. A photographer arrived with a wink and a nod and played the role of being from the Barossa Times.

Murf, Gerry and Austin arrived, and champagne flowed. I introduced our celebrant as a 'journalist' with the photographer. Her moment came, and she spoke, summoning all the oratorial finesse of Dame Maggie Smith, to say:

'I am also a marriage celebrant. Would anyone here like to get married today?' To which Brian and I pronounced in unison, 'Yes, please'.

Jaws on the floor, photos captured, and on we went to our quiet little ceremony at the Adelaide Hilton, where our love was originally fomented.

As part of our vows, I read lyrics from a Robbie Robertson song, 'Broken Arrow':

Do you feel what I feel?
Can we make that so it's part of the deal
I've got to hold you in these arms of steel
Lay your heart on the line
This time
I want to breathe when you breathe
Then you show me a sign
This time
Here we go ... moving across the water
Here we go ... turning my whole world around

Sadly, many people were missing. One was in spirit with us. I brought the framed photograph of Billy Thorpe taken by Stuart Spence. Having him there with us seemed fitting, as if he was indeed giving me away.

I could not have been sure of his approval had he been in person.

Back in Santa Fe, an old married couple, we were not home for long before touring commenced for us both.

In the preceding January, David Bowie had passed away. The Sydney Symphony Orchestra's commercial director, Mark Sutcliffe, approached me to create a show in celebration of Bowie's remarkable work. We were now on our second leg of touring around the country with each state orchestra. The show was a beautiful musical mélange of Australian talent, including Tim Rogers, Deborah Conway and iOTA.

We wound our way to Perth in the week of the American presidential election. American politics is not usually a big conversation in Australia, but this year was different with democracy at stake.

Hillary Clinton looked way ahead, but the orange-headed problem child was gaining. The brilliant journalist and podcaster Michael Moore had been banging on the media gates for months. Trump was gaining too much ground and would steal the election.

The night we performed 'Nothing Has Changed' by David Bowie in Perth, he did just that.

In dress rehearsal, I was out front directing the show.

My eye was on a news feed, not the stage. The moment the election was called in Trump's favor, to the world's shock and horror, I called a halt and told the assembled cast and crew the news. How could this be?

A verbally illiterate failed property mogul disguised as a reality TV 'star' was now the President of the United States? The show must go on. My mind was elsewhere in the reality that we were now living in those un-United States, and I was wondering what on earth was to come in the next four years.

Within days of the election shock, we were throwing a party for Brian's 70th birthday. Not a party, a gig. Held at St Kilda's Memo Music Hall hundreds of guests anointed the birthday boy, predominantly with whisky.

Following speeches by Glenn Shorrock and Chuggi, I took to the stage to introduce a special guest …

After Brian's beautiful endorsement of our love at the ARIA Hall of Fame, it was my turn to laud him and pronounce how happy we were on our American adventure.

I hoped to fly Brian's son Nick in as a surprise, but his schedule didn't work. The same could have been offered for his daughter, but she would not respond to my request. This was doubly sad given she and Brian shared a birthday.

With world events and our move to the US of A, I could not pass up the opportunity for a dig at American politics. I found a Donald Trump impersonator. The stage manager was in on the joke. The 'Star-Spangled Banner' filled the speakers. People didn't know where to look … and then out he came. 'Donald Trump' spoke of Brian's achievements and welcomed him into the bosom of 'Make America Great Again'. It was hilarious. Brian was dumbfounded and went on to perform at his own birthday celebration.

I started writing contemporary music shows for Mark Sutcliffe and the Sydney Symphony. The 30th anniversary of George Michael's Faith was approaching. Having seen the Bowie show regenerate catalogue sales, Sony was keen on a collaboration.

Olivia called me on Boxing Day morning. Had I heard George Michael died overnight? It was unexpected and an immense loss to the music world. The show would go on.

I flew back to the US ahead of Brian and went to Nashville to secure him a management deal.

Brian and I arrived back in Santa Fe with our lives about to begin a hopefully exciting phase. The house in Tesuque was magnificent. However, I feared falling into the same old trap — buying homes that were too large for us 'empty nester's'. For us, the heritage of New Mexico got under our skin as we learned more about life in a new type of America.

This Trumpian era was radically different from when Brian and I had lived in Los Angeles or Nashville — in earlier decades, in different relationships and mindsets.

There is a Spanish tradition on May 5 called 'Cinco de Mayo'. It commemorates Mexico's victory over the French Empire in 1862 but nowadays is more a celebration of Mexican/American culture. We went out for drinks with friends.

I experienced inexplicable unnerving feelings during the day, silly skin-crawling thoughts like needing to close a door.

It is not uncommon for me to encounter extrasensory experiences throughout my life — many of which I have previously explained.

Returning home, after hearing Brian's phone ring, came an enormous crash. He screamed out in pain: 'Oh no, oh no!'

I ran towards him, down the corridor towards my husband, who looked like a cockroach on his back, unable to recover his balance. I could pick him up, like Humpty Dumpty, and put him back together again. How wrong I was.

His shoulder looked like it had separated from his arm. He had hit his head badly, but there was no bleeding. I covered him in a blanket and called an ambulance. The hospital decided relocating his dislocated shoulder was the best course of action. Note to self: at 2 am do not accept what interns in a hospital tell you is correct. After massive doses of every painkiller known to Michael Jackson, they wrenched Brian's right shoulder back into place. I could barely look. They told me to take him home; he would be fine in a few days. This was not the happy marital beginning either of us imagined.

After a few days it was clear he was not OK. The long search for a good surgeon commenced. After interviewing candidates, I found a remarkable doctor in Aspen, Colorado. Given it was spring, there was not a waiting list of ski-accident victims ahead of us. The only piece of good timing in the whole sad story. The drive from Santa Fe to Aspen was six hours. Back and forth we went for a month or so in preparation for the reconstruction surgery.

There was a high likelihood Brian Cadd would never play piano again. His arm's reach, even with therapy, was nowhere near adequate to play. His surgeon was a music fan and vowed he would resurrect Brian's career. The whole reason we had moved to America was to give his career a resurgence in that market. Here we were staring down the barrel of him not ever performing again.

Amongst this domestic turmoil, death entered my world again.

Gary Ashley passed away in late May. He sent me several emails, via his son Alex, before he died. Their content was politely scripted memories of our time working and loving together. Pushing my old lover's demise to the back of my mind, I emotionally recalled our first inter-office 'DOS' email exchanges decades prior. Gary will always be the love in my life that got away.

Another broken arrow …

I couldn't fly to London for his funeral, as I was dedicated to looking after Brian. A day I regret I missed, like others Gary and I could have shared. I made calls to our colleagues to deliver the sad news. One of them was lawyer Peter Paterno. I asked him to be the one to call Van Morrison. Without sounding indelicate, I reiterated my desire to create the show with Van, who stood firm, as Gary would have loved to see it happen. Never say never.

The George Michael shows were selling out, and I flew back to Australia for the tour.

The shows were fantastic with Paul Gray at the helm as musical director. Despite his own medical concerns, he gave his all.

We had a stellar cast: David Campbell and I had not worked together since It Takes Two. Diesel was a fantastic wild card. The great new artist find was Brendan Maclean.

I met an Aussie singer in LA called Sam Sparro, bringing him into the ensemble to cover the disco diva piece. Backed by a powerhouse of women — Jade MacRae, Carmen Smith and Natasha Stuart — there was no one else on stage when they appeared together. Totally dynamite performers.

It was heartbreaking to learn a short time later that Natasha had terminal cancer. Our industry lost both Tash and Paul Gray — the lights momentarily dimmed.

To raise our spirits, Brian and I put together a first wedding anniversary 'tour' with the nuptial triumvirate from Adelaide. Murf, Gerry and Austin all gathered and met us in New York. Austin was by this time in college in Montreal. We traversed New York, San Francisco and LA before ending up at home in Santa Fe. We drove from LA to San Francisco and stayed at the kooky Madonna Inn. The first time I had stayed there was with Clive on a similar drive to San Francisco when I realized I was pregnant with Olivia.

This time was a lot more fun.

Underneath it all, Brian was still not himself.

We did everything we could to keep him buoyant, but it became clear the trip was physically too much too soon. We went on to Portland to visit Nick, Alex, and the kids. We were so glad to see them settled in their beautiful ranch house we had helped them buy. Austin loved hanging out with Nick's kids, Mia and Emmy.

We were so proud to show off Santa Fe, so we gathered all our newfound friends for an anniversary party. There was still a reservation in Brian's outlook, which I put down to exhaustion from the trip.

Nearing Christmas, Olivia flew in, and we took off on a mother/daughter tour of California. Visiting Ira Yaeger in Calistoga and spending time in LA was a hopeful introduction to a potential life in America, much like we had tried years ago in London. Olivia's drug behavior was well past her now, and as a mother, it was all I could do to encourage her into a new, happier lifestyle.

Ira played a huge part in this and adored Olivia for her quirky outlook and vision. The only sad pall over our trip was the memorial for Gary Ashley in LA. Gary and family lived next door to another prominent Australian — David Hill. David's career started at the ABC and took off with his appointment as head of Fox Sports in LA for his good friend Rupert Murdoch in 1993. A boisterous bear of a man with a fierce intellect, it was a pleasure to be welcomed to his home, even on such a sad occasion. I recalled the only time we had previously met was on the set of Countdown at the ABC back when Molly was threatening me to dance or 'never work in this town again'. Hilly got such a laugh out of that. Such wonderful innocent days, and now here we were bidding a stateside farewell to our mutual friend.

Gary's ex-wife, Donna, asked me to say a few words. I had no desire for this to be a badly written scene out of Dynasty. There would be no revelations told. I spoke about Gary's enormous contribution to the Australian music industry, made some jokes about the Kylie/SAW years, and ended on how proud he was of his three children. Inside, as my heart swelled with grief as much from losing him to death as from not winning him in our much earlier years, I looked at his children and knew in that moment the reasons we were never meant to be.

We saw in the new year at home in Santa Fe, just the four of us: me, Brian, Olivia and Austin. I felt as keenly as Brian did the absence of our other family members. But we vowed to stay resolute to our decision to conquer America for his career and his new album, Silver City.

Meanwhile, my mother was turning 100.

There was a fine line between knowing how much my mother would comprehend of a large gathering and literally overdoing it. I had been gathering letters of congratulations from the Queen, Prime Minister and Governor-General. These salutations do not come of their own accord — you must request them on behalf of the recipient. I created one great amusing moment for the gathering. Our friend Gerry Connolly is well known for his impersonation of HM Queen Elizabeth. Who better to hand Elvie Hill Pelman her personalized card, direct from Buckingham Palace?

Austin, in on the surprise, wrangled Gerry Connolly's arrival. At the appropriate moment 'God Save the Queen' blared out of the speakers. 'Her Majesty' strode into the room to a round of incredulous laughter. Elvie thankfully got the joke, rounding out a marvellous afternoon. Serge Thomann took beautiful photos for The Age — always a PR, remember.

Brian was on the mend back in Santa Fe with a male carer I had installed before my departure. There was no doubt in my mind the fall he suffered would have long-term effects beyond the repair of his shoulder. His mental health was also shattered. The not knowing if he could play piano again was a burden we both bore. These harsh realities were certainly not how we envisioned early 'married' life.

I realized my health was also suffering. I had been diagnosed with a blood disorder, and the Santa Fe altitude was compounding the issue. It was clear we could not stay living here. The ghost of Brian's accident was all too real — along with the punishing effects of the altitude.

Austin was now in college in Boston at Northeastern. We made a temporary diversion to try life in Boston and resolve our next move. During

Austin's college spring break, we took a road trip. Nothing as dangerous as our time in Egypt!

This adventure was akin to throwing a dart on a map to find our next, never forever, home. I loved this kind of challenge and the excitement of the geographic possibilities.

We roamed around the great state of New York, having already decided Massachusetts was too staid for our vibes. From the outer-suburban Westchester counties to the snobbery of The Hamptons, nothing took hold. We took some time in New York City, but Brian was averse to living in 'the big smoke'.

Then he said the magic words: 'Why don't we visit Woodstock?' One of life's great light-switch moments.

We turned the car onto Levon Helm Boulevard, and the town wrapped its hippie arms around us. We were sold.

How had the beauty of upstate New York evaded me?

I had flirted with California and New Mexico, but this was visual nirvana. Brian was about to commit his real estate 'faux pas' once again — just like entering Byron Bay.

At the second house he yelled, 'SOLD!'

I couldn't help but laugh and concur, as it was a beautiful home. Once again buying a huge house with the assumption our extended family would visit.

Thanksgivings would be ours, and laughter would ring through the halls over Christmas. The fact we were the furthest thing from a Norman Rockwell family painting seemed to be forgotten in the moment.

I always held out hope. Always.

As history repeats, Brian went to Australia on tour while I settled into our new home. It was lonely in a big ol' house but there were bears outside to keep me company. Big black bears herding their cubs across from Overlook Mountain. Simply enjoying their freedom, post-winter hibernation. The late snowfall itself was joyous, the silence in the air as I walked and imagined all the possibilities this new life could bring.

Being apart while one of us toured had never been an issue in more than 15 years. The distances in Australian touring meant we were never apart for longer than a week or so. Within the time we had lived in America, this became a bigger geographic and emotional issue. I knew I couldn't cope with the separation much longer and finally started to place demands on our marriage.

I have never been in a relationship or marriage where I placed financial or material demands on my partner. This was partially due to the luck of being financially independent. Live day to day and be happy; everything will work out.

My demands now were simple — less time spent apart and more love and respect between us.

We met in Paris, our happy place.

My 'legendary' rock star husband was inwardly a shy man of few words. For a guy who wrote songs for a living he had precious little to say when it came to real life. We wanted the same thing — life lived large — but that creeping feeling of detachment emanated from him.

Our restorative sojourn in France included celebrations with friends in the Ruinart champagne caves in Reims, followed by days swimming in warm Mediterranean waters. Most importantly, it included our revisit to Hérouville — the Château that got away. The French producers who secured its legacy had done limited renovation, and it broke our hearts to imagine what it could have become. Sting had filmed a TV special in the master recording room, but nothing much else was happening. Never say never.

My career desire for repeating and celebrating music history would rear its head and translate to another continent soon enough.

I phoned my centenarian mother to check on her health and buoy her with travel stories. She lived vicariously through me from her rocking chair. Her mind was muddled, but I gave her a glowing report of how marvellous my life was, thanks in part to her. What more can we impart to our parents in their final years but our love and thanks? Especially if they have had the temerity to stick around until 100 years of age to see how we ended up.

I was not to know this would be the last conversation we would have.

I sat in a sumptuous Provençal palace gazing out at the verdant hills, wondering how much longer she would live. Indeed, how much longer would I live? Didn't I have a duty to myself and Brian to ensure we lived our lives together to the fullest?

No sooner did we arrive home to Woodstock than the call came — Elvie Joy Hill Pelman had shuffled off her mortal coil.

My daughter Olivia broke the news. Childlike, she repeated the words, 'Mummy, she's not breathing'. She could not summon the word 'dead'.

The task at hand was how to farewell my mother, Australia's earliest Haute Couture designer. I found a cosy casket made of wool, like a baby's blanket with beautiful stitching. Before the service, as I gazed upon her face for the last time, all I could exclaim was, 'Oh, you look SO beautiful'.

You will understand if you have ever experienced the face of someone you have known so well, gone. The manner of 'gone' is hard to explain until you witness its ethereal beauty. All the animated life that has disappeared seems to retrieve some inner beauty. Maybe that beauty was always there but ravaged by time and circumstance.

I put my father's casket of ashes in with his beloved wife and sent them off together. My children and I decided to cast them to the wind in various places relevant to their lives. It was a truly cathartic moment.

On a happier note, Brian was being honored with the Order of Australia.

I had instigated the application many years before, guided by previous recipients as the recognition dictates. Above all, I was happy his mother lived to see her eldest son receive this high national achievement.

Our return home to Woodstock was still filled with doubt and uncertainty. Brian had completed his album 'Silver City'; an American release had to be planned. I knew emphatically I didn't want to be a part of his management decision-making any longer. Our relationship had to come first. We flew his Australian manager over to accompany him to Nashville. I could only hope they would make some success out of the very costly project.

Now came time to look at my own career and the impact moving to America had had on me. Historian Geoffrey Blainey coined the phrase 'the tyranny of distance' — a perfect description for the negative impact our move had on my professional options. I had to look locally in America and find a fulfilling path forward.

Ira Yeager in Santa Fe

Mick Fleetwood in Hawaii

George Michael Rehearsal

Signing Tangier deal at Sony w Chuggi and Billy Thorpes family

Wedding #4 with Thorpey included

Partner in orchestral crime—Mark Sutcliffe

Elvie's Farewell
Elvie Joy Hill Pelman
7th January 1918 - 30th July 2018

CHAPTER 12: BY THE TIME WE GOT TO WOODSTOCK

From the first time we discussed the idea of living in Woodstock, I remembered my association with the tiny artist colony town.

Michael Lang, founding father of the Woodstock Festival, had been Joe Cocker's manager in the 1980s when Joe was on Mushroom's Liberation label. My relationship with Mister Lang back then was limited to faxes and phone calls; now, more than 30 years later, I figured I would get in touch.

Word was out around town that Michael was creating a Woodstock 50th Anniversary festival.

We planned to meet up.

Michael walked into the café; his abundant charisma and aura acted as a beacon. He walked like a light-footed Peter Pan as people turned their heads. It was evident the town's population gave him his celebrity space.

This moment felt symbolically reminiscent of my days with Ed Bicknell and Dire Straits nearly 40 years earlier. It was like Michael Gudinski interviewing me at the start of my Mushroom Records' career path. The feeling was a combination of pivotal moments in my time with Michael Chugg and Billy Thorpe. Everything in my professional mind coalesced in that moment in front of Michael Lang.

I knew in my heart this was where I was meant to be. I could not know for how long and to what depth this moment would take me personally and professionally. I simply fell hopelessly into his orbit — then and there.

This was third time lucky for me. My third Michael.

There are a handful of times in all our lives — personally and professionally — we count as heartily triumphant. I was diving headlong into my next one.

I started work with Michael Lang and the Woodstock brand the next day. There was no formality, purely a knowing between us. Something magical was being created for the 50th anniversary of the greatest music gathering in modern history — a pinnacle of music history to be revisited.

Our only impediment was time being against us. After much negotiation, Michael had secured Japanese media conglomerate Dentsu Aegis to sign off on a $USD43.4 million budget to present the festival in August 2019.

The trouble was we were already in November 2018.

Day One: no pressure — we don't have an office, a staff or a system. It appears there is just one production guy and me.

Firat was a burly Turk, a soft-hearted giant who had worked with Michael as production manager through the '94 and '99 festivals. He had continued following Woodstock's pied piper, and here we now were trying to find each other's mettle.

Rolling on, Michael and I drove most days into Manhattan. This we did from our respective Woodstock homes — only a few miles apart. His driving was terrifying.

Seriously, there are New York drivers, and then there was Michael Lang. He found my squealing 'you're going to hit it!' amusing.

His signature giggle constantly tells me to chill out. Like it's 1969.

One day we had a lunch meeting with two people whose provenance was not explained to me. The woman launched herself out of the hotel elevator — a botox-benefited, bouncy brunette. She was all over Michael like a rash. Then there was a short, quiet, preppy guy who sneered. It was clear none of us knew 'who was who in the zoo'. Social etiquette was not Michael's strength.

Susan Cronin and Greg Peck were license holders for the Woodstock 50 festival. They had previously been married but were now purely business partners in hotels, and now an iconic music festival. Susan was a friend of Michael's from Los Angeles.

She was dynamite smart with a touch of sociopath. Greg appeared like he would no sooner marry Susan's type than wear a non-ironed Ralph Lauren shirt. They were yin & yang, good cop, bad cop — all of this I gleaned from our first meeting.

After lunch, we visited the lawyer's office. Michael Lang had the same lawyer as the Mushroom Group back in the '80s. It had been many years since I had met entertainment lawyer Paul Schindler. As we congregated, Paul came towards me with arms thrown out, and we embraced. My new employers could not fathom how this newly met Aussie girl was familiar with one of New York's top music lawyers. Michael Lang knew and smirked proudly.

Our early history had Paul Schindler concur with Gary Ashley on signing Indecent Obsession to MCA. We three sat in Paul's office laboring over royalty percentages, territory by territory. If I wasn't going to win final say in exploring a New York-based pop label for my Brisbane band, I was adamant about keeping the Asian royalty pool as high as UK/Europe. Just call it gut instinct, given that was where the band made the highest sales impact.

Here we were decades later, a different Michael in the box seat, but my commitment was just as strong.

Big girl pants fully pulled up — check.

No distractions — well, maybe the odd Old Fashioned and a joint with Michael.

Job at hand — set up an office and build a festival.

We found a quaint building in the middle of Woodstock for rent. It had been an art gallery, a landmark in an otherwise unremarkable street. It was big enough to house our office that would undoubtedly grow in numbers. It also had apartment accommodations for partners Susan and Greg when they travelled frequently from LA. I went into nesting overdrive and built the space around my new feathered friends. Those friends grew exponentially day by day.

For Woodstock 1994, Michael had formed a professional friendship with John Kocis, then marketing director of Pepsi, who sponsored the event. John and his team at C1 Marketing came to Woodstock, and we got down to business. Much of Michael's business style was based on assumption and had not changed from the 1960s ethos.

I had to read the room quickly, daily.

One day a mild-mannered team from London arrived at Michael's home in Woodstock. Prior to my arrival, Michael had committed to writing a book commemorating the 50th Anniversary. Publishing schedules being what they are, our position nine months out was critical. I took compiling photos and writing text as if we were expectant parents!

It was brilliant working with Reel Art Press, navigating Michael through the book's genesis. Our first euphemistic baby.

Venturing into the home Michael Lang had occupied for 40 years evoked similar feelings to arriving at Molly Meldrum's house decades earlier. There was an Aladdin's cave moment; in my core I felt personal reverence and respect. I wanted to go and make tea and tidy up. I did both times — different decades, different countries. In Molly's case I knew no wife was going to jump out and ask what I was doing. Here outside Woodstock a laidback lady named Tamara appeared and introduced herself as Michael's wife. I later learned she had been his assistant at the '99 Festival and they had twin boys now aged 18.

I was not backward in coming forward in submitting my husband for the Woodstock 50 lineup. Like all festival A&R puzzles there were hundreds of artists submitted for consideration — decisions to be made between the promoters and the talent bookers. Gary Spivack was the booker in charge from Danny Wimmer Presents (DWP). Michael and I flew to Los Angeles repeatedly for a series of meetings with the talent agencies to present the case why their superstars should grace the stage at Woodstock 50.

Young agents representing top-line talent did not necessarily remember the groundbreaking Woodstock 1969. The original peace, love and music festival may have inspired a generation to go into the music business, but they were not the influencers we currently face. Most agents aged in their 20s and 30s were not cognizant of their parents' musical era. Spivack did his magician-like presentation, featuring glorified posturing towards the festival-almighty: Michael Lang.

As we made our way across Los Angeles and New York into the offices of the top talent agents, Michael enjoyed Spivack's pitching adulation. Hundreds of artists were submitted, and the patchwork quilt of who would grace our stages commenced.

Upper mind for these agents — you could see the thought bubbles above their heads — were the burning, literally, images of Woodstock '99. And to a lesser extent, 1994.

Let's start with Woodstock '94.

The 25th Anniversary was held in Saugerties New York, close to the town of Woodstock NY. To this day, hundreds of weekend visitors travel to Woodstock in Upstate New York asking where the festival took place. They are geographically way off as Bethel was sixty miles west.

The 1994 incarnation was held over two hot August days and billed as '2 More Days of Peace and Love'. The original 1969 logo was reconfigured to show two doves on the guitar headstock, and the headstock reversed to be an electric guitar. Simple, effective, brilliant re-interpretation of Arnold Skolnick's original design. Arnold created the enduring 1969 logo at the 11th hour before the festival's artwork had to be committed to print. His visuals became a prime example of valuing what you contribute to and create for the long game.

Woodstock '94 featured several artists from the original festival — Crosby, Stills & Nash, John Sebastian, Santana, Joe Cocker (who Michael managed) and Country Joe McDonald. Headlining were Aerosmith, Red Hot Chili Peppers, Bob Dylan and Peter Gabriel.

All was at peace.

Then came 1999 — the 30th anniversary. Still buoyant from '94, Michael Lang entered an enterprise at an abandoned airfield upstate in Rome, New York. An age-old adage applied — Rome wasn't built in a day. This festival was plagued with the same weather and attendee issues as 1969. Relative to the era, negative outcomes sprung from the end-of-century angry music.

Limp Bizkit's frontman Fred Durst actively encouraged the audience to rebel and riot. This audience was made up of mostly angst-ridden Caucasian males and young girls trying to impress them all. Havoc broke out on the last night with fires everywhere.

These flames were ironically lit by a not-for-profit charity handing out candles for a peace circle. The result was far from peaceful with the National Guard being brought in to quell the rioters and stop the looting of food trucks and property damage.

Nearly 20 years on, what was Michael Lang thinking when he ventured into the festival space again? Many people asked us that question late in 2018. But before the unforeseen fall, there was only peace and hope in Woodstock 50.

The international festival space had taken on a huge corporate life of its own in the 20 years since Woodstock '99. Indeed, Coachella had built out from that very year, and another music festival behemoth, Glastonbury, was entering its own half-century orbit.

The company backing our event was the Dentsu Aegis Network out of Japan, a corporation that billed itself as 'Champions for meaningful progress', with the slogan:

'Through radical collaboration we make insight a reality that moves businesses forward'. I had to wonder how much people got paid to come up with such nonsensical corporate drivel.

In this iteration they were funding $USD43.4 m to relaunch Woodstock the brand as a festival for the people by reinforcing the credo that launched it in the first place:

3 days of peace, love and music.

John Kocis and his team had done the hard yards of due diligence to get Dentsu to the table. Michael and I certainly valued his opinion and intel above anyone else in the mix.

The Dentsu pot was stirred by two of their corporate divisions — MKTG and Amplifi. Headed up by Charley Horsey and DJ Martin respectively, these guys made the Three Stooges look competent. MKTG handled marketing and publicity streams, while Amplifi was the media investment arm.

It was clear from the outset they were punching above their weight, starstruck by Michael and the celebrity world they were entering. In early conversations regarding talent, they displayed no working knowledge of viable touring artists.

Charley, in all seriousness, asked why I would want Miley Cyrus as a headliner when she was merely 'Hannah Montana'.

DJ frequently queried why we couldn't resurrect Crosby Stills & Nash and … even Pink Floyd.

Our total budget for talent was around $US20 million for a three-day festival.

Back to the agents and pitching for talent. Calls with Gary Spivack in LA became almost hourly as we raced towards a December 2018 finish line to get artists secured. This was very late in the standard industry timeline for booking a festival. Way late.

Industry protocol demanded that artists be paid in full prior to public announcement of their inclusion in the festival lineup.

Each day the yes, no, maybe from agents became like water torture.

We secured Miley Cyrus, then very quickly Jay-Z came on board. Then The Killers and Imagine Dragons. Balancing new artists with the 'old guard' was essential.

We knew from the literally hundreds of thousands on our database that the festival audience demographic was going to span the Boomers and beyond!

John Fogerty, Santana, Melanie and John Sebastian represented original '69 alumni. The only artist inclusion argument Michael and I ever had was over David Crosby.

I had seen 'Croz' with The Lighthouse Band for the launch of his Here If You Listen album. He was in great shape, but Michael had some aversion to his inclusion. I never let up. I won.

The other act I won was Brian Cadd's inclusion, along with fellow Aussie Courtney Barnett.

Some 'new finds' emerging from Gary Spivack's excellent A&R skill had us excited. They were boygenius, Larkin Poe and Reignwolf. Michael and I witnessed a showcase with Reignwolf in Los Angeles and were blown away.

My top picks were Brandi Carlile, Janelle Monáe and Greta Van Fleet — a diverse musical trio but fitted across the Woodstock audience. The act I was sad not to secure was sister trio Haim. Real new kids on the musical block, their father manager could not be convinced.

Up to this point, Greg Peck had little to do with everyday organization.

He started to appear from LA frequently as tension mounted with Dentsu and Amplifi. Susan moved her family, cinematographer husband Alan and three children, to Woodstock to navigate our torturous timeline. She was accompanied by her righthand pixie buddy, Ronnie. On the surface Ronnie was a sweet, unassuming Israeli kid but cracking his shell, there was a super-smart entrepreneur inside. I adored him. He was rarely let off Susan's leash, but when he was, we had some fun.

Michael's birthday in early December was an insight into his broader family. By now Michael and I were joined at the hip.

We had lunch in New York City at the French patisserie Ladurée.

We shared a love of all things French. He had spent much time there post the '69 festival. Michael did not share my love of celebrating birthdays. His innate shyness would creep in on these occasions and give me further insight into what made him tick.

A date was set for the launch of Woodstock 50 in March.

I reveled in beating a deadline and accumulating the tools for success along with a stellar team of people. The only moment that matches that build-up is watching audiences as a show becomes reality.

Somehow in all the months of planning Woodstock 50, I could never figuratively 'see' that audience materialize in my mind. I spoke about this later with John Kocis and he had had the same feeling.

One magnificent person entered our unregulated playpen at this time.

Kii Arens was an artist in LA who had originally approached Michael to complete artwork for the '99 festival. His approach then was totally unique, as it was again 20 years later. He created designs using spin art — seemingly simple in the execution but a truly delightful 'spin' on albums and turntables and all the glory of bright colors flying around the insignia Bird of Peace. The team at C1, headed by Bill McBrayer for design and branding, did a fantastic job of translating Kii's uniqueness into our logos. They were incredibly patient with me as I was a perfectionist in this field.

Luckily, so was Michael, and we agreed almost 100 per cent of the time.

There was still a mountain of work to complete with permits and regulations. Negating all the production incidents of Woodstock '99 became a touchstone both inside and outside our camp. The production company Michael had chosen were arrogant from the outset. Their ageist disregard of Michael and his opinion was disgraceful. Neither Amplifi nor MKTG appeared to take our side.

There was one defining meeting in early February in San Francisco. The tension in the air felt like a prisoner's electrocution about to happen. It was, in retrospect, the first inkling that our funding partners were switching sides.

Good ol' Charley and DJ had no agenda other than covering their collective reputation, taking credit, and ultimately having a great time at Woodstock 50 wearing an AAA laminated sheriff's badge.

Launch day approached at Electric Lady Studios in New York City. The last time Michael had been inside this hallowed recording ground was with his friend Jimi Hendrix.

It added credence to holding the press function there, along with Creedence Clearwater Revival's John Fogerty.

Afternoon rehearsals were a collection of nerves and high hopes for a good media reaction to the final lineup announcement.

Michael completed back-to-back interviews all afternoon inside Electric Lady. I stood on the side of the stage as John Fogerty completed the soundcheck. I reflected on my nine-year-old self, hearing Cosmo's Factory, the album containing hits John was now singing beside me.

As I have acknowledged, I am not a starstruck individual. My feeling was an acknowledgement of the trajectory that life takes us all on.

Never underestimate where your beginning may meet up with your end.

Assembled media acknowledged the strength of our Woodstock 50 lineup — we were, as Joni Mitchell said, golden.

The event itself was brilliant, for its surroundings and overall reaction. A packed room held media and sponsors clamoring to know the final lineup – given the conjecture over preceding months that we couldn't get it together.

The studio room emptied with a sharp intake of breath as Michael read a list of 77 artists names, ending with Jay-Z.

There was one bizarre moment prior to the launch. The MC for the evening was David Steinberg. David was best known as a comic on Johnny Carson's Tonight Show and writer on Seinfeld, Friends and Curb Your Enthusiasm. A dinner was held the night before the launch to brief David and his wife Robyn. Michael and I, Susan and Alan, and a few other personalities had a lovely evening in true New York City style. Excitement for our launch was palpable. I had learned enough trying to make funny with the Little Britain crew and Woody Allen previously to shut up and just smile and laugh appropriately with this famous comedy writer.

We said our farewells and headed back to the hotel. An early-morning phone call told us David Steinberg had suffered a minor heart attack overnight and would not be our coveted MC. Michael and I immediately started reflecting on the night: we didn't indulge THAT much.

The launch event complete, a celebration dinner followed while we watched the audience reaction across our social media numbers. It was stellar, and the team took a well-deserved sigh of relief.

In exhausted silence Michael and I arrived back at our hotel, ready to take on the world of worries ahead, inside days drawing closer to showtime.

Suitably absent — my husband.

After our launch, I was metaphorically launched back into a time with different Michaels. I received a welcome call from Michael Chugg to announce he and Michael Gudinski had reunited. Frontier and Chugg Entertainment were now one and were to be bought by AEG in the US. The thought of them back together was not just great business but a great result for friendship that stirred a true feeling of industry solidarity.

I loved all my Michaels. I hold no favorite, no preference, just a world of wonderful memories.

CHAPTER 13: CONFUSION HAS ITS COSTS

While our Woodstock teams worked diligently to secure sponsorship licenses, media partnerships and the rest, Michael Lang was rolled out as the poster child and elder statesman for peace.

We were in no doubt about the message that Woodstock 50 was sending into the music community and beyond: one of determination to draw attention to the ails of the world.

Many not-for-profit companies came on board so we could deliver their message to what would be a worldwide audience.

One relationship was with 'March for Our Lives'.

Started by survivors of the Stoneman Douglas High School shootings in Parkland Florida on February 14, 2018, these young adults were galvanized and brilliant. It was clear that the message of Woodstock, both past and present, was for peace and unity above all else. I conducted many discussions with their team and was personally moved to assist their cause. The jingoistic nature of gun ownership in America is baffling.

As we watch the far right wield those guns as modern-day swords, the more terrifying it becomes. A case in point came years later with the January 6 post-election insurrection.

We reached out to a young woman that was making political and ecological waves across the planet — Greta Thunberg.

Conversations back and forth revealed she may indeed have been in the United States in August and able to attend Woodstock 50 as our special guest. The truth was that Greta chose to travel in a mode least intrusive on the planet's fragile ecological system — she wouldn't get on a plane. Her team was in the middle of putting together an Atlantic crossing, so arrival dates were a little sketchy.

For many reasons it didn't happen, but I still hold a candle up to those remarkable global efforts in rallying her generation into action.

Brian had made no headway in promoting his Silver City album in the US. Instead, he spent months on tour in Australia — reverting to the 'same old, same old' that he rallied against in championing our move to America.

I held onto an agreement with myself that I would not harass Brian when he was on the road. I would not be the woman that called every day to check up, not in, on him. It was his professional space. I never questioned if he was having a better time than his liver should allow. Maybe having previously been in an 'open marriage' gave me a different perspective, but I don't believe so. The stage was, and remains, his happiest place, so why put any clouds of doubt over that space? For either of us. The same cannot be said for many of his musical cohorts' wives — and many of them had solid reason to make daily inquiries.

I missed him and the home life we built over so many years. It was clear my 'demands' of a year ago, to not be apart for long periods, had not sunk in. Communication became fractious as his conflict-avoidant nature sat silently during our phone calls.

My work life with Michael Lang stretched into a social life as well.

We seemed to be in similar personal circumstances. We talked openly with each other, revealing that — from Stephen Stills' lyric — confusion does indeed have its costs.

Our regular car journeys tended more to the north of New York from now on. Marketing meetings in the city gave way to frenzied logistic group events at Watkins Glen — venue site for the festival. Hundreds of team members were students of 'building a Festival 101'. The complexities were enormous. Months filled with permits, police, and paranoia.

This Woodstock event was being held for the fourth time in New York State. The memories of 1969, 1994 and 1999 held strong, even if the players had changed.

Michael stood by choosing Superfly as the production company given their festival history. They were the successful promoters of the Bonnaroo and Outside Lands festivals. Despite the confronting conversations in San Francisco in February, the band marched on, and in Watkins Glen everyone got down to business, though delays were created with the grounds being frozen between December and February. Getting any real topographical layouts for the stages, production, camping and parking had been near impossible.

The last time this racetrack had been used for a large event was in 1972 for the Grateful Dead. These were different times with an expected audience wanting to camp on-site in glamping, tents and RVs.

By late March, tension was palpable amongst the logistics teams and local authorities. A Town Hall meeting was held for locals to air thoughts and grievances. Many people wanted to know how to maximize the event to their fiscal advantage — fair game. Local vendors approached us, as did community initiative organizations. One submission struck me as particularly innovative — a group that would create an area of 'Safe Space' for people who were sober or struggled with addiction. We scheduled to give them a large space and priority in our messaging.

Michael spoke eloquently at the Town Hall while I managed media outlets all keen to carry the story in a positive manner. To the last, the American media only ever supported Woodstock 50's development and messaging. I had crews from Holland, France, India and Australia's Seven Network come to interview us about the festival development. The goal of keeping Michael Lang forward face of the festival would never falter.

Post Town Hall, along with Firat, we drove back to the hotel for dinner with the Amplifi and MKTG teams. For once I was at the wheel. I pulled out some of my home-baked (laced) cookie goodness, suggesting it would take the edge off before dinner with the uptight faction. To my surprise, Firat also indulged. Our 6 foot 4 inch Turkish production manager did not drink alcohol let alone other indulgences.

The Watkins Glen hotel had become our team's second home.

Susan, Michael, Firat and I joined DJ, Peter Office and Charley. Peter Office was, in my opinion, one of the good guys. He worked out of Woodstock several days a week representing the finance teams. Michael always had suspicions of him being there as a spy. Adjacent tables held groups from Superfly and various other players.

DJ motioned to me: 'Please sit beside me so I can talk to you and not have to talk to Michael'. So, I sat, with Michael the other side of me. Peter looked across at me and pleaded, 'Can I have some of what you're having?'

I granted his wish and whispered in his ear, 'Fasten your seat belts, it's going to be a bumpy night', stealing the line from Bette Davis in All About Eve.

The comment could not have been more prescient.

Then there was Charley. He had already creeped me out with a tacit 'I'm watching you'. I recalled my Woodstock neighbour, who had previous professional dealings with Charley, referring to him as 'the smiling assassin'.

These guys had such a toxic distrust of Michael. In my opinion, this irrational behavior was borne out of knowing in the corporate world they could never achieve a legacy like their nemesis had done in 1969.

Conversation rallied between the tone at the town hall meeting and issues with the venue and production team. At one point, Michael inferred he had been 'blindsided' in some way. This set Charley into a psychological tailspin.

I was counting the wine bottles on the table to calculate how bad this could get. Susan regressed into a foetal position on her seat! She wasn't under my 'calming influence'.

The conversation was getting ugly as Charley went to lunge across the table at Michael. Peter was so disgusted with Charley's behavior he stood up to leave. I certainly don't blame him for taking that stance, as he was caught between his boss and his upstanding moral beliefs. As Charley's yelling attracted most of the other diners, DJ tried to talk him down off the lunatic shelf.

Michael Lang was a pacifist in every sense of the word. He would not have yelled back at Charley under any circumstances; giving fuel to this idiotic rage was not going to happen. Of course, that is the worst thing you can do to a drunken raving lunatic — ignore them. Susan and I were by now close to tears, pinned to our chairs, dreading any outcome.

Our big burly Turk, Firat, tapped me on the shoulder and leaned in close. Too close. I realized, he was almost falling off his chair. He told me he was so stoned his legs wouldn't work. All he wanted to do was get up and hit Charley. I was immediately thankful I gave him the cookie; otherwise, the night could have ended up with several people in jail or hospital.

The Mexican standoff — Charley was not going to be the first to leave as, loving the sound of his own voice, he had hours more of inane stupidity to spew from his drunken mouth.

DJ idolized Charley, so he was far too weak to step in. Michael nodded at me, we retreated. Susan shielded Michael while I struggled to steer a six-foot-four stoned Turk from the room.

After ensuring Firat made it to his room, I re-joined Michael and Susan, and a bottle of bourbon. No amount of analysis could have led us to believe this was the beginning of the end.

This was not new territory for Michael Lang. He had weathered these storms three times before over the preceding 50 years. All these slings and arrows had defined his character from the age of 24. He was not about to give up now.

Our professional relationship grew with every day's battles.

And happier times took a diversion into recreation. Days after 'Charley Gate', we drove home from New York City and took what Michael called the 'beautiful way home' through Peek-a-moose Trail.

On a stunning spring evening, light dappled through the trees, and silence was our music. I had not experienced this beauteous upstate New York route. Michael explained it was his preferred road home from Bethel in '69. I drew in the moment beside him, imagining how his perception differed between today and 50 years previously.

Our silent joy in the landscape and that shared experience will resonate as one of my life's greatest moments of reflection.

I broke our silence to query, 'Where are the bears?'

'Oh, don't worry, they are out there', came his cheeky response.

I arrived home hours later as dusk fell on Overlook Mountain.

Outside, my back garden shimmered, but a noise penetrated the peace.

In the blink of an eye, I realized a black bear was breaking into my porch room.

Be careful what you wish for.

Thankfully, the bear was not so far inside the house that I was in physical danger. Minutes later, and it could have been a very different scene. The huge 300 pounds of black fur and beady eyes clambered down an adjacent tree.

I shooed him away, shouting a stern warning not to return.

I was home alone, in the woods of Upstate New York, a pioneer woman from Brighton, Victoria yelling at a potentially murderous black bear.

Who knew?

Amongst the madness came one glorious night in New York City.

We were treated to a night at The Apollo for a jazz benefit concert. Brian had returned from touring in Australia. I sensed he felt uncomfortable around all of us as — now such a tight knit Woodstock production unit. He had been away for so much of the festival development. So used to being the headline act in the room, Brian found it difficult competing for space with Michael Lang and the Woodstock juggernaut. This would become symptomatic of the downfall of our time in America, for us both. But on this auspicious evening we were treated to performances at the Apollo by Savion Glover, Ben Stiller, Bernie Sanders and the sublime Tony Bennett.

We sat rows from the front of the stage with Tony Bennett looking straight into my eyes — the mark of a true performer is to make you feel like you are the only person in the room. My heart stood still remembering my mother's love for this incomparable performer. I desperately wished she were alive to hear my retelling of the moment.

In lieu, I blew him a kiss on her behalf.

Days later we headed to Boston for a symposium on Woodstock's 50 at Berklee College of Music. The event had been planned for months as a get-together for the core group of 1969 pundits — Michael, publicist Rona Elliot, Lighting Designer and MC Chip Monck, Audio Engineer Bill Hanley, photographers Henry Diltz and Elliott Landy. I had not met Rona before. Post Woodstock '69 she went on to a stellar career as journalist and publicist. She, more than anyone from the original crew, retained a close friendship with Michael. The images Henry Diltz shot of her in those hot August nights of 1969 showed a cherubic-faced pixie girl beginning life's journey. In this college room in Boston 50 years later, I recalled the first time I saw that sweet face — all hippie beads and flower headbands. Oh, how I wanted to emulate her as I grew out of my pre-pubescence into predicted 'Fabulousness'. It was the same attraction I had felt to Patti Mostyn's aura 40 years before these days.

Rona did not disappoint. Her generosity to all that were gathered exemplified earlier times of peace & love they collectively created in 1969.

It was a great way to spend my birthday weekend, especially as Brian and Austin were with me.

Chip Monck was known to Brian and me, as he lived in Melbourne and was active in the music industry. He had flown in for the event and turned up with a gift. He acknowledged my birthday with a beautiful gold locket that had belonged to his dear departed wife, Camille. By way of an interesting contrast, that birthday my husband gifted me a wheel of cheese.

Rona and Henry Diltz were close friends, both living in LA.

I was thrilled to meet Henry, knowing how close he had been to David Cassidy and the Laurel Canyon set. Our paths would cross again. Elliott Landy lived in Woodstock and still sold his candid photos of Bob Dylan and Van Morrison in their idyllic Woodstock backyards. Elliott had graciously loaned us a bunch of his photos to adorn the walls of our Elwyn Lane office. He and his wife, Lynda, were their own picture of laid-back Woodstock serenity.

Sound designer Bill Hanley was the elder of the tribe. Known as 'The Father of Festival Sound', Bill was already 82. He made everyone laugh on stage mocking his own deafness. He went on to write a wonderful book called The Last Seat in the House.

Tension was still high with multiple unresolved festival production issues as April proceeded.

The morning of April 15 I was sitting in the office with CNN for company. Incomprehensible images burst forth of Paris' beloved Notre-Dame on fire. The hideous reality unfolded over the next hours as the world held its breath, praying no total collapse would occur.

Weeks later, our festival world started to collapse, without any fire or brimstone.

Earth Day fell on April 21. It had been planned as our ticket on-sale date. Amplifi had stalled while we went back to the drawing board for the umpteenth time to assess how the delay in our on-sale would impact the festival.

At 11.55am on April 29, Michael and I were alone in the office.

Ben Sisario from the New York Times called.

Ben had written an excellent exclusive launch piece on the festival in January. Time stood still when he said, 'Michael, can you comment on an embargoed press release we have which is due to go out at noon — in five minutes. Can I read it to you?'

This eminent journalist rattled off the protocol and carefully constructed legalese as we both sunk further in our chairs.

Ben Sisario read on: 'As a result, after careful consideration, Dentsu Aegis Network's Amplifi Live, a partner in Woodstock 50, has decided to cancel the festival'.

Michael paused and simply uttered, 'Jesus'.

Ben's obvious question was, 'What's going on, Michael?'

Michael kept repeating, 'This is news to me'.

We hung up and promised to call him back.

Within the next ten minutes, after the Japanese company dropped the media bomb, we had sixty calls to return. Michael and I took a beat. We sat together at his desk, staring at each other, entirely incredulous in the moment.

What the actual fuck just happened?

Shock is multi-layered. While your mind scrambles to fathom reality, it also sifts through a 'needs/must' immediacy list.

We broke the daze and divided up crucial first phone calls to inform the broader team.

Susan and Greg hopped a plane from LA but not before briefing New York attorney Marc Kasowitz.

The fight started out expensively from that first phone call, but no one on our side was in doubt we would win the day, and the right to stage the festival.

Mr Kasowitz was an unlikely fan of a 50-year-old hippie rebellion, but the gentleman acted as Woodstock 50's greatest frontline defense. The fact that one of his other key clients was then-President Donald Trump did not endear him to the cause in the eyes of many media pundits, but we knew he had Woodstock 50's back.

We prepared a press statement. We sent an email blast to 300,000 people on our database who had ticked the YES box for interest in the festival.

The wider team remained incredulous that Amplifi had decided to take this totally illegal gamble as their unilateral standpoint. None of it made sense. All the artists had been paid 100 per cent of their fees upfront. Amplifi had already shelled out more than $20 million in artist payments. The agreed budget was more than $44 million. There was still $17.8 million in the bank account. And then there wasn't. To add insult to injury, Amplifi cleaned out the bank account, which in and of itself gave Team Kasowitz a prize fight.

Numb at the end of that day, I went home to tell my husband the news. 'The festival appears to be cancelled'. His response hit me with as incredulous a wind as the day's first phone call.

He merely asked, 'What do I tell my band?' Out of the thousands of supportive and caring comments he could have made, his only interest was as a selfish musician.

That well-worn penny that was his narcissism dropped one more level down to the ground around me. Confusion had been the call sign of the day. Now it truly had its costs.

Days later, Austin flew to Australia with a stern message of support for his beleaguered mother: 'I will see you at the festival, now go and tidy yourself up'.

Brian also left on tour. I was, again, alone.

My husband's parting words were less witty than my son's. I needed some emotional support to hang onto, but none was forthcoming. We knew this was going to be a tough separation for us both. It is all very well to be professionally occupied 24/7 but not having a calm voice of reason and kindness at the end of a day threw me into emotional turmoil.

I was supremely unhappy.

This manifested itself in angry outbursts on the phone and, as Brian was fond of saying, 'Angry is not easy to love'. He had had some prior experience in that emotional playing field. I made a repeated point of defining the difference between 'upset' and 'angry', but my husband was, in that space, a card-carrying, conflict-averse, avoidant-natured old man.

It was just over a year since we moved into this beautiful Woodstock home, yet it seemed we had traversed a lifetime of emotional disharmony. There was nothing intrinsically wrong with our love for each other. Conflict generally arose in regard to other family members, my inability to accept bad behavior, and Brian's inability to correct it as a parent. I was raised to ensure manners and civility took precedence in any family circumstance – witnessed by the fact my father and his ex-wife maintained a healthy relationship. Brian's children had not been reared with the same set of principles. This was not solely his fault, having been an absent father most of his life. But from day one of us living together, and me welcoming his offspring into our home, I had made it clear that manners would prevail. Too late, she cried.

Brian was in Australia doing the things he loved most — being on stage and spending time with his family. I should have seen the writing on the wall. I was too mired in my own human frailty and trying to keep a sane professional head under the circumstances.

Michael Lang and I did our consoling together.

Our code words became 'pink gin honey?'.

By early May the first Woodstock 50 vs Amplifi court cases were held in the New York City Federal Court. It was decided by the stakeholders that it was better for Michael to not be present in court each day. This would undoubtedly raise the ire of Charley, DJ and the rest of the corporate sycophants — pleading their case to the judge.

By all accounts, DJ and Peter Office both performed poorly in front of the judge when cross-examined and certainly did nothing to strengthen their case for the heinous betrayal they had committed.

Michael and I spent harrowing hours at our hotel and awaited word. We were often accompanied by Susan's husband Alan, the videographer. Word came that only measured justice had prevailed — we won the right for the festival to proceed and be fully produced. The court ruled that the unilateral cancellation by Amplifi was indeed illegal. Huzzah!

However, Woodstock 50 was not awarded the return of the $17.8 million taken from the bank account. This would mean no liquidity with which to mount an already past-due-date festival. Our suspicion on how long this coup had been in the planning was confirmed when Superfly also announced their 'resignation' from producing the festival.

Our saviour appeared in the guise of Sir Richard Branson.

The irony was not lost on me that this was the company I had nearly jumped ship from Mushroom to work for in the late 1980s. The Virgin team in Los Angeles were class operators, and the remaining team felt secure in this appointment. There was, however, the matter of them getting paid a producing fee upfront.

Greg and Susan had a huge network of people to target for funding. They had already sunk millions into the license and development of the Woodstock 50 brand, so they were personally not liquid.

I made a unilateral decision in minutes.

I would stump up for the Virgin payment.

Michael's good friend Bobby joined me in the fight. I became Woodstock's Joan of Arc. Like the Maid of Orleans, I was guided by the voice of St Michael, under a different kind of divinity. Knowing full well I could end up burnt on the stake as she was, this would be financial rather than literal.

On the surface it appeared as madness, but if all went well, it was a lay down misère. I'm not sure who was more shocked by my offer — Michael Lang, Greg Peck or Susan Cronin.

Greg prepared the paperwork while Michael grinned his cheeky grin at me and said, 'So, how is this producing role panning out for you so far do you think?' Another pink gin aided in the nervous laughter.

We had to laugh; there was no time to be reflective. That would come later, as it turned out, on August 17.

Our first meetings with the Virgin team took place at Watkins Glen. These guys beamed cool business sense while also being in the pocket with what had to be achieved. None of the corporate uptight bullshit of the Dentsu employees.

Team Virgin and Woodstock 50 achieved a level of professional simpatico quickly. Behind the production scenes, everyone was busy trying to raise funds to ensure the show could in fact go on. John Kocis from C1 was a stalwart. Day after day we churned out financial documents to support our efforts while Michael doused the media with his calm conversational coda.

He doused someone else — the President and CEO of the Dentsu Group, Mr Toshihiro Yamamoto.

The Dentsu Aegis Network, as a Japanese-owned firm, adhered to a culture of importance in honor and corporate fidelity. Michael wrote with an open heart and mind, always.

After laboring through several iterations, this is what we ended up sending. It is important that his words are reflected in full here to understand fully the situation we faced.

Dear Mr. Yamamoto,

I am the producer of Woodstock 50. When I was 24 years old in 1969, my three partners and I brought the Woodstock Music & Arts Festival to life in upstate New York.

Over the last 50 years, Woodstock has grown to be called not only a popular cultural icon but an iconic worldwide emblem of Peace and Love.

Many months ago, I was introduced to members of the Dentsu Aegis Network in New York who were proposing to represent the sponsorship and media sales for the 50th Anniversary Celebration of Woodstock, a music festival to be held August 16–18, 2019, through their MKTG

division. Eventually, MKTG together with Amplifi USA offered to finance the Woodstock Festival. Despite interest from several other organizations and even individuals, we agreed to move forward for both sponsorship sales and financing with your groups.

Initially, I had some concerns about linking an organization like Dentsu to Woodstock. Corporations are not always the right match for certain creative endeavours, but I learned that Dentsu has pursued various social initiatives after certain tragedies and scandals that Dentsu faced which gave me confidence that your company would be an ethical and honorable firm to partner with.

Your officer here, DJ Martin, Chief Commercial Officer, reassured me that Dentsu would not interfere, and equally important, could embody the special meaning of Woodstock.

It would only be in a supportive financial role to ensure our mutual success.

Shortly thereafter, I was presented with a contract which said Amplifi Live would be a coproducer as well as a financier. I raised my concern to Mr Martin who told me this was for optics only because of international investment law but that I should not worry.

We at Woodstock 50 worked together with Amplifi and Dentsu to create a first-class talent lineup and were working to obtain all necessary permits. In fact, on the morning of April 22, 2019, Earth Day, we were granted conditional approval by the State of New York for our mass gathering permit, along with certain conditions we felt we could meet by working as a team so that we could have tickets go on sale as we had promised the fans and the public.

Your team blocked this sale for no apparent reason. Together, our organizations faced a question of cash flow since Dentsu had not been successful in selling sponsorships for the Woodstock Festival. To fill this void, my side had been working to obtain completion financing and based upon the feedback we had been getting, we were confident we would be successful.

We communicated this to your people. We had also been working on value engineering the site to improve the economics. By Friday, April 26, 2019, we presented multiple plans illustrating a slight profit and substantiated these plans with supporting documents. However, for reasons not explained to us, it seemed to fall on deaf ears.

Three days later, on Monday, April 29, 2019, your team lead by DJ Martin, Charles Horsey and Lucas Cridland sent notice at 11am EDT that they had taken control of the festival (which they have no legal right to do) and at 11:15 EDT advised that they had cancelled the festival (which they had no legal right to do). This same team had also already notified the press without any advance notice to me or my team. While we were on a call together as a group at 12:00 EDT, the media had already begun reporting that Woodstock was cancelled. I then learned that Amplifi illegally swept approximately $17 million from the festival bank account leaving the festival in peril.

These actions confirmed my worst concerns about partnering with your company. These actions are neither a legal nor honorable way to do business. Adding insult to injury, since your team announced that the festival was cancelled, I have received multiple reports and evidence that Dentsu has directly contacted all stakeholders, including the venue Watkins Glen International, insurance companies, producers, vendors and business with me, and violate their contracts with my company. Your team has gone so far as to promise indemnification to these contracted parties should they back out of our contracts.

We also have evidence that Dentsu representatives have gone so far as to say that should the talent back out of Woodstock, they would be seen favorably by Dentsu and that this could result in their performing the 2020 Summer Olympics in Tokyo, where Dentsu is a major organizer. In these actions too, Dentsu has acted not only without honor, but outside of the law.

The consequences of these unjustified actions are far-reaching and mind-bogglingly significant.

Your company's actions will impact all those who have been directly involved with the festival, including my colleagues. It will impact all of those who are indirectly involved with the festival, including the public who has been clamoring to be a part of this historic event. It will impact the local community that would have received a much-needed economic boom. Finally, and in many ways most significantly, it would effectively mean that Dentsu would be known as a company that had acted to attempt to destroy an American cultural icon.

Your actions not only affect my company, but tens of thousands of fans. Fortunately, we have renewed interest in financing and remain confident that Woodstock 50 will take place as planned. In fact, the events of late, while not planned, have caused a groundswell of support for Woodstock in every conceivable manner, making the prospects of having a successful event a virtual certainty even after the actions your company has taken.

In 1969, Woodstock was not just a music festival. It was a movement, carried out not by me and my partners, but by the people. It was in many ways a reflection of the times. We faced many obstacles at that time in putting on the event. We successfully overcame those obstacles, through great perseverance, because we believe in the movement. Today, we feel that there are real issues facing our society, which reminds us in many ways of 1969. We feel we need Woodstock now as we did 50 years ago. We fought to overcome those obstacles then and we feel a similar obligation to overcome those obstacles now.

We only would ask that you honor the law and your obligations, stop interfering with our efforts to put on this wonderful event and return the $17 million you improperly took.

It is one thing if your company, Dentsu, wanted to back out of its commitment to Woodstock because it would not make as much money as it had hoped, but to try to suffocate and kill Woodstock so that we could not have a festival for our Golden Anniversary without you is puzzling for any company, let alone one that claims reform.

I bring this matter urgently to your attention because as I read your own corporate statement, it seemed to me you must be unaware of what treachery has taken place by your company.

Your words below do not line up with the actions taken by your team towards Woodstock:

Ideas that reach beyond the imaginable.

Technology that crosses the bounds of possibilities.

Entrepreneurship that surpasses the expected.

Three sources of strength,

Driving our innovation,

Bringing positive change

to people and society.

In the end, since Dentsu has already abandoned Woodstock, all I ask for is that Dentsu walk away peacefully and allow me to deliver to the people a 50th Anniversary Festival.

Again, I respectfully ask that Dentsu stop its obstructionist actions with the talent and stakeholders. We feel we now have a window to come together with you to peacefully resolve this matter and create a wonderful and special festival.

Indeed, many good partners have come forward with a desire to help as we all recognize the importance of Peace & Love in today's world.

Woodstock seeks to help heal the planet and the people on it.

I hope to hear from you soon on this matter.

Thank you for listening,

Michael Lang

In Michael Langs honorable nature we did not disclose this private letter to the media. It remained a private exchange. The actions of its recipient became known to us only later but sadly did not affect the corporation's outcome.

Our attention was diverted late May by another business opportunity.

Woodstock New York is renowned as an artist colony curating more than 100 years of artist heritage.

It became a geographical beacon for the bohemian demi-monde as far back as 1902 with the arrival of Englishman Ralph Radcliffe Whitehead who created the Byrdcliffe Arts Colony. There remains another local compound that speaks volumes to the contemporary musical heritage of Woodstock.

In 1963, Albert Grossman moved to Woodstock. By 1969, he had built the Bearsville complex and recording studio. His clients included Bob Dylan, Janis Joplin and Richie Havens. The studio later became known as Utopia and was home to Todd Rundgren.

Albert Grossman died on a flight to London in January 1986. His legacy lived on as the home to Woodstock Radio, the Little Bear restaurant and, most importantly, The Bear Café. All locals would convene there to hang out in the evenings. The current owners had been trying to sell up for some time. Being a real estate hotel developer, Susan Cronin saw and shared our vision for the possibilities. I was ecstatic at the idea of us all becoming joint owners and developing the Bearsville legacy.

Michael, Susan and I had dinner with the owner and paid a holding amount to prevent the site going to auction. We walked the grounds together and imagined the theatre rebuilt to its former glory. It was close to derelict; the site had been badly maintained for many years.

I recalled the excitement I felt walking the grounds at Château Hérouville outside Paris, imagining the same reinvented legacy. Maybe that French due diligence was a trial for what was meant to be here in Woodstock New York.

Albert Grossman is buried on the Bearsville land. His wife Sally lived next door until her death in 2021. We visited his grave; Michael being the only one amongst us who knew Albert intimately as a friend. Susan, never prone to sentimentality, broke the karmic reverence of the moment and said to Michael, 'So, are we going to bury you here next to Albert?'

I told her not to be so ridiculous, our youthful illustrious friend Michael Lang would be the one to see us all buried before his time came.

By the end of May another piece of the festival puzzle fell on the floor.

A meeting of all departments — law enforcement, medical, local government, site management — took place at Watkins Glen. For some 'oversight' reason, Amplifi and MKTG sent Peter Office as their representative to report their position in the attempted cancellation. He spoke for two minutes inside a two-hour meeting, only to say that Amplifi remained 'in control' of the festival. The sting was real as this was the first time Susan, Greg, Michael and I had confronted someone who we genuinely believed was a supporter of the cause despite working for the now 'enemy'.

I admit I could not look him in the eye. Michael, on the other hand, stepped forward to shake his hand.

By the end of the week, the racetrack had also pulled out as our venue.

Still not deterred, we sought alternate venue sites. We were excited by Citi Field, home stadium to the New York Mets.

It was available for our dates, production was possible. Being in the New York City precinct contravened the artists' radius clauses — to our detriment, not theirs. They still had the money upfront. Another bridge to cross, amongst many.

More confusion, and its costs …

We had a laugh as we walked baseball's hallowed halls. Michael, in times of incredulity, repeated his favorite quote. I always thought I heard him say this philosophical insight was from Yogi Bear. The quote was apt to the bookend festival circumstances of 1969 and 2019:

'It's déjà vu all over again'.

As we walked, Michael stopped at a plaque commemorating one of the league's great players — Yogi Berra!

It seems you can take the girl out of Australia but not so much the other way 'round. I had no idea who Yogi Berra was. I felt so stupid. I confessed I thought we were talking about Yogi Bear; he said it made me even more loveable.

The office was still in a flurry trying to secure financing, a venue and hold the artists' agents close, in our belief the festival would go ahead. Each day was more difficult, but we were resolute. For another four weeks we re-examined every facet of probability for getting on stage in August. There is no doubt other third parties — agents, artists, media, PR — were all starting to mark us insane.

This is Woodstock, people! It is exactly what happened 50 years ago! Michael Lang did not give up then, and we were not going to give up now.

The next venue possibility was Vernon Downs, a clapped-out racino — racetrack/casino — further upstate in New York.

In Oneida County it was in the same jurisdiction as the infamous 1999 Woodstock in Rome, NY.

The Virgin producing team flew in and agreed it could work if we got the final permit in hand within days. Council and town meetings were held. The owner of the racino, Jeff Gural, also owned the land under the Empire State Building.

He was no slouch and wanted us to create a famous festival on this site as a precursor to annual events. The town supervisors had other ideas. We were completely shut down. By this stage the Kasowitz legal team had put a PR company on to assist us with all external messaging. Sallie Hofmeister from Sitrick & Co in LA became my buddy and ally. She was experienced in crisis management and we swung through the daily hoops together.

June turned into July.

With each passing day it seemed more improbable we could get this event off the ground, especially as no ground was secured. The land surrounding Vernon Downs was owned by the Oneida Indians. They themselves owned a highly successful casino close by. Their CEO Pete Carmen was helpful. He agreed with Michael that having the level of crowd input Woodstock could present to the area was valuable to them. We drove the surrounds marking out parking, camping, etc. This became a constant head-butt with the Virgin guys and County teams.

It came to a head at, yet another, town meeting and we were shutdown. This truly felt like the end. Sallie and I sat writing the final press release. Susan was an emotional wreck and after a couple of drinks fell into a lament: 'Whatever happens, we are family! I love you guys'.

John Kocis, Michael and I veered towards pragmatism.

It came as a surprise the next day when Greg and Susan announced we were going to keep trying to secure a venue.

Ludicrous? Insane?

Somehow, humoring them seemed less destructive than not. They needed a venue with its own production infrastructure and ticketing system so we could go in with a reduced lineup. Unsurprisingly, some acts had publicly distanced themselves from now being involved with the festival — The Black Keys were first. Others remained resolutely on our side — Bob Weir from the Grateful Dead leading that pack.

The desire to not allow Dentsu's unilateral cancellation to win was pivotal at this point.

Susan and Greg both had their wheels spinning, in different directions. He was still securing financing, she was ordering thousands of lanyards, branded media-kits and VIP bags! The only thing more insane than their behavior was the two puppies that she bought and installed in the office. The barking and chewing phone lines was as overwhelming as Alan still acting as videographer every moment of the day.

It was truly a scene out of The Office. Our entirely dysfunctional office family was a home movie TV show.

With the arrival of Susan's broader family unit, Greg moved into my home in Woodstock. It was better for his mental health as his business partner, and mother of his son, was baying for blood. He was directly, if unfairly, right in the firing line.

Recognizing I needed support, my caring daughter Olivia flew in to help in a time of heavy lifting. Olivia is great with children and stepped right in to care for Susan's tribe.

Media speculation grew daily. Dave Brooks at Billboard seemed to be gunning for our downfall. He wrote that no one had contacted the artists and agents. This was untrue, but his comments were responsible for more artists pulling out. I was daily posting questions to Susan and Greg about material conduct and constantly getting shut down.

They were still spinning their wheels and would not allow rational discourse to poke a stick in the spokes of those wheels. John Kocis and I spent untold hours trying to find a way to make them see the end was nigh.

Firat drove the three of us up to Syracuse to check out the Fairgrounds. On the long drive, Michael composed a letter to Governor Andrew Cuomo that we sent on the fly, trying to enlist his support in securing an 'eleventh hour' venue. The Fairgrounds were too big an infrastructure rebuild.

In just another moment of madness, Michael and I flew to Washington DC to check out the RFK Stadium. While we flew, Firat, Alan and Ronnie drove down to meet us. On the way they stopped at the Merriweather Post Pavilion outside Baltimore, Maryland. It was deemed a perfect solution to a reduced mode festival. The promoter Seth Hurwitz did everything to make it happen. Susan and Greg drove down and spent the weekend crunching numbers.

Michael declined to join, fearing the lunatics had now truly taken over the asylum. He knew there was no way the artists and agents would agree to such a geographic pivot.

On a lighter note, the book we had been working on with Reel Art Press was ready for release. Rizzoli bookstore in New York City held a launch Q&A with Michael and Henry Diltz.

Meeting Henry again after all our communication editing images for the book was now a happy buzz. He was a tried and true 60's dynamo, just like Michael. How these guys had navigated and survived to their age was impressive beyond measure. I loved keeping up with them!

Publishers Tony Nourmand and Dave Brolan flew in from London, and it was a packed house at Rizzoli NYC.

Like meeting David Cassidy back in 2002, here was another childhood memory emanating in real life. As I watched Henry and Michael banter on about the good ol' days, I saw myself transported back to the Brighton newsagents buying American fanzine Tiger Beat. All the photos taken by Henry Diltz graced the walls of my bedroom until the sticky tape could no longer hold the weight of Cassidy imagery.

Henry's history in visually chronicling the emergence of the Laurel Canyon music scene was unprecedented. I had already started writing a show concept based around Laurel Canyon, and we agreed to talk more about it once the festival issues were resolved.

Henry and Michael were a natural talkfest together. They repeated the appearance at Henry's representing gallery in New York and LA, the Morrison Hotel Gallery.

All the appearances and documentary shoots Michael had agreed to participate in took on a different tone, given the uncertainty swirling around Woodstock 50. My illustrious leader soldiered on like it was 1969, appearing not much older and certainly not weary.

As his 75th birthday approached he did not carry his years heavily. He was still a mysterious Peter Pan with all of us lost boys and girls following him, hopefully away from the crocodiles!

Michael and I spoke privately, acknowledging our festival dream was over.

There would be no Woodstock 50, anywhere. But he had a duty of care to his partners, so we kept working while their wheels kept spinning in opposing directions. I tried to keep Michael, who was my priority, and myself from being dragged into the undertow.

On July 30, the axe finally fell. It had been over in our minds for weeks but, on this night, Greg finally saw sense. Financing incomplete, artists gone in droves. No venue secured.

Greg was not a seasoned drinker. Two whiskies and he started a rally cry in my kitchen that he could secure Alicia Keys 'just like that'. They had been neighbours in Long Island growing up. We stifled our laughter and waited for him to add Duran, Duran to his miracle-go-get-list.

There was nothing to laugh about. It was over. Period. Everything we had all worked towards in the ugly face of adversity was for naught.

How would the Woodstock brand ever recover from this defeat?

Days later I remained numb with the reality of it all, unable to resolve how this could have happened. Susan, Greg and their tribe, including the destructive dogs, had hightailed it back to Los Angeles.

Firat and I went to the office to pack up and Michael came to help. We were tired and teary. No amount of pink gin could help mend this loss.

What made it worse was imagining the evil triumvirate at Amplifi gleeful at our demise. It was with some delight to later discover they all got the sack for their miscalculated roles in the Woodstock venture.

Brian, Olivia and I headed into NYC for a couple of days R&R. We saw The Rolling Stones at the MetLife Stadium in New Jersey. Michael brought his twin sons along and we had a brilliant night. Despite being a devout Rolling Stones fan, Brian was sullen and withdrawn — I presumed still uncomfortable around Michael. In hindsight there was clearly more on my husband's mind about the future.

On the August dates when we should have been consumed with festival activity, we spent evenings inside the original home of Max Yasgur, adjacent to the original site of the 1969 Woodstock in Bethel. Sound designer Bill Hanley and his wife had remained close to Max and Miriam Yasgur after their tumultuous entry into the world of rock 'n' roll.

Max passed away in February 1973. Miriam re-married an accountant in Monticello and lived out a good life until passing away in Florida in 2014.

Sitting in their kitchen was just another surreal moment in our festival fiasco. A half-century later, how could we ever have predicted that this was where we would end up 'celebrating' 50 years since the original three days of peace, love and music?

There was music to be had outside as the current owners of the property put on their own side event each year to commemorate 1969. Bill Hanley, Rona Elliot, gathered in the home of the man who ensured Woodstock '69 took place.

There is historically as much reverence for Max Yasgur as for Michael Lang, John Roberts and Joel Rosenman. And rightly so. If at the eleventh hour in '69 Max had determined Woodstock Ventures was just a bunch of hippies trying to make trouble, fight the war and espouse peace, the gathering would never have taken place. Max was a staunch Republican, he was a dairy farmer, he didn't know from some bunch of longhaired twenty-somethings in the music business taking over his land! We can always wonder if he had fathomed ahead of time how many people would eventually attend the gathering, would he have allowed it to go ahead?

In Joni Mitchell's eponymous song, written as she watched television reports of the festival:

'By the time we got to Woodstock we were half a million strong'.

Sadly, we would never know how many people in 2019 would have joined us to experience 'everywhere a song and a celebration'.

The dream was well and truly over.

Brian, Olivia and I flew to California to visit our friend Ira Yeager and his husband George Hellyer.

I tried to 'decompress' at their holiday home in Sea Ranch. I was still very much on edge. This manifested itself in unnecessary arguments with Brian over everything and nothing. I craved emotional support and understanding, 'pandering' if you will, but my errant husband did not have the empathy gene.

Brian and I had our third wedding anniversary at Francis Ford Coppola's Winery in Northern California. But I was so emotionally drained I didn't feel like there was much to celebrate. Our time in America had been fraught with problems over the past few years — my blood disorder, Brian's accident, the strain of moving several times, his album not being widely released, and touring opportunities not eventuating. And the final icing on the cake — the demise of the Woodstock 50 festival.

With another Australian tour cycle looming for Brian, I railed against having to endure more months apart. What was the point of us being in America?

I recognized now how detrimental it was to our relationship. It was time to contemplate a move back to Australia.

Before Brian left, I booked tickets to see Graham Nash. A date night. I was looking forward to putting our angst behind us, enjoying each other's company.

As Nash sang 'Our House' I reached for Brian's hand and gave him a knowing smile to acknowledge how we felt that song reminded us of ourselves.

He was cold and unresponsive. I sunk into a depressive reality and on the drive home asked why he was so distant from me. For the first time in many years, this conflict-averse, emotionally passive man snapped back. He yelled that it was only a song; it had nothing to do with us.

This was so out of character. I did not know what to do. All I was seeking was support and understanding. He left to go to Australia under a cloud.

I was at my lowest ebb.

Austin was turning 21, so I hopped a plane to Melbourne to surprise him.

I joined Brian for his show at Crown Casino with Glenn Shorrock and met Glenn's new girlfriend. He was in the throes of divorcing his wife of 40 years, and I felt a certain sadness knowing how unfaithful he had been to her.

No one knows what truly goes on inside a marriage.

There was no marriage of any longevity in our music industry inner circle that had not weathered many storms. I never felt any level of discomfort with Brian in this area. He was not a one-night-stand kind of guy. I was confident I was not fooling myself in that supposition. After all, I had always said if he was unhappy with me, he could go without any fear of reprisal from me. My marital history attested to this moral belief.

During my somewhat 'conjugal' visit, Brian was performing at the annual Golden Stave fundraiser lunch. This year's theme was Woodstock, which I found only mildly amusing. I arranged for Michael to tape a video message to Golden Stave — which we ran before Brian's performance. I felt like I was in a vortex — none of the people at this event cared less that the 50th anniversary had not transpired. It all felt a million miles away from home, which it was in many ways, both geographically and culturally. Wining and dining with our Sydney friends gave a sense of missing those connections. The conversation still never arose that we should have given up on our American dreams and moved home.

I did the complete opposite.

I flew home to Woodstock thinking only of the financial reality facing me from the demise of the festival. I turned to the extra-curricular job I do best — flipping houses. It became clear the big house I bought was never going to be filled with children and grandchildren — just like the myriad houses before this one where Brian hoped to keep the dream of his integrated family alive.

I found a tiny cottage with a lovely view over the Ashokan Reservoir. It was a 1950s nightmare ripe for repair. Michael lived a mile down the road, so I asked his opinion. We stood in an early snowfall, in the rain, and he determined it was a good bet. For the first time I started to feel like a 'local'.

The mythology in Woodstock is that you are only a local after 20 years, so I was kind of jumping the queue with his approval.

Michael and I met regularly for catchup cocktails and optimism. Far from spending our time brooding over lost opportunities, we spoke enthusiastically about future endeavours. One of which had sadly disappeared from our grasp.

After the dissolution of Woodstock 50, Susan Cronin had lost her appetite for taking on the resurrection of the Bearsville complex. Instead, Michael and I met with the new owner, Lizzie Vann. He offered her sage advice on local folklore, Albert's original intentions and many other elements. If actual ownership or stewardship had escaped our grasp, we knew we could be involved at a local level with Lizzie to realize our Woodstock Nation mutual dream.

Brian remained in Australia over Christmas with the part of his family where I was not welcome. Jessica and family moved to the Gold Coast and were joined by her mother from LA. To say this hurt would be an understatement.

Austin and I frolicked around New York City with friends. My clever son headed back to college in Boston.

I took possession of the little cottage and started on the road to happy home renovator one more time.

Having spent so much time apart, we decided on a short vacation to Mexico with Austin in the first week of March.

I had experienced Mexico on the western coastline. On the eastern side, facing the Caribbean in Tulum, we 'Three Musketeers' were reunited like old times. Our Byron buddy Vinnie Rae had moved here and was as magnificent a presence in Tulum as he had been in Byron at his eponymous Rae's hotel.

After a relaxing week, we flew back to New York. On the surface this was an unremarkable journey, but people in Cancún airport were wearing masks. Travelling in Asia this can be the norm, but it was strange to see it here. The woman next to me on the plane was in full PPE gear. I presumed she was a germaphobe.

Three days later the whole world changed.

Everyone has their own terrifying recollection of that moment when we globally tried to fathom 'lockdown', wearing mandatory masks and no toilet rolls on the shelves. Madness. Wasn't 'pandemic' a word from 1919, not 2020?

I started renovating the cabin on the property in preparation for Olivia joining us. This space was charming — a sturdy fireplace, kitchen, bathroom and bedroom — I converted the attached garage into a living room space while we were in Mexico.

With the reality of coronavirus becoming more frightening daily, Austin's campus closed. I drove quickly to Boston to collect him.

Then came the mad scramble of decision-making, whether we would remain in Woodstock or hightail it to Australia. We decided to stay and sit it out in the wilds of Woodstock — thankful we were not in a city environment where things were starting to look grim.

The universal reality that life as we knew it would never be the same started to infuse into everyday life, from simple precautions like washing vegetables to obscenely frequent Amazon deliveries. Forbidden to undertake visits to restaurants and friends, Zoom became our lifeline. God forbid if the internet would have gone down. A truly remarkable time marked uniquely different by each of us across the globe. The long-reaching effects will not only be the millions lost to the virus' vicious grip but also the lost education, industries and livelihood across generations.

In our microcosm, Brian and I settled into a stagnant routine so unlike our normal lives as active, productive people. I recognized a growing anxiety and paranoia in my husband and vowed not to let him fall down that rabbit hole.

If this pandemic had happened earlier, I may have taken on a different attitude to his reporting COVID death numbers, almost hourly! As in potential strangulation. In this new space, I took on a 'yes, dear' mantra and kept the Chardonnay flowing.

In our blissful upstate New York countryside setting we sat out the summer of 2020 by the swimming pool with occasional gardening. Daily distractions and positivity were my goal. I could not have been more upbeat if I tried. In hindsight I am sure this positivity was somehow borne out of the loss of the Woodstock Festival. 'Always look on the bright side of life …'

And so, 2020 flew by until plans for our future had to be made. A rescheduled tour for Brian was getting closer.

By January 2021, Australia looked under pandemic control, shows were on schedule. Getting him on a plane was going to be a gargantuan effort logistically and emotionally.

The days before Brian's departure were doubly saddened by the death of his mother Jean. We had both been raised by strong stoic women, and Jean made her own decision on when she wanted to cast off her mortal coil.

Our drive to JFK Airport was silent and filled with angst. I drove cautiously and clutched my husband's hand in some vain attempt to inject assuredness that he would not fall victim to COVID-19 on the journey. As I turned to watch him disappear through the departures queue, I was filled with an overwhelming sense of dread that I would never see him again. I drove home feeling my world was coming to an end, totally unrelated to potential virus-induced mortality.

I could not put my finger on it, but intuition told me something bigger than my feelings had just died.

During enforced Sydney quarantine, I would keep Brian's spirits up each day through Zoom. Being alone in the dead of winter in the cabin did not concern me other than being apart from him again. We agreed these long months of separation had to end. In retrospect it would have been the best thing for our marriage, as all the touring inevitably fell apart due to COVID as the months unfolded.

To compound my anguish during our separation, Brian developed more medical issues. My primary nature is carer: always has been, from children to friends to husbands. By now it was impossible for me to get to Australia, as the border closures were firmly in place. Our virtual conversations became more painful by the week.

My 60th birthday was approaching and in the waning days of 2020, prior to Brian's departure for Australia, we had collaborated on ideas for parties in Melbourne, Sydney or Byron Bay. All ideas gone to dust by not being able to fly to my original homeland. This may seem a glib complaint given the hardship so many people encountered during these times. As the months moved on at a snail's pace, our situation became even more perplexing.

Our physical separation became only part of a bigger problem. How many relationships have been compromised or destroyed due to elongated global separations? Thousands. As Humphrey Bogart posited in Casablanca to Ingrid Bergman, 'It doesn't take much to see that the problems of (three) little people don't amount to a hill of beans in this crazy world'.

In this despair, it seemed ironic I was sitting at a Woodstock bar reiterating these words to the son of the man who wrote them. My friend Peter was the son of Howard Koch who wrote 'Casablanca'.

Michael Lang and I continued to meet to discuss next steps on various projects — from TV series to documentaries, exhibitions to Broadway scripts. He remained my closest friend and ally. Around March he was complaining of back pain and other medical issues. My course of action was to cook him another batch of chicken soup, along with a side serving of 'cookies'.

Despite having turned 76 years young, Michael was undoubtedly starting to physically feel his age. His youthful attitude was in stark contrast to my husband. Brian wears his age like a thorny crown. The thorns on that crown turned inward around this time as his depression escalated. I felt powerless to help him climb out of the black-dog hole. Cadd family members treated me like I was unduly concerned about my husband's welfare. My innermost thoughts traced back to the same type of dismissal from Damien's family ahead of his bipolar disorder diagnosis. I could not stand to go through losing another husband to diminished mental and physical health, but this time I was faced with it from thousands of miles away.

This was not how I planned to celebrate my 60th birthday.

Turning 60 has personal intuition and repercussions for each of us.

I did not feel I had leapt any detrimental mental hurdle, far from it — my ideas flowed freely in so many professional directions. Physically was maybe another reality — I had begun to resemble my Scottish grandmother rather more than I had hoped. Stooped and drooped. Had being married to a man 15 years my senior hastened my own ageing?

While I contemplated the so-called 'Final Act' of my life, I was hit with a curveball. My guru, my friend, the 'Prince of Youth' himself, Michael Lang, was diagnosed with non-Hodgkin's Lymphoma.

I felt all the air suck out of my lungs. There was no possible world I could imagine without him in it — for so many reasons. This information was private. I could not share it with anyone outside his family and two of his closest friends. I vowed to uphold his privacy and continued making vats of chicken soup.

He only talked in the future tense: he would beat it, come what may ...

I made a swift decision to travel to Paris for the summer.

The weight of remaining in Woodstock without my husband, and with Michael unwell, was overwhelming. Internally I was crumbling under the weight of uncertainty.

My son was on vacation before graduation and accompanied me on this spiritual sojourn. Austin has been my emotional support in multiple scenarios, homes, and countries. Every day I acknowledge my luck that he arrived in my universe. He is so much more than my son. His kindness and intelligence are both lauded by our friends far and wide, especially his Godfathers Michael Idato and Tim Lawson.

Michael Lang encouraged me to travel and rather liked the idea of living vicariously through my photos and videos of the Paris we both loved.

I visited him in the hospital the day before I flew out. Despite his visual appearance, the Peter Pan in him was still present. We held hands and talked of future endeavours, which he underscored with, 'I will beat this, promise me you won't worry, send photos of what you experience in Paris'.

The memory of walking out of that hospital room still fills me with heartache. Penetrating summer heat in the Poughkeepsie air suffocated me as I gasped in the reality of the situation. My mind's eye could only envisage Michael and I driving 'the beautiful way home' along Peek-a-moose Trail and the happiness in our plethora of shared experiences.

Summer was filled with European travel fun for Austin and me, albeit with the unspoken absence of Brian in any form of communication. I would attempt phone conversations, only to be met with stony silence. Short, sharp emails claiming he had 'no answers' about our future were confusing to say the least.

And confusion has its costs …

As all summers do, this one came to an end, mercifully without any of us catching COVID. Austin returned to Boston. I went to London to work with RGM Productions.

Borders were now open, so I decided to travel to Australia and meet up with my husband to discuss our next steps.

All marriages go through emotional phases within each partner and the individual's cycle of life. No couple is immune from doubt and altered emotions towards their respective partner. Navigating these times is often put in the hands of a third party. That had spectacularly failed for us in the past with Zoom counselling. I was determined we would sit and talk, or not talk, just sit — and come to terms with where we both were in our lives.

Was there a future for us as two individuals recalibrating our life together as a couple?

The first meeting in a year with my husband was overshadowed by enormous loss.

Michael Lang lost his battle with cancer, making his decision to stop treatment. He passed gently, into that good night. I thought of the words of Dylan Thomas:

Do not go gentle into that good night,
Old age should burn and rave at close of day
Rage, rage against the dying of the light

The day was stained with both physical and emotional loss.

My jetlag-addled brain jolted into reality — I had lost a loved one and a marriage in a single day.

Rona Elliot was our glue. She did Michael Lang proud in her friendship, giving succour to so many of us who were grieving. Less than a month before, Michael's inner circle had sent videos of birthday love to him in hospital — compiled by his daughters, Lari Ann and Shala.

The sense of duty I still felt sent urgent notes to friends and colleagues whom I knew should not learn this sad truth via the oncoming media circus. His illness had remained private to the very end and his memory, along with his dignity, had to be upheld.

Amongst it all, I was rendered mute in disbelief he would not be there when I returned home to Woodstock. What indeed would Woodstock even 'look' like without him? I had to remember all the intimate times we shared, in our love of music, peace and each other.

I could not be present at his funeral. Shiva was conducted on Zoom, COVID still restricted travel and his closest friends spread far and worldwide. So much shock and sadness.

I spent days walking on the hot Australian beach sand feeling discombobulated. No future direction presented itself. Rail at the moon … yell pleadingly to the dead … no one is going to show you a way forward other than your own inner self.

My husband's rhetoric on our situation vacillated between zero and one on a rational intelligent scale. Physically being in each other's presence, it became clear he had made a unilateral decision to remain in Australia without consulting me. And just as shockingly, without me.

I limped back to Woodstock. Friends became everything. Rona was my spirit animal. I had my bestie in Melbourne Fiona with her @Fi'Advice on speed dial. I had my Woodstock 'sister & brother', Ami & Spoony, on ground.

I cannot enunciate enough the importance these people played at this time in my life.

This was indeed a new life to navigate after 20 years in a relationship that was for 'always'. My lust for life would not be diminished by his descending darkness.

Then came clarity.

Paris.

CHAPTER 14: PARIS, SOMETHING GREATER

A renewed joy for life revealed itself in an apartment overlooking Notre-Dame Cathedral. A tree planted in 1604 creates a breeze through its leaves that enters my windows as I write.

The few friends I shared my new location with continued to ask, 'why?'. There was a simple answer — I choose to live through my eyes.

Anywhere I wander in these Parisian streets is a visual feast. Just like Ernest Hemingway wrote, my chosen city is 'A Moveable Feast'.

I live on the street of the famed bookshop Shakespeare and Company, where 'Papa' Hemingway spent so much time with owner Sylvia Beach. The second owner was American George Whitman, who termed his part-time employees 'The Tumbleweeds'. This referred to anyone passing through who fancied themselves a would-be author. They were able to stay in the store overnight in exchange for a few hours of work and reading a book of choice each day. The only rule in this bohemian enclave was discussing the Tumbleweeds' chosen novel with Monsieur Whitman.

The store is now owned by his daughter Sylvia, a remarkable woman who has turned the bookshop into a tourist attraction. She has introduced new generations to authors who began their careers living penniless in Paris – Ernest Hemingway, F. Scott Fitzgerald and James Joyce amongst them.

I can sit in the store's soft chairs for hours, reading and imagining decades-old energetic conversations on literary merit.

After years of uncertainty and confusion, elements of happiness started to creep back into my life. I begin every day with a brisk hour-long walk across the Île Saint-Louis and around the Latin Quarter. I wave to my artist friend Laurent.

I bid 'bonjour' to the Quai Bourbon guardian of a Hotel Particular. I lament at the homeless tents under the Pont Marie while feeling proud to live in a city that provides for these needy individuals.

Je suis une Parisienne.

I buy baguette from Isabelle's, direct from the oven. I smile while breaking a piece to devour on my way home. This is a local tradition.

The local market operates three days a week. My 'fromager', Manu, and I simply refer to each other as 'Darling'. There is no need to repeat my order each visit — he knows after so long that Comté 'dix huit' is my cheese of choice. And don't forget the beurre demi-sel.

Inside this new happiness came hours of dark reality.

Coming to terms with the end of my 20-year relationship, I had to rationalize my financial position.

Brian had left me in the same way he had his previous marriages — walk out the door and don't look back. No care and no responsibility.

It was lucky I had a thick skin and had managed everything to do with our financial life during the relationship.

I realized my beautiful home in Byron Bay had to be sold.

My estranged husband and I visited the house on my return to Australia. Walking into what had been our 'forever home' felt cold and impersonal. Gazing out at the ocean held none of its initial appeal.

I was shivering. My shaking in dread was a physical manifestation of the reality confronting me. This was no longer home or an option to be one for me again. Brian was adamant he had no interest in living there again — with or without me.

We would meet again by coincidence in an airport lounge, boarding the same flight to Melbourne.

At the end of the flight, we walked out of the airport together. He said only one thing: 'What is written on your jumper?'

I unfurled my woollen scarf to reveal in red letters the word 'AMOUR' – French for love. I muttered to him, 'Always hopeful', as he turned to leave the terminal in silence.

That silence, like so many other times I had not realized, spoke volumes.

He couldn't get any plainer than that.

Until he did, through a Brisbane law firm.

The shock of his hostile move was multi-layered. I had been civil in all the times we met to come to terms. From the paperwork it appeared he had appointed these legal sharks' months before I came to Australia to discuss our marital position. He had never mentioned any of this.

So began a 2-year legal case of pure greed. Many of his friends, and some family, rallied around me in disgust at his blatant cash grab.

From the day Brian returned to Australia, he moved in with his daughter.

The picture became crystal clear. Jessica's 15-year 'ghosting' of me had amounted to getting Daddy back in her arms. And have him buy her a house.

The losers here were my children. Olivia and Austin had spent 20 years of childhood and early adulthood with Brian as their stepfather. In this brutal ending, he had disassociated himself from them — without a word.

There are many things to forgive at the end of a marriage, in retrospect. But my husband's behavior towards my children can never be forgiven. Over two decades I gave his children homes and heart; only one of them has repaid me with any kindness since the dissolution.

The nightmares dissipate; the sadness dissolves over time.

I have no bitterness left at the way Brian behaved towards me because I now recognize it as his pattern. He is a flawed human being with no empathy. I chose to spend those 20 years with him, so any naivety on my part that he would not repeat that pattern was on me.

A writer in New York I wholeheartedly admired, David Brooks, wrote in his book The Second Mountain:

'Marriage defies anecdote and sometimes is felt most powerfully after it has gone'.

It becomes more apparent with age; days grow shorter. Be it in winter while building a fire in my apartment loft or in summer clipping the yellow-headed daisies on my terrace. There are only so many hours in a day and a myriad of ways to spend them. Then comes the night when Paris lights up and people walk and talk in multiple languages around me.

On the corner of my street is a renowned nightclub that played host to Josephine Baker decades ago.

On my first night here, I ventured to the club — hungry and tired after my move from a world away in Woodstock.

I was placed at a table beside the piano player.

He started a conversation with me in between sets.

Côtes du Rhône lubricated our conversation in broken French and English.

I had found a friend in my first trepidatious hours in Paris.

All I could think was, 'Please God, not another piano player …'.

I have never had trouble meeting people and making friends.

Paris has proved no exception.

I hold monthly 'soirées' where I take on a kind of Gertrude Stein open-house philosophy. People of all nationalities and walks of life join with friends of friends, and the circle widens.

This gives me great joy.

I live by words scribbled by George Whitman, the motto of

The Shakespeare and Company bookshop on my street corner:
'Be not inhospitable to strangers, lest they be angels in disguise'.

This has been variously attributed to W.B. Yeats, or as a quote from the Bible.

I created a painting with those words in 2003. It adorned my front door in Woodstock. There is no way I could have known over 20 years ago how relevant that sentiment would become in my everyday life and geographical location.

Amongst local liaisons, many friends from overseas are regular housemates. My magnificent children have both moved to London and visit Paris frequently, as I do them.

I may not have the big, rollicking family Brian falsely envisaged would be our future.

These people who join and comfort me now are above and beyond the definition of family.

It was with both irony and joy that the notaire I chose to sign my divorce papers was on the Ile St Louis. His office is merely footsteps away from the apartment Brian and I shared in 2005 on our first trip to Paris. I run past it each morning and breathe a deep sigh of relief.

Full circle in a life that has not yet completed its true fullness.

Paris with Clare O'Connell, Tim Lawson, Jordy and Madoc

Summer fun with Brett Price in Mykonos 2024

Austin's 'God Pappy' Michael Idato

Writing this book with the help of Angus George on Rue Cler

The Good Life in Paris

Cruising La Seine with Chuggi, Maam, Russell & Donna Morris

Pals in Provence

Snail Eaters in Paris

EPILOGUE: A GIRL LIKE YOU

I am striding through the Paris Metro on an autumnal evening on the way to dinner with new friends. The station at St Michel is strangely empty this evening.

We are holding hands, my lover and I. We are swinging our arms in unison, skipping through the Metro halls like children. In our shared headphones he chooses a song by Edwyn Collins, where he sings:

'I've never known a girl like you before'.

The song in this moment makes my heart fill with happiness. I stop and twirl in a dance that reminds me of being on the set of Countdown, dancing for Molly Meldrum. Only 40 years have skipped past.

I've still got the moves.

My lover chooses the soundtrack of my life now — every day a new song as I take my morning run along La Seine. The first song he gifted me was 'Something Greater' by Parcels.

My life has indeed become greater in many ways.

Never say never.

In the final act of The Circumference of My Being, I have found and connected deeply with that young girl hanging from a Paris window with her hope for a FABULOUS future.

She found four of those predicted marriages; maybe a fifth is on my future horizon.

None of us knows what tomorrow holds.

Billy Thorpe echoed life's choices and possibilities in 'Since You've Been Gone':

'Forget your dogmas, your religions and your creeds
Forget your mantras and your 'oms'
There are no methods to this crazy life we lead

No secret paths to walk upon
Just hang love's portrait in the cathedral of your heart
And warm the landscape of your soul
Sow the seeds a child can reap
And smile if we should ever meet
Cause just like you, I'm all alone'.
And to close this circumference …
Jonathan Larson wrote profoundly in 'Rent':
There's only us
There's only this
Forget regret, or life is yours to miss
No other road, no other way
No day but today

For more photos in full color, scan the QR code.
www.AmandaPelman.com/gallery

My Parisian Window

www.ingramcontent.com/pod-product-compliance
Lightning Source LLC
Chambersburg PA
CBHW040302170426
43194CB00021B/2868